Palgrave Studies in Accounting and Finance Practice

More information about this series at
http://www.palgrave.com/gp/series/16220

Sean Stein Smith

Shifting from Accounting Practitioner to Academia

Tactics, Tips, and Strategies for the Transition

palgrave
macmillan

Sean Stein Smith
Department of Economics and Business
Lehman College
Bronx, NY, USA

ISSN 2524-8251 ISSN 2524-826X (electronic)
Palgrave Studies in Accounting and Finance Practice
ISBN 978-3-030-67545-5 ISBN 978-3-030-67546-2 (eBook)
https://doi.org/10.1007/978-3-030-67546-2

This Palgrave Macmillan imprint is published by the registered company Springer Nature Switzerland AG
The registered company address is: Gewerbestrasse 11, 6330 Cham, Switzerland

Preface

This book project was a very personal project for me, as it is a topic that I feel is critically important for the continued success for both higher education and the accounting profession at large. It would be difficult to select an industry or sector of the economy that has experienced more dramatic change and disruption than the accounting and broader financial services industry. Since I have had the wonderful opportunity to work in the accounting industry prior to my transition to higher education, I felt that I had a unique perspective to offer on the many issues driving change in these professions. Having had a first-hand experience of how accounting tasks and roles have evolved, even just over the past several years, the importance of having an educational pipeline equipped to address these changes is essential. In my time as a student I had the great privilege of having instructors from every background, and having that diversity of instruction and expertise equipped me to succeed in a rapidly changing workplace. This is something I strive to replicate in my endeavors, both in the classroom and with private sector institutions.

To that end, this text should not be seen as a definitive or authoritative guide for how practitioners can transition to a non-practitioner career path. Put simply, there are just so many different factors that come into play, and such a wealth of options for accounting practitioners to consider, that no single book could possibly address this array of choices. Rather, this book should be taken for exactly what it is; the reflections and observations of an individual who has successfully managed what can be a fraught decision-making process. Accounting and accounting education might not have been traditionally thought of as a partnership or ideas that go hand-in-hand, but they truly are partners oriented toward the same goal. Educating and preparing the professionals and leaders of tomorrow is an obligation and task that will increasingly require collaboration and cooperation between higher education and the private sector. What this book should illustrate and highlight is just how many different ways these collaborations occur, and some of the ways in which practitioners can access these opportunities. Higher education and accounting are both traditional businesses and sectors that are in the midst of radical changes; this book was written to help educate, empower, and encourage both constituent groups to work together and move forward successfully.

New York, USA Sean Stein Smith

Acknowledgments This book is dedicated to my family, who always encourage and support all of my endeavors and projects.

Introduction

Higher education is a dynamic, fast moving, and rapidly changing space of the economy and general conversation. Especially following the Great Recession, the conversation and dynamics around higher education have certainly changed; increasingly people are questioning whether or not there is demonstrative value connected to higher education. In other words, the very same forces that continue to reshape the economy on an almost daily basis are the exact same forces influencing changes in the higher education arena. This may not be the association or message that you have previously connected higher education with, but it is undeniably true; higher education more closely resembles a fast moving economic sector rather than the stodgy ivory tower that might usually come to mind. Although higher education is usually steeped in tradition and has a track record of being slow to change and evolve, assuming that higher education will remain this way represents a partial and incomplete view of the situation. Education is, clearly, at the core of many initiatives and projects that have otherwise been launched and discussed both in the United States and overseas. Cost, course content, or the stratification and bifurcation of income or household wealth that different levels of education can result in, have become hotly contested points of debate across the political spectrum with individuals on both sides staking out strong positions. Within this context, and including the conversation around economic inequality, as well as the renewed debate between supporters of free market forces and those advocating increased government regulation, is the backdrop against which this book was written. Bringing this conversation back to a more grounded level, this book is also told from a single individuals perspective, complete with all of the anecdotes and hindsight wisdom that provides.

If you had come to me 5 years ago and said I would be a tenure trackfaculty member at the one the largest university systems in the world, teachingaccounting, that would have seemed to me like a strange or bizarre idea. That said, it is also important to note that my journey is not as unusual or unique as it might seem on the surface. Connecting private industry and corporate employees with the higher education landscape is a trend and topic that has been developing and maturing for many years at this point. Possibly taking the form of adjuncts or contract-based faculty, but usually consisting of individuals that had previously worked in the private sector before retiring, this cross-pollination has occurred consistently for years. What has changed now, however, is the fact that many professionals—including myself—have made the transition from private sector work to academia in the middle of a career. Especially in the business departments and course settings, this is indicative of several large structural shifts that are underway and that are driving change in the marketplace at large.

First, the demands and expectations of higher education continue to change and evolve in response to what the marketplace increasingly expects of higher education. It is simply no longer enough to prepare students from text or other source materials; students, potential future employers, and the institutions at large increasingly expect some real-world applications and examples to be featured as a part of the conversation. Building on this increased need and expectation is also the reality that students are competing in a global marketplace; education and the faculty that provide this education must be equally as well prepared to contend and deal with global trends and market forces. In fact, much like how international work experience is usually seen as a positive in the corporate sector, it is not unreasonable to forecast that this trend will continue and permeate within the higher education space as well.

Globalization, despite the headwinds it faced following the COVID19 outbreak and subsequent political discourse, is an underlying trend that is here to stay. What this means from the perspective of the higher education can be distilled into several broader trends and directions that will be analyzed within this text. Firstly, technology and digitization will only become a more inclusive part of the educational process. Pushback aside from M.B.A. and other more costly programs, the potential for remote learning is difficult to understate. Second, this shift and increased usage of technology has the potential to highlight existing inequality and disparities that already exist. Institutions of higher education will need to take care, that as online offerings and other non-traditional programs gain prominence, that all students are able to equally participate. Both of these subtrends have the potential to revolutionize and transform the higher education from the top down. As with any large-scale disruption and innovation, however, there are going to be winners and losers as a result of these widespread changes and developments. Practitioners, in whatever capacity they enter the academic conversation, have an important role to play as institutions across the broad adapt, evolve, and expand to address these multifaceted and far reaching changes.

It is also worth pointing out that the very same trends that are dominating the business landscape and economy at large will also have an impact on the higher education space, including the increasing digitization and automation of many underlying business processes. Compounding and accelerating these trends, as well as recognizing the fact that these forces are not fads but rather represent fundamental changes to the marketplace means that institutions, administrators, and faculty will have to keep pace. This book, written from just one person's perspective, will hopefully shed some light as to how these trends can be addressed, dealt with, and incorporated into course development, faculty development, and student engagement. Higher education continues to change at an accelerating pace, and practitioners that are making the transition to higher education and uniquely well positioned to leverage experience and deliver value across the board. There is a lot to cover in this rapidly evolving arena, and since you are reading this book the idea of making the switch from more of corporate role to one in higher education has, at the very least, crossed your mind.

Let's get to it.

Contents

CHAPTER 1

A Changing Profession

Introduction

It would be difficult to analyze or present a profession that has experienced more dramatic change during the last several decades than the accounting and broader financial services landscape. The causes of these dramatic changes have not always been generated as a result of positive news or forward-looking changes, but rather a combination of positive and negative headline news. Whether it was the failure of Enron, the global financial crisis, the failures of numerous institutions during the aftermath of the Great Recession, or the still emerging repercussions of the COVID-19 pandemic, it readily became apparent that the current status quo of managing, reporting, and disclosing accounting and other financial information was insufficient. These failures, however shocking and destructive to the economy at large, were merely indicative of several changes and forces that were otherwise driving change and innovation throughout the business landscape. While no listing of business changes or disruptions have the ability to be all inclusive or entirely comprehensive in nature, it does appear that these are definitive forces that professionals and educators need to be aware of.

S. Stein Smith, *Shifting from Accounting Practitioner to Academia*, Palgrave Studies in Accounting and Finance Practice, https://doi.org/10.1007/978-3-030-67546-2_1

Changes Coming to the Profession

First, and something that has occurred outside of the accounting and financial services profession is the development of personalized, customized, and real-time services available to customers. Whether it related to Netflix, Uber, Amazon, Facebook, or other technology organizations, is would seem to be an underlying reality of business that information and data will increasingly drive the decision-making process going forward. Outside of the technology field, however, this is also a trend that continues to manifest itself in the real-time delivery of mobile information, just in time delivery of coupons or other discount information, and the ways in which that services tend to learn and improve the more that they are utilized. Fascinating as this is in its own right, these ideas and trends are the topics that could generate an entirely separate book. Rather, this text attempts to bridge the gap between the current state of accounting and financial information, and where the profession needs to end up. Additionally, and hopefully by sharing some personal anecdotes and pieces of advice, this text will provide practitioners considering a transition to higher education with practical and actionable advice.

This expectation of real-time information connects to the accounting function in a relatively logical and straightforward manner; the current delivery of accounting and financial information is not delivered in a real-time and continuous manner. Periodic reporting and disclosure of information have long been a mainstay of the accounting process, but the expectations of stakeholders continue to evolve and change. Expectations, regardless of what geographic region or industry is in question, continue to shift toward the need for information to be delivered, reported, and analyzed on a real time—or at least continuous—basis. Organizations increasingly leverage tools like artificial intelligence, robotic process automation, machine learning, and deep learning to handle the large amounts of data produced internally. These same tools can, and should be, harnessed and leveraged to assist with the processing of reporting financial information. In addition to reflecting the reality that the accounting data functions and practices should evolve and keep pace with other trends and industry forces, these trends also create opportunities for recently transitioned practitioners.

Second, and even though there are numerous technology tools that can—and are—being leveraged and harnessed with the production and reporting of real-time information, several fundamental obstacles and challenges remain that may prevent educators and practitioners from fully maximizing the value of these tools. Put simply, there does appear to be a skill, technical, or knowledge gap between what many academics feel comfortable teaching and the skills that students need to succeed going forward. This is not stated to place any blame or fault on any of the associated educators or administrators. Rather, this is stated to acknowledge and articulate the reality that this space—both inside financial services and outside of it—continues to evolve and develop, possibly even already beyond the and scope of what initial organizers and users had planned for. Given this reality, and the fact that new entrants continue to disrupt and generate new applications and use cases, it is not a surprise that many programs find themselves struggling to develop content fast enough to satisfy client and customers. As opposed to viewing this as a challenge, these developments should be viewed as an opportunity moving forward.

Building on this third and final point, however, it is truly important that educators understand how much of these changes and expectations are derived from customer demand and input. At the end of the day, accounting professionals and firms are not hired to provide coding or programming expertise aligned with certain software packages or solutions, but to rather provide business advice and insights to business owners. None of the technology and business changes that will be discussed in this book or in other materials have developed alone or in a vacuum. Rather, these technological changes are an indication and symptom of changing expectations on the side of business owners and clients. To fulfill these expectations, and to meet the needs of clients now and going forward, it is reasonable to expect that education and educators will need to evolve in a similar manner.

Clients, to put it simply, want to have access to data, financials, and financial forecasts as soon as they are produced and updated. Pertaining to this information, and no matter the good the personal relationship between the firm and client is, it is always better to receive the relevant information as soon as possible so it can be the most helpful to the decision-making process. Given the fact that such capabilities do already exist outside of the accounting and financial services space, it is perfectly logical that clients and customers expect a similar experience with their financial data. Meeting the needs of clients and end users is not something that is unique or specialized to the accounting or broader financial services space, but it does represent an area where it is increasingly evident that the status quo is unsustainable. The sheer volume of information and data that needs to be handled by an organization on a day-to-day basis leads to the following reality. In order for the accounting professionals of the future to be able to meet and even exceed client expectations, said professionals must be able to be conversant and hold productive conversations about these technologies. Taking a step back, a however, and truly understanding the technology itself, this seems like as good time to specific and outline several examples of these emerging technology tools. Prior to some definitions, however, it is even more important to understand the ultimate impact of this increased technology integration. In other words, just understanding the tools themselves is only one part—albeit an important part—of this process

A New Way of Doing Accounting

Ultimately the goal of any accounting project, process, or function is to provide consistent, comparable, and timely information to the marketplace, and this holds true no matter what institution of higher education is assessed, what specific topic is being analyzed, or the industry in question. As digitization and automation permeate the broader business landscape, it is critically important that the end result of these technology trends are understood and incorporated into the course offerings. Put simply, the traditional methodology associated with accounting, the periodic reporting and analysis of information, is not enough to keep pace with the production and dissemination of information by organizations. Technology, automation, and the expectation of real-time data available on an on-demand basis are trends that do not seem to be passing fads, but rather seem to represent a fundamental change to how businesses operate as well as how data is processed. Breaking down the current fields of specialization in accounting, the three primary areas of expertise—tax, audit, and advisory—seem equally well positioned to experience dramatic changes and shifts in both how work is accomplished and the skills that employers will require of new hires. Taking a look into some of the specific changes, it quickly becomes evident just how much the profession will evolve, and how dramatic the education of future professionals will need to evolve.

First and foremost, there is increasingly an expectation that information and data will need to be available on a continuous basis, but at the same time that information will need to be secured and protected as well. In other words, even as the marketplace increasingly expects information to be available on an as-needed basis, the level of data integrity and security must also be maintained. The current state of the profession, even equipped with current levels of technological automation and integration, does not seem well positioned to fulfill these expectations. Educators and institutions of higher education are in a unique position to not only fulfill the needs of the current marketplace, but can also play a dominant role in the development of the accounting profession in the future.

Second, the very business model of higher education seems to be impacted by this shift toward a digital first or digital only business environment. Online courses, digital education, and virtual learning have long been mainstays of the education space, but this trend and shifting dynamic is not one that appears to be a fad. Rather, the pivot and reallocation of resources toward virtual learning, digital resource, and a remote-based learning experience seem to be indicative of a fundamental shift in how education is provided, how information is consumed, and the process by which associated credentials are verified and confirmed. As ever-increasing amounts of education, and the associated personally identified information, are stored and transferred in a digital-only manner, the practitioners of the future will need to be prepared. This entails two distinct, yet equally important facets. Practitioners will need to not only understand the emerging technologies from an end-user perspective, but also be able to understand and articulate just how these new technologies will influence the audit and attestation processes.

Last but not least, the very nature of education looks positioned to change. Specifically, the trend in education seems to taking the form of continuous learning rather than a one-and-down event. Whether this takes the form of certificates, continuing education programs, or other types of continuous learning and education, the underlying trend is clear. Educators and the institutions involved in the educational process will need to round out and augment current offerings and programs in order to keep pace with market demand. In other words, the very nature of how education is thought of, marketed, and refined going forward is going to need to evolve as a direct result of these emerging technology trends. While not every class, course, or program will need to focus on emerging technology tools or trends, it is reasonable to expect that these topics will need to be integrated in an ever-increasing number of educational offerings. Having that context in mind, it seems a good time to take a look at some of these technology trends themselves.

Big Picture Technology Trends

It is true that technology integration and technological developments are nothing new to the accounting and financial services space, but it could be argued that the sheer pace of change and development has accelerated rapidly. Accounting professionals, and the educators tasked with preparing the next generation of professionals and practitioners, have long made the integration and adoption of new technology tools and applications a mainstay of the profession. Different technological advancements, including the computer, tablet, Internet, smart devices, and iterations of accounting software, have allowed the increased automation of accounting functions. Such automation and the integration of technology into accounting and financial services functionality allows practitioners to be freed up to focus on higher margin and higher value services.

This exact same integration and freeing up of resources, however, also presents a fundamental change to virtually every aspect of accounting, financial services, and financial reporting. It is true that technology represents automation and the ability to redirect or reallocate resources to higher margin and more accounting focused activities, but also can lead to several large-scale changes. First and perhaps most importantly is the reality that as accounting practitioners and accounting firms are able to engage in new and different services there might be numerous conflicts of interest that will arise. This can manifest itself in a manner of ways, but perhaps the most obvious is the fact that as accounting professionals enter into new service areas the independence and objectivity so prized by external end users may end up being potentially compromised. Whether or not the independence of the accounting and financial profession is actually impacted or not, even the hinting at, or possibility of, reduced independence could wreak havoc in the profession for years to come. This is a topic that will be revisited throughout this book, as it is something that needs to be incorporated into curriculum development as the profession and educational content evolves.

Secondly the increased technological integration among a range of organizations—accounting focused or not—means that not every organization is going to be as interested in traditional accounting services. For every opportunity that technology creates, it is also worth noting that there are going to be instances and situations where some roles are not as necessary. Blockchain, robotic process automation, and artificial intelligence may be the buzz words and hot topics of the moment, but those are symptomatic of the changes in the profession rather than a cause itself. In any event, and regardless of personal opinion or perspective, technology and technological services are going to play an ever larger role in the education of future professionals as well as the tasks performed by those currently in the workforce.

Blockchain—all that blockchain represents is a decentralized and distributed manner by which network members can share data and other information between each other in an encrypted manner on a continuous basis, and to so in a manner that is nearly immutable. There are many different iterations of blockchain that currently exist in the marketplace, and these different options can sometimes prove less helpful than one may have initially thought. As the ecosystem around blockchain continues to mature and evolve, there does seem to be one truth that remains unassailable. Although not an accounting system at the core of the idea, blockchain is well situated to revolutionize how accounting information and processes are handled both now and going forward.

Robotic process automation—while many organizations, led by management teams that have seen the potential of artificial intelligence represented in movies and other forms of media, might want to skip ahead to a full-blown artificial intelligence implementation, the reality on the ground is far different. Due to a lack of appropriate controls or workflow management issues, the only end result of comprehensive automation projects is oftentimes larger quantities of mismanaged, inaccurate, or incomplete information. Robotic process automation, framed in that context, can best be thought of as a halfway point between current automation levels and a full-blown implementation of artificial intelligence. In other words, robotic process automation—which can assist in both accounting and non-accounting functions—enables existing and new technologies to improve the efficiency of existing processes and operations.

Artificial intelligence—an umbrella term used to outline and define a category of information technology tools that can either augment or render obsolete the need for human oversight and interactions throughout specific processes. Specifically, and pertinent to any educational conversation on the matter, is the differentiation between the various forms and types of artificial intelligence. For an accounting program, department, or school, it might make more sense to emphasize certain types of artificial intelligence over others. A term that is bantered around quite a bit in both the practitioner and academic press and media, artificial intelligence does seem to represent a trend and force to be reckoned with in terms of its eventual impact on both the profession and business at large. The accounting professionals of the future must be able to work with, train, and understand just how AI templates and platforms function, as well as how they change the workload of the profession.

Cryptocurrencies—perhaps the most well-known application and use case for blockchain technologies, most cryptocurrencies are not FDIC insured. Even though a certain emerging class of cryptocurrencies—stablecoins—represents financial products that are advertised as a method to reduce price volatility, much remains uncertain about these assets. Specifically, from an accounting, taxation, and disclosure perspective there are numerous questions and considerations that still need to be addressed and resolved before said assets can scale to a mainstream level. This ambiguity, although frustrating for some practitioners, also creates an opportunity for those same practitioners to play a definitive role in shaping the conversation.

Automation—although this is perhaps the most discussed and analyzed topic in the financial services space during the last several years, a large amount of work remains until these automation tools are well prepared for mass introduction. Not a new concept by any means, the trends and forces that have driven automation forward, however, have continued to accelerate as the cost of producing, using, and upgrading these automation packages have continued to drop. Whether to do with sourcing lower-cost materials, operational efficiency gains, or simply the compounding of Moore's law over time, automation is the underlying force behind many process improvement initiatives and projects at organizations.

Cloud—the idea of working in the cloud does not seem like a radical or innovative concept, but it truly does change how the data that is so critical to accounting and financial services is processed, treated, and handled by both accounting and other financial professionals. Taking this into account, and realizing the fact that many firms have already migrated to the cloud, it is also important to recognize the fact that the movement into the cloud does not eliminate data custody or cybersecurity risk. Conversely, the very shift to the cloud that—on paper at least—reduces or helps eliminate cybersecurity risk—may actually end up amplifying these risks.

Specific technologies will surely change and evolve over time, and these specific tools and terminologies that are currently dominating the accounting and educational conversation will in no way resemble the disruptive technologies that will eventually drive change in the higher education field. The specific tools themselves, framed in that light, do not matter as much as the willingness to understand both what the tools are, and the impact that these tools have on the conversation. Accounting professionals might be in the midst of a disruptive period of change currently, but these changes and associated ripple effects have long been occurring in different areas of the economy. Aside from any specific tool, however, there is also an underlying trend that continues to create challenges and opportunities across different economic sectors; the increasing digitization and automation that often accompanies increased technological adoption.

Connecting to Higher Education

Adapting to a continuously changing landscape might not be the first thing that comes to mind when higher education is discussed, and that is because for a long time not much has changed. The model of instruction, with an expert lecturing to a hall or classroom of students absorbing information, has not changed. A scene can be cut from any film or TV show depicting classroom instruction, and different fashion styles or technology tools notwithstanding, it would be difficult to determine which scene was from which era or time period. This model of instruction and classroom engagement has remained unchanged and that is for a good reason; students are there to learn and acquire knowledge from someone who possesses said knowledge and expertise. Despite the putting forward of alternative models, including but not limited to the concept of a flipped classroom, this traditional model has for the most part remained unaltered. Simply put, and despite the efforts of some educators to change the conversation, it remains a challenge to have a student-led instructional conversation on a widespread or systemic basis.

Many ideas have been put forward, headlined by the idea of a flipped classroom or some other sort of student-led engagement and instruction. In theory, a flipped classroom results in the students leading the conversation and classroom discourse, with the instructor serving a role more akin to facilitator or subject matter expert to answer specific questions. In most cases, however, students are enrolled in a specific course because they wish to learn more about specific technologies, subject matter areas, or other forms of information from a subject matter expert; the instructor. Even if students are able to allocate time to pre-read and pre-prepare the materials necessary for the class itself, the ability of them to do so in a manner that will help lead to productive and meaningful conversations is most going to be hampered by a lack of understanding of the content itself.

Clearly, there are some course and areas where a more prominent role for students makes more sense such as master's level or doctoral level classes, but for the majority of college classes and instructional cases that just will not make sense. Technology is enabling this desire, to transform education from more of a lecture to something closer to a conversation, by enabling students to review materials before class, engage and interact with the material in a number of different ways, and leverage other non-textbook resources to assist with greater understanding and reading comprehension. Now this is by no means a guaranteed tactic or way to increase student engagement, but this greater digitization of educational resources means that it is more possible than before to drive change in how materials are covered in a number of different courses. That is not to say that every class should be focused on integrating blockchain and other emerging technology tools, but that these topics and tools should be part of the conversation. Not only should these tools and technology platforms be identified, but if possible, these tools should also be integrated into the course itself.

This is also an opportunity for practitioners that are making the transition from industry or public accounting to higher education; higher education is a business and is increasingly assessed as such. Bringing in some of the financial discipline and analytical rigor that is associated with private enterprise to academia is not only something that should be encouraged, but is increasingly something that will become mandatory over time. Disruptive innovation has come to virtually every industry sector in the world, and it would be illogical to assume that higher education and academia will be exempt from these trends. Education is no longer in the ivory tower and must become more integrated to the needs and realities on the ground in terms of what employers are expecting, as well as what employees are expected to be aware of. Technology might be the headline news story at this time, but as opposed to being the singular driving force, it should be thought of as a symptom of much larger trends and changes. One of the most obvious and high-profile symbols of this large change and shift is the increased integration of technology into virtually every subset of accounting and financial services.

The Intersection of IT & Financial Services

Whatever specific technology application is presented or analyzed the point in the same; technology and technology tools lie at the center of the future of financial services. Students, both current and future, will need to be familiar with and able to understand how the tools that are entering the marketplace will be adopted and utilized by various organizations the world over. This technology trend means, in essence, that the current topics and themes covered in accounting and other finance courses will be insufficient going forward. In addition to the increased training, hiring, and integrating of established faculty members with expertise in these areas, this increasing integration also represents a potential opportunity for practitioners to play a leading role.

Technology forces and trends, from the iPhone mobile applications, tend to be adopted and implemented first in the private sector before permeating other areas of the economy. While it is true that many initially disruptive technologies, including the leading role that DARPA played in the development of the Internet, were supported and led by the government, the playing field seems to have titled increasingly toward the private sector in recent years. Bringing the hands-on experience that practitioners have with both emerging technologies and procedures is an invaluable aspect that hiring professionals that aspire to educational roles can bring to the table.

These technology forces and the disruptions that they are continuing to generate represent both an opportunity and a challenge for the profession. On the one hand, there does not seem to be a large enough pool or talent and intellectual capital currently available to handle the influx of data, information, and workflow changes generated by these technology shifts. Such a shortage is caused, at least in part by, the lack of educational expertise in the higher education arena. Put simply, many faculty have been out of school, and at least partially out of the skill acquisition mode, for several years. This is absolutely not the fault of anyone involved, but does create an opportunity for practitioners to both create value for institutions of higher education and have a fulfilling career pivot and shift and virtually any point in a career.

One of the most commonly cited issues in higher education is that there does appear to be an imbalance between the number of college students and the number of trained and able faculty to educate. Especially when analyzed at a national level, and not just the most top tier institutions, this gap only seems to grow larger. Due to any number of factors, including demographics, comparative pay scales, and the robust job market for accounting professionals outside of higher education, an educator shortage has been a problem that has been discussed for years. Across the spectrum, and in both the higher education as well as the practitioner space, programs and scholarships have been launched to help plug this marketplace gap. The specific of these different initiatives and efforts differ, but the underlying goal is the same; to try and entice current students or current professionals to transition to academia. Whether or not these programs ultimately succeed is a subject for a different book; the purpose of this text is to help explain that a solution to this shortage already exists.

Higher education, particularly education affiliated with accounting and other financial services professionals, does not merely consist of learning and practicing technical skills and concepts. In addition to these skills and knowledge, students must also learn how to professionally interact with clients, solve complex problems, and be able to contend with an ambiguous business landscape. These are the traits, be they referred to as leadership or soft skills, that can often play a differentiating role in the career of a professional. Individuals who have either recently left practice, or are still employed in practice to a certain extent, posses not only these skills but the ability to convey this information. Technical skills and concepts may change, and these are also concepts that practitioners can convey, but the value and benefits a practitioner can provide extend far beyond merely providing FASB updates. Technology, leadership, and the ability to work with others are facts of professional life that (1) students need to be made aware of, and that (2) practitioner individuals will be able to provide them in the classroom.

There is a famous graph depicting the rate of change that is currently underway in the marketplace versus the pace that humans can deal with change, and the illustrating is shocking. Widely cited and discussed, the primary takeaway is that as different technology tools and directions continue to accelerate in terms of adoption, the ability of people to adapt does not accelerate at the same rate. To put it simply, the pace of technological change is already outstripping the ability of humans to contend and grapple with the range of change disrupting the business landscape at large. Change is obviously a core component of any business and economic landscape, but the pace of change currently underway in the accounting and financial services landscape is reflected in how quickly and completely higher education continues to change and evolve. Discussed throughout this book, the same trends that are buffeting accounting professionals and practitioners, including automation, digitization, artificial intelligence, robotic process automation, and the array of blockchain applications, are simultaneously driving change in virtually every aspect of the business landscape. But so what, some might say, higher education is not a traditional business in the sense that institutions are not judged in terms of profit and loss, nor cash flows, nor the rate of dividend increases that are delivered to the marketplace.

That view, however comforting and reassuring, only presents a partial and incomplete view of just what higher education represents in the current economic landscape and marketplace. Higher education, in all of its various formats and iterations, represents a multi-hundred billion industry in the United States alone, and on a global scale is a trillion-dollar enterprise. In addition to the sheer sums of capital that are allocated, invested, and utilized in this space, there is also the implications that higher education has for many students; a pathway and guide path to a more successful future. Framed in that context, it becomes clearer as to just how these emerging technology themes and tools are connected no matter if accounting or higher education is being examined. As these connections become clearer, however, it is also important to recognize the reality what these connections mean for the future higher education and the practitioners employed therein.

Something else that should be kept in mind and on the front burner is the fact that many of the same tools that drive efficiency and cost savings in the private sector and/or are creations of the private sector should also be leveraged in the educational space. In addition to discussing and instructing students about these different technology tools, applications, and platforms, it is also important to take advantage of emerging technologies to drive change within the institution itself. An expanded conversation around disruptive innovation and innovation at large will be conducted toward the end of this chapter, but it stands to reason that if emerging technologies are being covered in the classroom that they will also be implemented at the institution at large.

The Profession of the Future

At the risk of stating a potentially controversial fact, the primary reason why many individuals embark on a higher education journey is to become equipped with the necessary skills and information to obtain jobs and positions, both now and in the future. Education is seemingly facing something of an existential crisis. On the one side are proponents of a more traditional educational outlook and mindset, which is focused on a liberal arts education instead of specific technical skills. There is certainly some merit to this position, as colleges and universities should be focused educating the whole students versus simply preparing students to obtain some specific types of jobs. Trade schools, vocational options, and other educational choices have an important role to play—some would argue an even more important role going forward—but should not entirely replace the traditional liberal arts model.

On the other hand, and especially in nations where the cost of college is becoming a hotly contested economic and political issue, colleges and universities cannot ignore the reality that students (and parents) expect an education to also lead to a position and even career. This blending of more traditional education with more job or career-focused tracks and options is both a challenge for educators and institutions, and an opportunity for practitioners migrating into higher education. The simple reality on the ground is that employers are not always entirely satisfied with the skills and preparation that students enter the workplace possessing. In order to remain competitive and viable moving forward, institutions will need to work with, learn from, and leverage the insights that former market participants can bring to the table.

A Word About Disruption

When the concept or idea of disruptive innovation is brought up, or blue ocean strategy, or any of the other numerous strategic planning terms there may be some combination or eye-rolling, questioning, and skepticism. This is not entirely unfounded; there are innumerable jokes about buzzwords, catch phrases, and other business terms and jargon that have become so commonplace and routine that they have become cliché. Jokes aside, however, the accounting profession is well situated for a bout of disruptive innovation and dramatic change, even if some members of the profession have yet to realize the fact that this trend will cut across all sectors and areas.

Taking a higher-level perspective for a moment, the idea of disruptive innovation and disruptive change leading to massive change in the accounting profession should not be viewed as a surprise, but rather an inevitable step in the evolution of the profession. By reviewing an accounting textbook—for any level of instruction—it rapidly becomes clear how repetitive and consistent certain processes, tasks, and accounting operations actually are. Account reconciliations, bank reconciliations, audit confirmations, tax filings, and even an array of advisory service offerings (technology implementation and planning, for example) consist of nearly identical steps. It should come as no surprise, in that case, that product and technology experts continue to make investments and inroads into the accounting profession.

On top of the repetitive and periodic nature of many accounting, taxation, and reporting functions it is also important to point out that for many years the accounting profession has had a relatively unchallenged position in terms of accounting, taxation, and financial reporting work. With this established reputation and market position, there was also a relatively easy byproduct of this dominance; pricing power and pricing leadership. One merely to analyze the margins of various accounting and business services, and acknowledging that some of them such as audits are loss leaders, to see how this manifests itself.

The end result of these two forces—the repetitive nature of accounting and business tasks and healthy profit margins associated with them—is that the accounting and financial services industry is ripe for disruption. While this might initially seem like an abstract or radical idea the reality on the ground is not nearly as radical as it might appear at first. Automation and digitization of current accounting and financial services practices and routines have been happening for decades. Even seemingly ubiquitous tools and products such as online trading, mobile apps, and accounting software are a direct result of these dual forces; an attractive marketplace indeed.

Forces such as these have been ignored nor have they gone unnoticed by other non-accounting or technical organizations. An attractive industry with healthy profit margins and limited competition for clients and customers has led to a bevy of new entrants entering the space. Whether it takes the form of trading platforms based entirely online and running on artificial intelligence platforms, or accounting software organizations that are entirely constructed and managed by non-accounting personnel the effect is the same. Ever-increasing amounts of accounting and financial services work are being performed by non-accounting or financial individuals or organizations.

What this means from a practical perspective is that the future of the accounting profession, while not ominous, is certainly going to be different than it might have been otherwise. There is any number of fully automated, technology-infused, or otherwise augmented organizations that are encroaching and financial services space; this does not like a trend that will dissipate anytime soon. Rather, and especially as virtual and remote work continue to become more accepted and more mainstream in nature it stands to reason that an increasing number of organizations will operate in a remote and virtual manner. On top of the obvious implications for physical locations, this will also have implications for the nature of the organizations operating in the space. These changes will also directly lead to changes in how content is taught, and what type of content will be covered.

Simply teaching the same concepts and ideas over and over again will not lead to any improvement, differentiation, or benefit for either the students involved or the institution in question. In order to have programs and students that are equipped with the necessary information to succeed and thrive in such a competitive landscape, the topics and ideas covered in accounting and business curriculum must become as innovative as the forces driving these changes. Disruption and disruptive innovative forces are already having a dramatic impact on the profession, and it stands to reason that accounting education will need to evolve and change as disruptively.

The Takeaway

Disruption might not be a topic of concept that is routinely taught in accounting courses, but it is a force that is going to have dramatic changes on the profession as well as the educators that prepare the students of the future. Kicking off this book by touching on this topic or idea might initially seem like an unusual approach to take, but that misses the larger point and perspective. Disruption is rapidly coming to the higher education sector, and the role that practitioners can play in the successful navigation of these trends should not be underestimated. From bringing practical advice to the conversations around budgetary requirements, new courses and programs that are being developed to market, heading up various programs, and playing a key role in instructing various new courses and certificates are just a few of the ways in which practitioners coming to higher education can have an impact. Disruption will be something that will invariably create winners and losers over time, but those institutions that move quickly to embrace disruptive innovation and disruptively oriented ideas will benefit the most.

Wrapping Up

As this book progresses, there will be anecdotes from my journey sprinkled throughout, but there are trend and force that seems to be inevitable in terms of how it will impact higher education. Technology and digitization, taking the form of either online classes, certificates, or other technology-integrated educational offerings, appear to be taking a leading position at the forefront of how education is evolving and changing. In addition, these developments and changes are reflective of how technology is evolving and changing the business landscape at large. Addressing these changes will, of course, be a challenge and create difficulties for institutions across the board, but will be even more difficult for institutions seeking to do so without the assistance of practitioners from industry. Practitioners, and especially practitioners with an accounting, business, or broader financial services background, can certainly deliver value and insights that are beneficial to all types of institutions.

With all of that said, however, it is also important for practitioners to approach this conversation and transition with a levelheaded and objective view of the situation at hand. Although there may be many areas in which this transition and relationship may be beneficial to all involved parties, it is equally as important to realize that there are factors that need to be assessed prior to making this transition. Higher education and the private sector operate quite differently, expect different things from employees, and reward different types of behaviors. After deciding that a shift or transition might be appropriate, it is even more important to assess which factors and considerations are most pertinent to the situation at hand.

While it is true that the accounting and broader financial services profession are going through a dramatic transition, it also should be realized that this these changes and events are not happening in a vacuum nor are they happening purely independent related to broader business and economic changes. There are also several bigger picture events and changes that are occurring outside of both accounting and higher education that will inevitably have a substantive impact on just how exactly higher education evolves and changes moving forward. Practitioners in and of themselves are not going to magically make this transition and change possible, i.e., just hiring individuals with prior work experience and expertise is not going to help with the development and successful rollout of certain programs, content, or other projects.

In order for both the accounting profession at large, and the educational pipeline tasked with producing the next generation of leaders and practitioners to succeed, there is a growing realization that the current educational structure and incentive structure in the profession are not getting the job done, for lack of a better word. Making sense of the multiple stakeholders that are involved in these conversations, the importance of what these stakeholders are most interested in, and what the goals and objectives of these multiple stakeholders are is an imperative for practitioners and administrators seeking to make sense of this environment moving forward. Coming from the private sector or corporate sector it is important for practitioners to remember that the conversation, guideposts, frameworks, and virtually every other aspect of how individuals are assessed and reviewed are going to be different. On top of these changing evaluative measures, however, there is also a more potentially nefarious trend and theme that any educators need to take into account as courses, programs, and institutions seek to keep pace.

Accounting and financial services, although not as unpopular as they might have been in the aftermath of the financial crisis, do seem to suffer from a negative reputational halo. Accounting consistently ranks as one of the most top ranked and respected group of individuals and institutions, but that does not always translate to effectiveness for attracting students or external funding. Financial services at large, to the contrary, continue to suffer akin to a hangover following the financial crisis, with poll after poll demonstrating the trend that many of the top graduates from various institutions are not interested in working at financial institutions. Regardless of what specific opinion is held as to whether or not top graduates should be concentrated in finance or not, the impact on higher education is indeed important for any practitioners seeking to make the transition. Blood is in the water for accounting and financial services, and everyone is aware of it; technology organizations—with mixed results—continue to make forays into the financial services, lending, and credit areas. Even if organizations such as Google, Amazon, and Facebook never actually make a dent in the lending or credit creation business landscape, the impact and threat of such new entrants is enough to keep incumbents awake at night.

In other words, practitioners that are reading this book, current faculty members that have picked it up, or administrators seeking to make effective decisions for their institutions moving forward need to realize that the need for greater practitioner inclusion in higher education is just one part of a much larger picture. Not every institution is equally as well equipped to contend with a changing business landscape, nor is every practitioner is going to be equally as able to assist institutions in a fast changing environment. Finding the right fit, in other words, is equally as important and applicable for higher education as it is in the private sector; that is something that this book will hopefully be able to assist its readers with.

Reflection Questions

1. What specific emerging technologies have had the largest impact on you, your colleagues, or your firm so far?
2. If given the opportunity to learn more, whether in a classroom setting or professional education venue, which technology would you select?
3. At this point, how would you rank the preparation that higher education provides students with regard to emerging technology on a scale of 1–10 (1 = lowest, 10 = highest).

Additional Readings

IBM Blockchain Basics (ebook and other resources)—https://www.ibm.com/blockchain/what-is-blockchain.

Accounting Today—"What AI Does for Accountants"—https://www.accountingtoday.com/opinion/what-ai-does-for-accountants.

CPA Journal—Cryptoassets—"Accounting For An Emerging Asset Class"—https://www.cpajournal.com/2019/06/21/cryptoassets-accounting-for-an-emerging-asset-class/.

Blackline—"Accounting Process Automation"—https://www.blackline.com/accounting-process-automation/.

The Brookings Institute—Top 6 trends in higher education—https://www.brookings.edu/blog/education-plus-development/2019/01/10/top-6-trends-in-higher-education/.

CHAPTER 2

Making the Transition

Introduction

Taking a step back from the theoretical and adding a dose of my own personal journey into the mix to add some real-world context and information is, I think, an important part of the conversation that is all too often overlooked or overshadowed by other factors. Simply wanting to undertake a career change is a great start and should be where this conversation begins, but that is by no means sufficient to successfully complete the process. One consideration that needs to be brought to the attention of anybody who is considering making a transition such as the one from practice or industry to higher education or academia is whether or not more education is something that should be looked into as a part of this process.

Something that also should be taken into account is that depending on the niche or role that an individual is seeking to engage in during the transition from private industry or public practice to the educational sector. Specifically, if an individual is seeking to work in a more traditional setting, obtaining more education and credentialing is something that should be seriously considered, and may even be required. If, however, someone is seeking to obtain a role at more of a corporate training provider or a role within a public-private-partnership type of arrangement, the existing credentials and education might be sufficient. Alternatively, if

S. Stein Smith, *Shifting from Accounting Practitioner to Academia*, Palgrave Studies in Accounting and Finance Practice,
https://doi.org/10.1007/978-3-030-67546-2_2

the education provider that you are interested in partnering with tends to be focused on emerging technologies, applications, and software an individual might be expected to complete existing product and service offerings. In other words, in order to be an instructor or partner with a for-profit provider or education company, that individual might have to complete some of the course they will, in turn, start teaching.

Making any transition from one economic sector to another sector is always something that will generate risk, opportunity costs, and a steep learning curve. Clearly, this will be different depending on the individual in question and the specific institution in question, but this is always going to be something that needs to be understood. The idea of an opportunity cost might seem like a rather abstract or strictly economic concept to include as a part of this conversation, but it is worth revisiting as part of both my journey and what you should assess as a part of this process. Let's drill down and examine just what an opportunity cost actually is and represents, both in concept and what it actually looks like for a practitioner making a shift and transition to higher education. For the purposes of our conversation, an opportunity cost can be summarized as the lost income, opportunities, or information that are given up to proceed with a certain course of action. These losses of opportunities, income, or information can be larger or smaller given the various situation, but there are always going to be tradeoffs that are part of this process. Let's walk down a few of the ways in which opportunity costs can and do manifest themselves for practitioners seeking to transition from industry to higher education.

Transition Factors for Practitioners

Firstly, the time and effort it will take you to educate, train, and prepare yourself to actually make this shift. We are going to be diving into some of the options available in terms of employer options and different types of roles that are available, but becoming well informed and educated on these topics is something that will take time and efforts that could have otherwise been allocated elsewhere. Other types of training and education and professional development will have to be forsaken in order to free up time and mental space to learn this new information.

Second are the costs and expenses that need to be contended with or incurred as a part of education or preparing for education are probably the most direct and simplest to understand cost of this process. Obtaining additional education, be it in the form of degrees, certificates, or other educational training programs, is virtually always going to be something that individuals need to be ready to embark on. These certificates, education, and trainings will cost money, incur time, and are a direct representation of the opportunity costs that you are incurring and opportunities you are giving up.

It is also worth pointing out that there are potential collaborative opportunities that are going to be given as a result of this transition and shift to higher education. If you are becoming part of the faculty at an institution of higher education you are not going to also be able to conduct the same level of type of professional roles that you would have been able to in other situations. In other words, and something that we will discuss later, many institutions do not allow—or curtail—external engagements by faculty members to some extent. On top of these rather obvious considerations and factors that need to be taken into account as a transition from private industry or public accounting is being considered or weighed is the fact that you will be entering an entirely new economic sector. Specifically, some of the factors that you might want or need to weigh when deciding whether or not the transition is worth the hassle include, but are not limited to, the following. Colleagues and former customers or clients might not entirely understand the rationale behind your switching up or career path or your embarking on a new career arc. This might manifest itself through the reality that you might not cross paths with your former colleagues or clients as often as you had in the past. While it is true that both private industry and academia have conferences and events throughout the year, the nature, timing, location, and frequency of these events can vary widely. Stated another way, you will most likely have to make new colleagues, friends, and networks.

Not attending the same old conferences year in and year out might not seem like that great a loss, but this can also present itself as the following. There is an (inaccurate) perception in some circles that individuals in the higher education space, especially at colleges and universities, are not as up to speed with emerging trends and market realities as practitioners might be. It might be true that practitioners that are actively employed either in business and industry, or public practice, are probably more well versed in specific technology tools and business practices that does not mean this is always the case. For that matter, especially at institutions that are actively involved in the development of cutting edge programs and topics, it is equally as likely that the members associated with higher education might actually be better informed than some practitioner colleagues.

Bridging this gap, and more importantly, changing the perception and associated with the higher education field and academia at large, is a role that practitioners making the switch from practice to academia are uniquely well situated for. In other words, by integrating and mixing more traditional academics—who may or may not have substantial practical experience—with individuals that have a background in practice who are coming to the educational side of things, represents the best of both worlds. Certain classes and topics, including introductory or more theoretically based classes, might be more dependent or in need of instructors with practical insights. On the other hand, classes and topics that are connected to emerging technologies, accounting standard updates, or other more timely topics might be better served with instructors that have fresher or more recent practical experience. Both have merit and deliver value to students, and by balancing both sides of this equation will result in a more comprehensive and robust educational process.

The Big Picture

Education is a tricky subject especially given the backdrop that this book and conversation are being written against. Much has been written and discussed the over-education that has occurred in some aspects of the economy and some generational groups, but taken at a higher-level perspective this is not as shocking or surprising as might initially be thought. Given that millions of individuals graduated from college as the economy was entering and contending with the Great Recession, it does make sense that many of the individuals that had graduated college at that point returned to higher education for the following two reasons. First the appeal of increasing your educational profile is usually a good idea; returning to college or staying in college to obtain additional certifications and degrees on the surface is always a good idea in virtually every instance. That said, it is important to make sure that the degrees and certifications obtained do meet the criteria of a traditional cost-benefit analysis. In other words, it is important to make sure that both the financial cost and opportunity cost are outweighed by the benefits that are attainable as a result of receiving this education.

Secondly, obtaining different and more advanced certifications and trainings are going to be necessary to stay competitive going forward; returning to college or university continues to make sense in this context. No matter what field or employment is analyzed, there is a definitive need and desire among employers to have a workforce that is continuously updated, educated, and trained to contend with emerging trends and forces. Lastly, and while this is not as cut and dry as some would have you believe, there a quantifiable benefit to obtaining a college degree in terms of lifetime earnings as per numerous research reports by the Bureau of Labor Statistics As per the 2019 statistics, holders of advanced degrees earned an average of $1559 per week, whereas individuals with only a high school diploma brought home $749 per week. In other words, advanced degree holders earn more than double that of individuals that only have a high school diploma. Now of course that is only one part of the equation, with the costs and opportunity costs of attending college and obtaining higher education also needing to be factored into the decision-making process.

These benefits have seemingly played out in the number of Americans who are attending college and higher education, with nearly two-thirds of high school graduates or GED holders enrolling in college during the first year of eligibility. Now this book is not about the undergraduate education space, but it is worth noting and understanding these bigger picture trends as your decision around a doctoral program and academic career path are being decided. Specifically, as the number of college enrollees increases over time there are bound to be more—in terms of numbers if not percentage of the population—that obtain and hold advanced degrees. In other words, the competition equipped with advanced degrees will continue to grow larger so this might be as good as time as any to investigate the obtainment of a doctorate in any case.

Even with the increasing debate around the value of a college of education in such as fast-moving and fast-growing economy, the benefits derived from obtaining larger amounts of education are quantifiable and demonstrated across socio-economic and geographic lines. The specifics of this additional education are going to be different depending on what the goal of the individual is, but the underlying message in the same. While the importance of certain college degrees may increase or decrease in importance over time, but the importance of credentials and other information does not appear to be fading or being reduced. Rather as the business landscape continues to develop and shift at an accelerating rate, the development of classes and courses will also need to evolve equally as fast. Practitioners making the transition and shifting to higher education should keep this fact in mind; as long as the business landscape continues to change and evolve there is going to be a need for educational products and services to make these offerings relevant, practical, and helpful.

While this difference does shrink depending on major and type of institutions that are examined, there is a wage premium paid for and associated with college education. This combination of forces has created, and continues to create, a powerful tailwind that has driven millions of Americans to obtain more credentials and education. That said, and as powerful as these trends are, higher education is not immune to bigger picture debates and conversations around the value of education. As these debates continue to make headlines and occupy mindshare of individuals across the political spectrum, institutions will need to make sure the value proposition of their offerings is clear. So as you consider this transition to higher education, will you need to obtain additional education?

The short answer is, probably.

Assessing Academic Positions

Before diving into the different types of academic positions, and different types of doctorates or other education might be necessary, it is worth taking a moment to understand just what these types of positions might mean for your career arc in higher education. Depending on which type of academia and higher education is most appealing to you, you might make a definitive decision or choice or position and institution. This might seem like a rather obvious fact, but the range of practitioner experience can result in certain individuals being more or less interested in certain types of roles. For example, a tax researcher or practitioner might feel more at home in a research-oriented role, even if on the surface the idea of being a "researcher" is not one that initially comes to mind.

Conversely, someone that has a background in business development or some other sort of business acquisition might be more interested or comfortable with a role more aligned with developing programs or working with corporate partners. Especially since there is an ever-increasing number of private sector organizations entering into the content and educational space, the ability of institutions (and professional employed therein) to "speak the same language" as they partner organizations will only increase in importance. In addition, if a practitioner is coming into the academic fold from an especially high-level role or position, these individuals might be more interested in leadership role. No matter what type of role a practitioner comes to higher education from, and what type of role is sought after in the educational space, obtaining additional education and training is most likely going to be required.

While not an entirely constructive answer, it really does depend on what type of position and what type of academic career is most appealing to you at this time. As I was considering making the transition, one of the first things I did—which in hindsight was actually a pretty good idea—was teach as an adjunct at a few local colleges and universities. We will get more into what exactly an adjunct is and where they fit into the higher education conversation later on, but that part-time exposure allowed me to figure out whether or not I actually enjoyed teaching or not. Following that, and coming away convinced that I did actually enjoy the educational and teaching process, I decided to obtain some additional education in the form of a doctoral degree. If making the move from industry to academia is something you are doing to set yourself for a medium to long-term career, many institutions are going to expect—and may even require—that you have some sort of terminal degree. The ominous connotation aside, the terminal degree in most fields is some sort of doctoral degree, but that is where this analysis can take an interesting turn.

Much like the field of accounting has an array of subsets and segments that can be explored by interested individuals, and one of the first decisions to be made is whether or not you want to pursue a traditional PhD or a professional doctorate. Before diving into what some of the differences are, it is important to stress that some institutions and some departments within those institutions tend to have a preference for one type of doctorate of the other, and that is something that should be researched as a part of this decision-making process. Once that has been completed, the remainder of the assessment can be started. The very first thing to do, and something that I wish I had done sooner in my research than I actually did, is to research and analyze exactly what the contents are of each program. Building on those findings, then it is possible to decide whether or not a traditional PhD or professional doctoral degree is the best fit for you.

The Different Types of Doctorates

It is true that when the term doctorate is brought up the baseline assumption among many individuals is that this means a PhD, but that is far from the only option. In fact, for many working professionals that are making the change to higher education, pursuing a non-traditional or non-Ph.D. program might make more sense. Especially for practitioners seeking to make a successful transition from private industry or public accounting to higher education it can come as something as a surprise to find out there are different types of doctoral degrees available. Let's take a look at some of the options out there that are not the "traditional" Ph.D. program and route.

First things first there are two general categories of doctoral degrees that can be used to organize the analysis process; theoretical and applied. A more theoretical doctorate will be a better fit if the plan is to have more a strictly academic career either as a full-time or part-time professor or instructor. An applied doctorate, which are analyzed in more depth below, will most likely be a better fit for individuals seeking to leverage the knowledge gained via a doctorate in more practical or applied settings. In any case, the requirements and expectations are going to be quite similar in nature, with both categories of doctorates requiring intensive research, writing, and coursework. Additionally, there is virtually always going to be some type of requirement for a committee to review the final product (the dissertation) of the individual prior to it receiving final approval.

Breaking down the three (3) most popular types of business doctorates, the following classes appear to be most commonly cited as the most popular for business professionals seeking to obtain terminal degrees. Kicking off this listing is the traditional Ph.D. program which is most likely the one that most individuals are most familiar with. Running in duration of between 5 and 7 years, this traditional or classic doctoral program focuses primarily two phases. In phase one, individuals focus primarily on course work and completing assignments prior to shifting toward the dissertation itself. Following the completion of course work and a final examination, individuals are then allowed the start and complete their dissertation. This bifurcated structure can sometimes lead to individuals getting held up after the final examination, leading to students not completing the doctoral process.

A Doctorate in Business Administration, to the contrary, is purpose built and designed for working professionals seeking to leverage information gained during the doctoral process in a corporate setting. Contrasted against a more traditional Ph.D. program, a D.B.A. program can be thought of as more applied and practitioner information rather than theoretical or conceptual in nature. This is logical given the fact that the idea of a D.B.A. is to imbue the learner with the information equivalent to a Ph.D. program, but to do so in manner that will be of help to a business setting. While the content and information covered will be similar in nature, one differentiating characteristic is that learners are often able to work on both their coursework and dissertation simultaneously. This approach often time means that learners are able to complete the program in a much shorter time frame than would otherwise be possible in a Ph.D. program.

Lastly, the concept of Ed.D. seems to represent a halfway point between a D.B.A. and Ph.D. program, with a more specialized focus on organizational leadership in the higher education space. In other words, an Ed.D. is a type of doctoral program for individuals looking to remain involved and embedded within the higher education space, but not as faculty; rather as an administrator. Clearly, the focus of a doctoral program focused on organizational leadership is going to be slightly different than other programs, which while they might have some components of leadership included therein, are not going to have that as the primary content area. An Ed.D., framed in that context is most likely going to be the best fit for an individual either already working in the higher education space, or someone seeking to enter the area through a non-teaching or research route.

Building on from this initial decision, it is then possible to analyze the program itself to understand what specific characteristics and traits work best with your career, goals, and the outcome you are seeking. Drilling down, but without presupposing to put together an all inclusive or exhaustive listing, the following do represent areas that any potential doctoral seeker should take into account. The first step in this process should be to decide what specifically to assess about the program itself, as well as the desired outcome you are seeking. Perhaps the most logical place to start this assessment is how the program itself is managed and run, both from a student perspective as well as an administrative point of view. For example, in the case of a traditional PhD program the entire process can take nearly 7 years from start to completion, and is usually broken up into two distinct areas. The first section is comprised of course work and classes, which may not seem all that much different from a Masters or other graduate degree program. This second component, the actual dissertation itself, only begins after the course work has been completed, which can lead many an aspiring PhD holder to instead end up as an A.B.D. (all but dissertation). Such an analysis also presupposes that the PhD student is also able to pass any and all comprehensive exams that take place after the completion of course work, but prior to starting a dissertation.

A professional doctorate, which may or may not have a different label depending on the institution in question, may take place and operate in a manner more akin to something a professional could manage. Whereas a traditional PhD is often a full-time endeavor that requires the student to attend classes on a full-time basis, professional doctorates are often designed with working people in mind. From a takeaway perspective, this means that most of the time an individual can pursue a professional doctorate while still working on a full-time basis, which is what I did. Understanding how the program is structured is (1) vitally important to the decision-making process, and (2) something that every program should be more than happy to share either via online FAQs or on-site visits. An additional consideration that should be part of the assessment part at the phase is also what graduates of the program or institution tend to go on to do. Are graduates mainly employed in academia, or is there a balance between academia and industry? What about the graduation rates of the program itself? Especially if you will be self funding this education, entering into a program with subpar graduation rates would not seem like a logical investment of either time or capital.

After determining what to asses about the program, the next step in the process should be to organize and develop and assessment plan, so let's take a brief look at what I did during this part of the assessment process, and hopefully what you can learn from the good and bad decisions that were made along the way. My own personal journey from industry to academia started the same way many other similar transitions have occurred; with a desire to do more, be of more value to the my colleagues and my profession, and to be more engaged with what is going on from bigger picture perspective. For some individuals, this would lead to them returning to school for and advanced degree, but in my case—and since I was already equipped with my desire to obtain a doctoral degree—this led me to instead focus on transitioning myself into an educator and an active part of the academic field.

During the due diligence and looking for programs, there was one thing that I had as a hard and fast rule; the program in question had to be built for working professionals. In other words, a traditional Ph.D. program—ranging from 5–7 years in length and requiring me to quit my job—was out of the question. I was coming to the process as a CPA and (more than) fully employed, but did not have the means to simply exit the workforce for an extended length of time. That base requirement led me to begin my search focusing on executive doctoral programs and distance learning program, which at the time (2012–2013) were still a relatively new product in the marketplace. It is also important to remember what time frame my search was occurring within; pretty much right after the Great Recession was finally starting to loosen its grip on the economy. Many of the for-profit programs that had offered these professional doctoral programs, some rightly and some simply as collateral damage, had suffered financial and reputational damage as a result of the aftermath of the Recession.

Decision Factors

With all of that said, I did ultimately end up settling on a distance learning program offered by a for-profit institution; Capella University. Distance learning programs may have had a substandard connotation or reputation at some point in the past, but with advances in technology and increasing demand these quality considerations seem to be receding into the rearview mirror. While the process did turn out well in the end for me, there are a few things I wish I had done differently during my search; while every individual and program is unique these core factors might be of assistance in navigating these sometimes confusing space. Instead of focusing on specific institution in question, focus on the program or type of program you are most interested in being a part of. Especially if you are transitioning after a break from education, I have found that it sometimes matters more if whether or not the institution and culture therein is a good fit for you and your schedule versus simply focusing on name recognition. Name and brand recognition are incredibly important, but they are not the be-all and end-all of this process. The volume and intensity of work and expectations for any doctorate program are going to be different (and elevated) from the work and expectations you have dealt with previously. Actually speak to someone at the program. This may sound ironic in a business environment dominated by technology and a lack of interpersonal contact, but sometimes the best way to get the answers you actually need is to pick up the phone and speak with someone at the institution you are researching. Online resources and interactive chat bots are fantastic tools that should be utilized at every opportunity, but there is something about the ability to speak with someone that can just be more insightful and rewarding that conversing with a bot. Conversations that are had between you and someone actually at the program or institution in question can also help you get a better handle on the tone and culture of the program. The phrase "tone at the top" is said so often it has become a cliché, but it does matter, especially if you are going to be investing large amounts of time, mental energy, and financial resources on this program. Additionally, and here is something that I cannot stress enough; speaking with a person can lead to tangential or incidental comments or conversations that can answer questions you didn't even know you had.

Take some time to chart out what you actually want to research and discuss at the core of your doctoral research. It may seem like you are putting the cart before the horse if you spend too much time focusing on dissertation topics before you have even started the program, but this is something that is vitally important. One thing that I experienced right at the beginning of my doctoral program is that my initial research idea was not appropriate enough to form the foundation for a dissertation. To my mind, my research idea was (of course) a home run idea that would certainly be a good fit for doctoral research, but upon more rigorous analysis it became evident that there would not be enough evidence, research, and information to support a full length dissertation. Especially for individuals transitioning from industry, this change in mindset is an important one to recognize. Specifically, something that might arise during this thought process is the following. Business professionals and accounting practitioners are used to, for lack of a better word, addressing and solving business-level problems, rather than honing in on one specific issue. Doctoral research, much to chagrin and potential punch line of many jokes, seems to focus one niche and very focused topics and ideas. Understanding that, and eventually becoming comfortable with this idea and approach, can make a tremendous difference in the doctoral journey.

Make sure you understand your obligations. The time and mental energy required of a doctoral program are going to be more intensive and time consuming that virtually any other project or academic initiative you have previously done. When considering what kind of program will work for you, the terminal degree you are striving for, and the ratio of in-person to virtual components, it is important to recognize the reality that—no matter what the case ultimately is—that you will be forced to allocate a substantial amount of time to this project. Making sure that are you are mentally and physically prepared for what this entails is not something that can be overlooked or taken too lightly. As amusing as this might seem it might be worth even consulting online communities and platforms of current doctoral students to see what the highs, lows, opportunities, and challenges. Time management is a skill and competency that is important for any professional, but is also critically important for the successful completion and fulfillment of the doctoral process. Many a potential doctoral dissertation or project has been derailed by a lack of time budgeting and planning on the side of the learner.

Possibly consider looking into your network to see if there is someone else whose experience you might be able to follow. For example, in my network, and due to my adjunct teaching in the past, I had the good luck to work with and collaborate with several academics whom had previously worked in the accounting industry. What this meant is that I did have some people I could speak to, compare notes with, and bounce ideas off of as I strove to make this project work for myself. Clearly not everybody will have such a network to leverage and make use, but it is important to make sure that every potential resource is tapped. Making this transition is a big deal regardless of where you are in your career, but that does not mean that everyone's journey is the same. Even if you do not personally know too many people who have previously completed a doctoral journey there are numerous online and virtual communities that can prove invaluable advice and insights on this topic.

Education is not always going to be the same for every individual seeking to transition to higher education and academia, but it is important for practitioners to recognize the fact that the education is most likely going to be necessary as a part of the transition. Even if a formal doctorate or some other form of terminal degree is not required for this specific situation, there is most likely going to be a certificate or training program that should be taken. Working in the professional landscape does generate an obligation for practitioners to take part in continuing education, but that is only one part of the story. Continuing education is, of course, a part of the professional and fiduciary obligation of any professional, but that does not mean that every individual will be seeking out, or even interested in, the same types of education or information. Realizing this, and understanding that depending on the type of role being sought out and the type of institution in question is simply one of the many decision and choices that practitioners are going to need to make. Seemingly a simple decision, these choices and evaluating the various options are just one of the many multifaceted choices practitioners will have to make during the transition from industry to academia.

Why My Story Is not Universal

While it is true that my name is the on cover of this text, and that you are hopefully reading this because my personal journey and story seemed of some interest to you at some level, it is equally important to realize that my story is not universal. From a higher level, it is obvious that every individual is different and will be approaching this conversation and transition from a unique angle, but that is merely scratching the surface at what is meant by saying that my story is not universal. In my particular situation, I had the good fortune to be embarking on this transition with very manageable student debt, a job that enabled me the flexibility, i.e., I could leave on time most days, and the support network to help me deal with the inevitable bumps and obstacles that came up along the way. Not everyone is going to be entering this transition period with an equivalent situation, and many of you may enter with a situation that is radically different.

No matter what the specifics of your transition are, there does seem to be a grain of truth to following; this is not a decision that should be taken lightly, and you need to truly understand what you are getting into as a result of this choice. Obtaining a doctoral degree is something that less than 2% of the United States population has a doctoral degree. Strip out medical professionals who need to obtain a doctoral degree to practice medicine and the number of non-medical individuals who have earned a doctoral degree continues to plummet further towards 0%. I am not mentioning these stats to be discourage you, or to cause alarm, but to rather illustrate how difficult and unusual the journey you are considering actually is. My advice may be helpful or not helpful depending on your specific circumstances, but either way I do think some of the themes, considerations, and topics that I point out will be of assistance as you make this difficult and long-term decision.

Depending on the specific facet of academia you wish to enter, the obtaining of a doctorate might not be necessary and might even be a misallocation of your time and resources. For example, designing industry-specific content and information across the business landscape might not require a doctorate but would definitely require that the practitioner be up to date and current as it pertains to industry norms. With colleges and universities trying to expand offerings while simultaneously trying to minimize or avoid the hiring of tenure track faculty when possible, the role of niche practitioners or individuals seems to be all the more important moving forward than they had been previously. Either way, and even if formal education is not considered or particular importance in the content of future employment any practitioner seeking to make the transition from industry to academia successfully will need to keep themselves current in order to succeed in a new field and area.

What You Should Consider

As we wrap up this chapter, and acknowledging the reality that you will be weighing a variety of factors as you ultimately make this decision, there are a few general categories that appear reasonable for anyone attempting this transition to consider and take into account. Perhaps the first and most obvious factor is the type of institution you are looking to be associated with as a part of this journey. For-profits, not-for-profits, distance learning, or residency driven (traditional) programs, all possess pros and cons that should be assessed, documented, and weighed as you analyze program options and choices. Second, determining what exactly you are aiming for in terms of an academic career is a seemingly simple decision that has major implications. Examined in more depth in the coming chapter, the career track and arc that you are hoping to obtain a result of this transition is something that needs to be factored into how exactly you evaluate the different options and choices that are available to you as you navigate the fast-changing landscape of academia and higher education at large.

There have been any number of texts written about the considerations and factors that should form a part of how professionals analyze professional transitions, and this book will ideally add something to this conversation. What makes the transition unique, and potentially more complicated and difficult than other professional transitions may be the very different natures of professional and academic work. Both, clearly, are work with respective opportunities and challenges, but the core responsibilities and expectations of this work are vastly different from one another. Incorporating that fact, and illustrating these differences throughout this text are the goals of this book, the facts cited therein, and the anecdotes sprinkled throughout this manuscript.

A discussion of the different types of work expected by academics is a topics that will be revisited throughout this text, and that is for a very simple and straight forward reason; different workloads and expectations have a large impact on both the quality of life for professionals as well as the likelihood of a successful transition. Balancing the workload is a requirement and expectation for all individuals across industry lines, but the dramatic difference between corporate and academic life can result in quite a shock and shift as individuals attempt to do so successfully. Throughout this book, there will be some examples and considerations that any professional seeking to transition successfully should take into account, and hopefully all of those examples do indeed prove helpful, informative, and potentially even a little entertaining.

This book is not meant to provide the one and only way to attempt this transition, or to put forward my experiences as the best way to do so, but to rather form the basis for more advanced and comprehensive conversation. Clearly every individual is different, possess different goals and objectives connected to making the transition to higher education, and must incorporate those individual differences into how the wide array of data connected to this transition is analyzed and connected. With all of that said, there are several universal truths and facts that are connected between the types of work available to individuals and the ability of aspiring practitioners to successfully transition to higher education.

Additionally, one item that should always be part of the analysis and conversation around the field of higher education and the transition that is necessary for individuals seeking to make it successfully is the underlying reality that things are going to change more often than you might initially think or realize. For example, my own personal journey has taken me to several different institutions, different types of institutions, and a few different roles along the way; that is perfectly fine and normal given how fluid business and education are on both a micro and macro basis. Although the phrase "the more things change the more they stay the same" does have some merit it is also worth noting that many things have changed and taken different forms over time, including how learning takes place.

Reflection Questions

1. Based on your own experiences, what is your current opinion of online education versus in person course offerings and does this differ depending on the level of education being assessed?
2. In assessing the different types of doctoral programs and options, where does the "traditional" PhD offering fall along the spectrum of applicability and relevance to the current marketplace?
3. Regarding continuing education, does it seem like a full doctoral program is truly necessary or would a combination of certificates and other courses be sufficient?

Additional Readings

1. Forbes—Disruptive Transformation, A Way to Change Higher Education—https://www.forbes.com/sites/barbarakurshan/2020/07/29/disruptive-transformation-a-way-to-change-higher-education/#7049225a3a4d.
2. InsideHigherEd—Ph.D. vs Ed.D.—https://www.insidehighered.com/blogs/gradhacker/phd-vs-edd.
3. US News—How Online Classes Work: 10 FAQs—https://www.usnews.com/higher-education/online-education/articles/2018-01-16/how-do-online-classes-work-10-frequently-asked-questions.
4. Elsevier—5 secrets to surviving (and thriving in) a PhD program—https://www.elsevier.com/connect/5-secrets-to-surviving-and-progressing-in-a-phd-program.
5. Wharton—How To Choose A Ph.D. Program—https://doctoral.wharton.upenn.edu/selecting-phd-program/.

CHAPTER 3

The (Career) Options

Introduction

Perhaps the best place to start analyzing the opportunities and possibilities connected to employment as a member of academia and the higher education space is the distinction between full-time and part-time work. Not only is this approach closest to an understanding and analysis of work in the corporate landscape, it also mirrors an approach and pathway that most people can seek to emulate and integrate into any specific career plan or arc. Last, but certainly not least, the distinction between part time and full time is also something that is connected to how I entered the higher education landscape and space. In addition, this particular path is how I continue to encourage other practitioners to experiment and attempt to understand just how different industry can be from other aspects of the workforce, including higher education.

As mentioned previously, my entry into higher education and academia began with the proverbial dipping of a toe into the education workforce as an adjunct, or part-time employee, which also represents a pathway that virtually anyone can follow as the transition is attempted and completed. Starting while I was still actually completing my doctoral degree, I had the great opportunity to be able to adjunct at several of the largest universities in the (great) state of New Jersey. Returning to my alma mater of FDU enabled me the opportunity to teach both in-person classes and fully

S. Stein Smith, *Shifting from Accounting Practitioner to Academia*, Palgrave Studies in Accounting and Finance Practice,
https://doi.org/10.1007/978-3-030-67546-2_3

online courses across multiple colleges at the university. Building on this also enabled me to gain invaluable experience in terms of dealing with students, running a class, and dealing with the, sometimes, contentious process of final grades (depending on how the student in question was performing).

Doing this for several years while still working full time in industry also enabled me the opportunity and privilege to see which aspect of my accounting career was most enjoyable, rewarding, and—to be honest—fun. Building on this exploratory aspect of my entrance into the higher education field also allowed me to expand my search and job experience to Montclair State University. While the courses at the FDU tended to be focused on undergraduate course via both in-person and online course formats, the classes at Montclair focused on MBA students. Teaching at this level, especially as someone who did not fit the "traditional" mold of a college professor, was a unique opportunity and a challenge. On the one hand, a challenge was ensuring that I could hold my own in a classroom where many of the individuals may have been my age or even older. An opportunity, related to this very same challenge, was the fact that this provided me an intellectual challenge and an opportunity to have in-depth conversations and dialogue between myself and my students. This may or may not apply equally apply to everyone attempting this transition, but it is something worth mentioning since—in any case—it is important to be aware of your audience. Students are, after all, your audience and your crowd so playing to their strengths would seem to be a logical course of action.

There is also the following that should be incorporated in the decision-making process; that although the stereotype of college students may be that most college students are aged 18–22, live on campus, and are relatively unencumbered, the reality can be far different. Given the importance of continuing education, expectations on the side of employers that employees will continue to upskill and acquire new information for the workplace, and other societal pressures these stereotypes are continuing to fade away. Different types of students, in and of themselves, will not make a specific class easier or harder to handle or instruct, but it is something that needs to be built in how courses and content are developed. Every institution is different, but that underlying trend—toward more non-traditional students filling classrooms—is something that does not appear ready to fade away or become less important. Put simply, it is important that anyone attempting this transition be aware of the constituent groups that, may or may not be as impactful on a specific day, but are important to the overall discourse.

An Alternative Approach

This is not to say that a traditional teaching-focused career is the only way to gain some experience and boots on the ground practice, and depending on the work schedule of the individual this may or may not even be possible. Some other options for practitioner trying to figure out if (1) this transition and changing career path is a good idea, and (2) what specific subset of higher education is the best fit at large include, but are not limited to the following. Coming in as a guest speaker to classes at an alma mater, working with local universities and colleges to come in as a representative of your organization are both good ways to gain exposure to both the university mindset and way of doing business, as well as the classroom experience.

Something else that can be used as an approach to experiment with more of an instructor role is to work with an external professional educational service provider. These are discussed in more depth later on in this book, but there are any number of options for individuals seeking to fill a role of a professional educator. While not an exact equivalent or match for the higher education space, several of the core components connected to preparation, delivery, and feedback received can be used as a proxy for how a transition might ultimately play out.

The Big Three

Any dialogue around careers in higher education must also take into account and realize that there is not a one-size-fits-all approach, nor is there even a one-size-fits-most approach that will work well for most individuals. The primary focus of my commentary on this issue focuses on what is probably the most well-known type of academic career; one that is primarily focused on teaching and instruction. While this might be the well-known career path for aspiring academics, this does not mean that it is the only one, the correct one for any given individual, or even the one that is most rewarding.

Teaching and instruction remain an important component of what every educators or institution affiliated with educational services will have to provide. Remember, no matter how stellar the research or how well run the program in question, if students are not properly educated and equipped with the knowledge they need to succeed, other facets fade in importance. The importance of teaching and instruction, even in the face of increasing pressure to publish and produce research, manifests itself in two distinct ways. First, every institution and service provider generally have some kind of way or ranking for the best, highest ranked, or most well-received instructor at their institution. Second, educational associations and groups routinely have regional, national, or subject specific awards that recognize highly accomplished or recognized instructors across the spectrum. Setting aside the teaching-focused career options for the time being, there are two other general categories of academic careers that might be of interest.

Research is always going to be a part of any career transition into higher education, and depending on the type of institution and type of work that is most enjoyable the ratio of teaching to research may vary somewhat. Research heavy roles, although not always traditionally linked to business faculty, certainly do exist in the business arena and take several different forms. Firstly, and perhaps most obviously, is the traditional idea of research that makes use of public data, privately obtained information, and/or survey information that is generated as part of original research efforts. This is most likely what comes to mind when the idea of research is mentioned, but is not the only way that research can manifest itself. An additional option is research conducted in conjunction or as a collaborative effort with a private sector or nonprofit partner organization. Such collaborations actually happen more often that might otherwise be believed, and can be quite engaging and interesting for all parties involved. Some of the most cutting edge research and publications that come out of the marketplace are a result of collaborative efforts between members of the university space and private sector organizations.

A third option or third way in which individuals can become employed in higher education with less of a teaching focus is to instead focus more on the administrative and running of an institution rather than the instructional area. Clearly the running and administration of a college or university is similar to the managing of any large enterprise; there are going to be personality conflicts, budgetary issues, and content considerations. One iterative step that might make more sense if the idea of a more administrative role sounds appealing yet daunting would be to begin this transition by focusing on the developing and management of a single program or program area. For example, accepting the responsibility of managing or overseeing a specific master's program or other facet of a school or larger program might be a good way to see whether or not such an approach is something you would enjoy.

The Constituent Groups

Prior to diving into the specific faculty options that are available to aspiring academics entering the higher education marketplace it is also important to acknowledge that there a wide array of individuals that are involved the conversation. Taking the different views and perspectives of these people into account is important for any number of reasons, but primarily for the impact that these individuals have on the educational conversation. From tenure, to funding, to grant requirements, to the holistic health of the institution as a whole, understanding the mix of individuals involved in the conversation is important. Let's take a look at a few of the constituencies that are universally a part of the dialogue that surrounds higher education and need to be part of any analysis connected to this career transition. This is not dissimilar to any business decision or analytical process; it is an unusual event that only one specific audience or group of individuals is consulted during a decision-making process. Think about, would any viable business enterprise remain viable for very long if it was unable to property identify who or whom its customer is? While the types of constituents will be different in the higher education space, which makes logical sense, the importance of balancing these different groups cannot be overstated. As reiterated throughout this book, the increased competition and crowded landscape for educational services make servicing these different groups a priority for all parties involved. Let's take a look at a few of the many groups that have an important role to play in this space.

First and foremost are the students that are actually at the institution in question. Beginning with the student body makes sense from any number of perspectives, but perhaps most obviously because without students there is no need for the institution at large. Being beyond this rather obvious connection, it is also important to examine what type of student body—commuter or resident—is present at the institution. These different categories of students are going to have very different needs, wants, and expectations of both the faculty and the rest of the institution. For example, commuter students are less likely—on average—to take advantage of office hours, tutoring services, and other academic services because they are not on campus as often as resident students. Integrating the breakdown of commuter versus resident students into course planning and what ancillary services you offer is something every aspiring academic should factor into syllabi and course planning.

Fellow faculty, administrators, and staff and colleagues. This is where the proverbial rubber meets the road in terms of actionable intelligence for you as a reader of this text. Examined in depth in the coming pages the different faculty categories are going to be held to different levels of expectations, but that is only part of the story. Regardless of what type of faculty is being discussed there are a few items that every academic is going to desire at an institution. Job security, the ability to research and publish in areas of interest without fear or repercussions, and teaching schedules that align with their schedule are all items that are going to be items that faculty are going to expect. A core conflict, although that might seem like a strong word, that can arise between faculty desires and student expectations is the fact that these two parties may have conflicting—or often opposing—scheduling desires. Linking back to the first point, understanding the student body is an important first step in making sure that these two constituencies are both satisfied.

Higher level administrators. It may be fashionable to assign the vast majority of blame or responsibility for the issues associated with higher education with the rise and growth of the administrative class, but a more nuanced approached may make more sense. Although in some cases there may be some acrimony between members of the administration and members of the faculty that is not always the case. From an administrative point of view, these individuals are tasked with balancing the often conflicting needs of students, faculty, and external accrediting bodies. In order to balance these needs, which may or may not be in alignment with the expectations and desires of other university groups. Whatever personal opinions or personalities or present, the faculty, staff, and administrators do need to work in conjunction to propel the institution forward successfully.

Scholarships, funding, and other sources of financing. The increasing cost of college tuition is not something that has happened in a vacuum; increasing costs is a virtually inevitable result of the multiple pressures and expectations of various stakeholder groups. In and of itself, increasing costs for a good or service is not a bad thing, but there needs to be a way to connect the price and value exchanged for the service. A primary reason as to why this connection seems to have broken down is the presence of the multitude of scholarships and other financing options available to students. This is not to say that these financing options are a bad thing; they serve an invaluable purpose to assist students who are either traditionally disfranchised or unable to attend for financial reasons. That said, the wholescale subsidization of college tuition and other costs by—in large part—the federal government does distort the price and volume relationship.

Employers, local organizations, and other businesses. This may seem like an obvious constituent group to be taken into account, but according to some market participants, colleges, and universities should operate without any influence or impact from the business community. Such an attitude, as appealing as it may be in some meeting rooms and conceptual debates, does not match up with the reality on the ground nor the need of students that are currently in the classroom. At the end of the day the goal for many students that obtain a college education or degree is to then leverage those credentials for a position in the workplace. Working with the business community, be it on a local level or a national/global level, is an integral part of how higher education will continue to evolve and shift going forward.

Balancing the needs of an array of stakeholders is not something that is unique to higher education, colleges, or universities in any way. Any large institution, be they governmental, private sector, or higher education in nature, consists of larger numbers of individuals that all have varying expectations, needs, and desires. What makes higher education potentially more difficult to effectively manage, however, is the fact that the ultimate customer of higher education can be difficult to accurately define. From my personal experience I had a professor in graduate school who would not label students (including myself at the time) as customers of the university; to his mind that cheapened the purpose of a university education. Depending on how one wishes to look at the higher education landscape, there can be several classes and groups that may classify as customers or end users. Students are clearly consumers of the educational product but classifying students as customers may potentially misrepresent the relationship between students and educators. Although students are the primary individuals that receive the educational services, they are not consumers or customers in the same sense that a customer of a retailer would be thought of. Instead of simply paying for a good or service and receiving a product in a transaction there should be a relationship between members of the educational community.

That is not to say that providing a satisfactory customer experience is not required or optional for colleges and universities; far from it. Framing the context and importance of placing students with careers and jobs, and jobs that are actually related to their areas of study and research at university, has become increasingly important alongside both the increasing costs of college and global competition. Students (like any other group of people), by and large, will almost have something to complain about or have something that forms the basis for gripes, but that is not the same as not providing a product or service that delivers what had been promised. Addressing the needs of both students and employers, both of whom should be considered customers and users of the educational experience, is something that needs to move from the back burner to the front burner going forward.

Who Is Your Customer?

A logical place to start the conversation is connected to who exactly are the consumers or customers of is with the students of the organization. Some academics, however, seem to bristle at the conflation of students with consumers or customers in a traditional sense; the transactional process often associated with commercial enterprises does not quite fit the model established by higher education. For example, when an individual goes to the movie theater and purchases a ticket and some snacks for the film, that is the end of the transaction. The consumption of the film and ancillary products is almost a byproduct of the underlying exchange of value; higher education is by its very nature different from other transactions. In an ideal environment, and what many educational advocates consider the best case scenario, is that institutions and their students have an ongoing relationship. This continuing relationship can take the form of alumni engagement, returning back to volunteer for on campus activities, or returning as a guest lecturer, but the importance is that both parties involved have a positive mindset and relationship even after graduation has occurred. Creating this symbiotic and positive ongoing connection is something that some institutions and individuals can struggle with from a business perspective; once a student has graduated there is limited up-front monetary value to be gathered from these individuals. Underestimating the value of this continuing relationship, however, can come back in the form negative externalities, a lack alumni engagement, and an artificially depressed fundraising or gifting environment.

On top of students being considered customers there are also other external end users and recipients of institutional data that are customers in other ways of the information and data produced by organizations;

accrediting agencies. Much like how food and other consumer facing organizations need to obtain certification and approval to continue operating in the economic landscape, institutions of higher education do need to obtain and retrain certification to do so. In order for this process to work, there is a periodic expectation and requirement that institutions will compile and report certain types and classes of information to the accrediting bodies. Framed in this context, it is reasonable to assume that these entities would also take the form of customers or consumers in the same way that regulators are consumers and customers of financial services information. This relationship, however, does have a unique attribute and angle that is unique to how institutions interact with the regulatory landscape and individual regulators; in order for institutions to operate effectively, to stay open, and as deliver services as advertised, regulators must be satisfied. Examining the importance of this regulatory-institution dynamic and relationship it also seems important to understand just what the impact of satisfying this end user group can entail for an institution. Depending on the regulatory requirements, the amount of work and documentation required and necessary for a satisfactory accreditation can occupy large amounts of faculty and administrative time. The sheer array and volume of accrediting bodies can further complicate the situation, so balancing the documentation and reporting requirements of these various regulatory bodies is a shared duty of faculty, staff, and executive leadership.

Speaking of external users, the governmental bodies that oversee the physical and geographic operations of a specific institution should also be factored into any analysis. Perhaps most clearly illustrated at the community college level, there is certainly a role for local, regional, and state governments to play in the educational conversation. Politics aside, although that is an inevitable side effect of involving local governmental groups; there are several ways in which regional or state governmental groups can exert influence over the institution in question. First and foremost, the institution might be encouraged to develop and support job training or other vocational programming in conjunction with local businesses, chambers of commerce, or other local business associations. Secondly, and here is where the collaboration between different partners can become tricky, is that either private or public universities might wish to establish pipelines to enable students—for example—to attend one community college and then transfer credits at some point to either a local private university or public university in the space. In any case, the collaboration or cooperation between different institutions and the governmental bodies in the area can generate additional layers of complexity that need to be considered.

Specifically, the connections and influence brought to bear on institutions of higher education by different external stakeholder groups—politicians, community residents, corporate partners, and other external constituents—is something that needs to be acknowledged. If any stakeholder is contributing financial capital, time, energy, or other sorts of resources it is not unreasonable that these stakeholders will expect their respective voices to be heard. Balancing these sometimes conflicting voices of various external stakeholder and membership groups represents a role for anyone involved in the higher education space. Practitioners, potentially even more so than established academics, have an important role to play with regard to navigating this multi-stakeholder environment. Amplifying this importance is the role and influence that the loan and scholarship industry play with regard to higher education. Put simply, the sources of financial resources, which can oftentimes include governmental institutions and parties, must be part of the conversation around financing higher education.

Something else that should be taken into account, especially is the development of new courses, programs, or certificates is being considered, is the impact that new offerings will have on the customer analysis. In a more traditional setting or conversation the customer analysis will generally follow the above outlined groups and format, but if there are programs, courses, or offerings that are being developed with a more job focused outcome as one of the criteria, this can create additional complications. For example, if an accounting firm—or any organization for that matter—agrees to co-fund, co-sponsor, or otherwise assist with the building out of a program or certificate, these partner organizations will have certain expectations. Specifically, there might be certain topics of ideas that the partner organization would like to see covered, taught, or otherwise included into the conversation

The Loan and Scholarship Industry

Prior to diving directly into a conversation around the role that loans and scholarships play in the higher education space, it is important to note that this space is changing rapidly. Student debt in the United States alone exceeds \$1.5 trillion, and as a direct result of that there are numerous alternative financing arrangements that have begun to emerge, in addition to various political attempts to cancel or otherwise reduce the burden student debt places on individuals. This section should be taken as an initial introduction and overview of this complicated, fast changing, and somewhat controversial aspect of higher education.

This might seem like a slightly out of place topic to discuss in a text attempting to serve as a guide and helpful resource for practitioners seeking to transition from industry to academia, but it is something that needs to be spoken aloud. In the United States alone there is outstanding student debt in excess of $1.5 trillion (and climbing) as of this writing; assuming that this has no impact on the decisions being made at institutions of higher education would be naive. Student debt, of course, is part of the educational process, and always has been something that all parties involved have had to be aware of. It seems, however, that this conversation may be reaching a tipping point and if one looks under the surface, this fact may actually represent one of the largest disruptive trends in the space. Put simply, if a product or service becomes so expensive that it is out of reach for the majority of potential customers, this does not set the industry or individual entity up for success moving forward. So, what does this have to do with practitioners making the switch or transition from private industry to higher education? Why should somebody considering this transition focus too much on the conversation surrounding student debt? Let's take a look at some of the second and third order ramifications that this—labeled by some—student debt bubble can and already is having.

First and most obviously is that the topic of student debt has reinvigorated the conversation and debate around the alleged value of a college degree. While it is a simple matter to look up potential future earnings associated with a degree, and this certainly holds merit, that is only the first part of the required analysis. Taking a next step approach to this analysis it becomes clear that the impact of increasing student debt can take several different forms and can actually alter the makeup and direction of an institution. Ask anyone how has ever taught a college course within the last several decades and the importance of enrollment confirmations will probably come up as an additional piece of compliance paperwork that is a necessary evil. Confirming that students have attended, and that they have participated in an academic activity, or engaged in the learning experience, is something that every instructor has to handle at some point during the semester. These confirmations, however, are not aligned with any educational processes, but rather the flow of federal funding connected to institutions and individual courses. Compliance and funding are part of every business, but some would argue that such an overt focus on these trends diminishes the focus and priority of learning.

Second, and something that has been documented in numerous books over the last several decades, is the somewhat predictable effect that the availability of plentiful funds at low cost has on the financial status of certain programs and institutions. Put simply, as the amount of funding continues to increase over time, there is going to something akin to scope creep that begins to manifest itself in various ways at institutions. This is not to say that ancillary programs do not add any value to the college or university in question, but these tangential ideas do represent potential competition in terms of funding and institutional support. For example, are rock climbing activities and walls equally as valuable to the educational experience as courses focusing on economics, literature, or computer science? Any practitioners seeking to make a transition from industry to academia must be aware of the growing number of programs and activities that might not be related to business programs. Even more so than other academic areas or economic sectors, business school and education is more conducive to continuous education, training, and programs that can be developed to meet market needs. Specifics will vary, but the development of certificates and other non-traditional programs seem like logical evolutions and outgrowths of this process.

Bringing my own personal experience into this conversation, I have personally had the opportunity to develop numerous certificates and programs at a number of institutions. These include, but are not limited to, some of the following. I led the development, creation, and instruction of a CPA preparation program, which I think is critically important for any accounting program. No matter what the personal opinion of an individual is regarding the CPA exam, it continues to be held at recognized as the gold standard for accounting professionals. Granted, the program that I led the instruction of did not attract hundreds of students, but offering the program was a rewarding experience that I have strived to replicate at any number of different places. Following my transition to my current role, I am leading the effort to develop, market, and offer a certificate and/or course program connected to blockchain technology for accounting professionals. In addition to representing a personal passion of mine, blockchain technology is increasingly being recognized as—potentially—the most game changing technology in accounting over the last several decades. Being able to offer education, training, and development opportunities connected to emerging trends and technologies will only increase in important moving forward.

Last but not least, are the increasingly hardnosed and pointed conversations that virtually everyone in the higher education space increasingly need to answer and address with regard to the cost-benefit tradeoff of attending college and university in the first place. The costs of higher education have been dissected and analyzed ad nauseam during the last several years, but it is an important part of the broader economic conversation that is happening. Practitioners may or may not have expertise related to the inner workings and machinations of the specific institution in question, but the ability explain and justify the current levels of budgetary spend and allocation should not come as anything new. Bringing additional financial expertise, familiarity, and comfort with regard to the discussion of budgets, costs, and associated benefits are certainly areas that practitioners can assist with from the very beginning.

With all of that set aside for a moment, we can start examining some of the specific job opportunities available at these different institutions.

Types of Academic Roles

Adjunct Teaching—Pros and Cons

As with any other job or employment opportunity there are pros and cons to adjunct teaching, and depending on the specific career path, adjunct teaching may be a better or worse fit for you, so let's take a look at some of these pros and cons. Like anything else in ones professional life, there are pros and cons, as well as opportunities and challenges that are connected to taking a new position. This is why many practitioners, including myself, tend to begin an academic transition and journey with some adjunct roles. While temporary and no guarantee of future employment, this subset of academia does allow aspiring academics to experiment with teaching and higher education, as well as trying to figure out whether or not they actually enjoy the process itself.

An interesting development regarding the increased utilization of adjunct instructors in higher education is the reality that in some cases adjunct faculty members have become quite involved in the operation of an institution. In other words, and despite the fact that virtually all adjuncts are compensated on a flat-fee, or course-by-course basis, that there may be additional expectations and work outside of merely teaching the class itself. Every institution is different, but this is yet another excellent reason to make sure you perform your due diligence on the institution before interviewing or accepting a position.

Starting with the pros, the first and most obvious one is perhaps the flexibility and opportunities that arise from adjunct teaching. Actually, one of my doctoral advisors at Capella had constructed a portfolio of adjunct teaching opportunities that had provided a steady, yet flexible, source of income that had persisted for several decades. Many professionals teach on an adjunct basis for decades, including some of the most interesting and engaging professors I had during my undergraduate and graduate career. My own experience as an adjunct was also relatively positive in nature, as I was able to teach at a number of institutions without tying myself down to any one specific institution or department. Gathering this breadth of expertise is important, as with any new career, because it allows you to gain the necessary "on the ground" experience to make the correct decision going forward. As with any opportunity or career option, however, there are cons that do need to be acknowledged and discussed in any book discussing the academic job market.

Adjunct professors, by the very nature of this subset of professorship, represent a flexible and on-demand workforce that can be flexed up and down in demand to enrollments. This very flexibility, referenced previously as one of the positives associated with adjunct work, can also result in a situation where institutions overly rely on part time or adjunct professors to teach the majority of classes. As someone who made the transition successfully from private industry to academia, I can certainly see the benefit of having individuals in the classroom that have professional experience. That said, and cited by numerous studies, it is increasingly apparent that some college administrators may sought to leverage this lower cost and more flexible pool of labor to augment course offerings as well as driving bottom line results.

A quick Google search and analysis of headlines related to the discussion around adjuncts yields several core themes, regardless of what source is actually cited and or used. First, it seems to be quite difficult—and this was verified in my experience as well—for individuals employed as adjunct professors to be hired as full-time professors in any capacity. In some cases this may suit individuals quite fine, but if someone is teaching as an adjunct following a doctoral degree with the hopes of a full-time position, this can lead to a very frustrating and demoralizing process of rejection and continuous part-time work. Throw in the fact that adjuncts are usually compensated at a small percentage of full-time faculty, and it becomes clear how a combative conversation and landscape can be created and sustained between different constituent groups.

Combative headlines aside, there are certainly benefits that can be generated for all parties involved through increased involvement of practitioners as adjunct faculty members. For example, an individual might not want to develop or have to instruct a number of basic, introductory, or more generalized courses, but this same person might be more than happy to build out, develop, and instruct a specialized or more focused course that is closely connected to areas of expertise or background. Adjunct faculty play an important role in the educational conversation, do tend to teach a significant number of courses, and often bring a much needed dose of reality and market experience to the classroom. As stated above many practitioners dip their toes into academia through adjunct teaching, and depending on where an individual finds themselves this might be an ideal place to begin the conversation.

Lecturer

Depending on the type of institution are most interested in, or the type of career arc you are planning for yourself, once you do successfully transition from industry to higher education, the idea of a lecturer position can be very appealing. In essence, and what the case is at many institutions, is that lecturers are considered almost a hybrid between tenure track and contract faculty (more on both of those in the coming pages). Many lecturer tracks are compensated at equivalent levels to other members of the full-time faculty, with the primary distinction being that in the majority of cases there is no publishing requirement associated with lecturer tracks. Instead, and differentiating this career track from other full-time faculty options is the focus on teaching; many lecturers teach between 4 or 5 courses during a given semester, versus the 2 or 3 (although in some cases 4) that other full-time faculty members are tasked with instructing.

On paper, and especially at first glance, the lack of publication and conference presentation requirements may seem to make the lecturer track an ideal position for someone transitioning from industry to academia. This position is not entirely without merit; simply being tasked with talking about topics that you already know quite a bit about can seem like a simple enough task. With all of that said, however, is it important to remember two important things about lecturer track faculty positions. Even though many lecturers successfully teach for years or decades at a particular institution, there is no guarantee of continued employment after the contractual period expires. In other words, and closer to other corporate positions, this type of role is dependent on continued renewal. Additionally, depending on when the courses you are teaching actually take place, you may end up working a near equivalent in terms of hours in your lecturer role as you might have at an industry position.

It is worth noting that there does seem to be a rising percentage of courses being taught by lecturers or contract faculty (discussed next) at many large institutions, and this continues to exist and grow for a few reasons. First, the lack of research and service requirements associated with lecturer positions does tend to appeal to practitioners who—frankly—might not want to invest the time and mental energy writing academic pieces and/or traveling to conferences. Additionally, there does tend to be less formalized or terminal educational degrees and requirements necessary to apply for and obtain a lecturer level position than tenure track or tenured position. Not meant to be disparaging in any way, but simply acknowledging the following reality; individuals with MBAs or other Master's level degree are usually quite a good fit for lecturer positions and the courses that institutions are looking to fill in terms of coverage.

Depending on the institution in question the role of lecturers can vary quite a bit, ranging from being—basically—supercharged adjuncts to a position and status closer to tenure track or tenured faculty. Ensuring that the roles, responsibilities, and other duties are understood upfront, as well as the opportunities for expanded engagement, are understood upfront is something that cannot be overstated when it comes to finding an appropriate role and position within an institution.

Contract Faculty

The idea of contract faculty was not a concept that I was initially familiar with, nor was it one that I had ever heard of before it became my entry point into the field of higher education. Boiling it down to the core essence of the idea, the idea of a contract faculty member is to provide both the faculty member and the institution with an increased sense of security and connection between both members and individuals. My experience as a contract faculty member, at Rutgers University, gave me a fantastic opportunity to land a position at a prestigious institution where I might not have otherwise been able to land a full time, tenure track opportunity. As a member of a contract faculty you have, pretty much, the same roles, responsibilities, and duties of a tenure track faculty member, with one important difference. Depending on the institution in question, there are an array of options in terms of contract length, from 1-year, 3-year, or 5 years. Personally, I am aware of multiple contract faculty members that have been employed for decades under this model, but this does not mean that this will also occur for every individual.

There are definitive positives to being employed as a contract faculty member, including the job security that comes with a multi-year contract, and this can definitely be an excellent stepping stone for newly minted doctoral graduates or individuals trying to transition from industry to academia. Specifically, this also enabled me to land a position at a great institution with fantastic individuals that helped me grow, develop, and become a more well-rounded faculty member. I still collaborate with some of my former colleagues to this very day! Building on the great work and collaborative opportunities I had at this institution also led me to obtain a full-time tenure track role. That said, that does not mean that there are no negatives or potential drawbacks associated with a contract faculty role. Perceived by some circles as a step down from tenure track faculty, at some institutions contract faculty are not as fully appreciated or as involved in faculty governance as tenure track faculty may be. Every institution is different, but that is something to take into account as you are analyzing the opportunities open for you.

One item to keep in minds is that in can be difficult, if not impossible, to transition from one faculty classification to another subset of faculty, and this is something that should be factored in when you are applying for initial positions. From a practical manner this means that the first institution you are able to apply to might not be the one that you are able to make a career at, and this is something that many aspiring academics—regardless of background—have a difficult time accepting. This is something that I had to realize on my own, and while frustrating at the time, I came to realize that is not uncommon in academia.

Especially after going through the rigorous interview process, which can stretch over months and multiple on-site visits, it can be frustrating to hit this proverbial wall—either implicitly or explicitly—as you try to evolve, develop, and grow into this new career area. Contract faculty or lecturer track faculty can hit this wall quite often under the following fact pattern. After starting at an institution as a lecturer or contract faculty, this individual decides to go back—usually while informing the department or school—and complete a doctoral degree. This individual may do so with the implicit or unspoken hope that this doctoral degree is the key toward being "upgraded" to a tenure track position, but this might not ever happen.

Such an arrangement might seem unusual to some, but actually is not as odd or as unusual as it might initially appear. In many cases, individuals that are seeking to get a promotion or otherwise elevate themselves have to either transfer internally within an organization, or even leave the organization for a new one in order to receive either the (1) increased compensation, or (2) higher level position that they desire. Framed in that content it should not come as much of a surprise that sometimes faculty members have to transition and leave the current institution at which they are employed to obtain the position or level they are seeking out. While this might be the ideal outcome or the outcome that is most desired, it is one that needs to be realized as a potential reality.

Tenure Track Opportunities

The conversation around tenure, obtaining tenure, and the processes by which individuals can obtain tenure is a topic that is going to be revisited throughout this text, and that is for a very straightforward reason. Tenure track opportunities and the associated implications of tenure have an outsized impact on institutions across the academic space because of the influence that tenured or tenure track individuals play an important role in the instruction, student retention, and governance of the institution at large.

Perceived by many as the top tier, golden ring, or otherwise end goal of any aspiring academic career track, a tenure track opportunity and career is also the position that is most coveted and difficult to achieve for many aspiring academics. Especially in some fields that are not growing as quickly as they previously had, or taking place at prestigious institutions, the competition for these limited number of openings is intense. Without diving too much into the nitty-gritty, these openings and opportunities are also heavily influenced by the demographics of the areas in which they operate within. Taking any analysis from a population, migration, or demographic perspective, there is one fundamental fact that cannot remain ignored; population growth and the growth associated with colleges and universities are oriented and pivoted toward the south, southwest, and western regions of the United States versus the northeast. Compounding this is the reality is that many of the oldest and most well-established institutions are located in the northeast, and continue to attract talent from around the globe. Not meant to be discouraging in nature, but it is a reality that should be factored into the decision-making process underway as institutions, programs, and roles and are analyzed; applying for a job requires equally focus on where as opposed to what opportunity.

The Tenure Journey

My journey toward a tenure track institution was one that took quite a bit of time to actually become realized, and hopefully some of the opportunities and challenges that have happened to me would be of benefit to you as your journey continues. First things first, however, is a separation between myth from reality in terms of how a tenure track opportunity functions and interacts with other aspects of the academic landscape. Many individuals entering the academic landscape for the first time may be surprised that there are so many different options and tracks for academic professionals. In conversations that I have had with people in and outside of academia, it comes as a surprise that not all professors or academics are the same in terms job responsibilities and obligations.

Something else that needs to be taken into account, especially if the aspiring academic or academic in transition part of one of the younger generations, is the length of time that the tenure process can take. While it might not take a full "ten years" to obtain tenure, it may take a much longer time than many professionals are used investing into a certain project, and that can be both a good and a bad thing. On the one hand, most professionals are used to dealing with periodic deadlines and assessments, but these assessments usually occur on a monthly, quarterly, or at the longest end, on an annual basis. There are pros and cons to this approach, the scope of which have filled management books for years, but the reality is that professional assessments, promotions, and feedback happening on a consistent basis.

On the other hand, academia tends to move at a much slower pace than most professional settings, which can of course give professionals and practitioners much needed breathing room to develop and mature as professionals. This slower pace of development and interaction, however, can also lead to some frustration among recently transitioned individuals; this level of frustration is amplified if tenure track opportunities and positions are factored into the equation. Frustration aside, this longer term during which an individual is evaluated and judged may require a fundamental shift in how a professional plans workload, interaction with other colleagues and institutions, and producing content to be reviewed by peers and superiors. Building on that, and adding to the general confusion that can all too often rear its head, there is also a substantial amount of confusion among practitioners and aspiring academics as to what exactly a tenure track opportunity entails. So let's take a deep dive into what exactly the tenure process entails, and hopefully do a little myth busting along the way.

Let's do some myth busting on some of the most common misconceptions about tenure track faculty as well as the opportunities and challenges that come with this type of academic opportunity.

> Myth #1—Everyone that is on the tenure track will automatically receive tenure and become tenured faculty.

This myth is completely false and is something that potential academics need to be very much aware of if they do select a tenure track path in their academic career. Simply obtaining a tenure track position, while certainly a victory in its own right, is only the first step toward a successful tenure track appointment. To amplify the pressure that such an appointment can bring to bear is the reality that, if tenure is not granted, the academic in question almost always has to leave the institution and seek alternative employment.

> Myth #2—Tenure track requirements are the same everywhere.

This myth is not completely false, but can lead to a false sense of familiarity or comfort with the tenure even if it is not entirely true either. Generally speaking, tenure requirements consist of a combination of factors that are taken into account, and include assessments connected to the service performed by the faculty members, teaching evaluations, and research. Even though these requirements and evaluative criteria are generally the same regardless of the institution in question, the specific factors and weighting of these factors are almost always different from institution to institution.

> Myth #3—Tenure track faculty are treated differently than other faculty members at the institution.

Tackling this myth can be tricky, because, as discussed there is quite a bit of conversation and debate connected to the future of higher education, the types of faculty employed at the institution, and how these debates connect to the future of institutions at large. Depending on the institution and department in question, however, there are differences depending as to how involved certain faculty members in different aspects of university and institutional governance. Compared to adjunct faculty, for example, tenure track and tenured faculty do tend to have a larger stake in the future of in college or university, and so are more likely to be involved in committee and over governance efforts.

> Myths, busted.

Myths about faculty, teaching, research, and the role that faculty members play in the current and future of an institution in question are numerous, so we just focused on a few of the more prominent myths here. Depending on the institution in question, which we are going to be diving into in more depth going forward, there are also additional considerations that needed to be weighted by the practitioner in question. Regardless of the specific myth or question that is raised as a part of this academic transition, the underlying message is consistent across geographic and institutional lines. The most important part of evaluating any type of career path or arc is what role or type of institution is the most appropriate or best fit for you.

The type of role that is initially sought after, or even initially obtained by an individual are indeed important, but do not mean that the role will be a permanent one. Although it may be difficult in some cases to transition from current roles to a new or different role at the same institution, it is certainly possible to transition from role to role as you also transition from institution to institution. In my career, for example, I was able to transition and move from an adjunct, to contract faculty, to tenure track faculty within a relatively short span of time. Admittedly I benefitted from the flexibility that my position in the workforce as well as my willingness to relocate physically, and move around the general geographic area in order to take advantage of said opportunities.

It is worth noting, and something that will be revisited and analyzed later on, that as the higher education landscape continues to change and evolve it is also relatively clear that the ratio of tenure track faculty to all other segments of the faculty landscape will continue to change and evolve over time. Although higher education has long been a business, and a big business at that, the approach and mindset connecting and surrounding the higher education conversation has remained relatively gentile and focused on the academic areas rather than the dollars and cents conversations. That said, and partially in response to external changes, but also partially in response to changes driven by both institutions and the students that attend these institutions, colleges and universities are becoming increasingly dependent on contingent, part-time, or other types of non-tenure track faculty.

Some bemoan the rise of increasing numbers of contract or other contingent faculty as the death knell of higher education, whereas proponents make reference to the power of the gig economy shaking up the staid educational landscape. The truth, like in most cases, lies somewhere in the middle. Temping and staffing agencies such as Robert Half have a long and successful history of providing contingent labor and staffing to any number of organizations over time. It would seem illogical to conclude or even speculate that higher education is so uniquely constructed and organization that it is unable to leverage these types of advances to improve performance. Additionally it is also worthwhile to take a deeper dive into the numbers and see just what exactly is going on with regard to the ratio of adjunct to full-time faculty members, both at the institution at large and in the specific department in question. On the surface it might seem that the adjunctification of the profession is continuing to accelerate, but that is merely a cursory view of the situation. Depending on the department in question, for example, adjuncts may have been hired in greater numbers than full-time faculty, but may only be tasked with teaching a relatively small number of classes. Another example of this may be actually analyzing which courses are being taught by adjuncts, i.e., even if there are dozens of adjuncts listed in the website there may only be a handful that are actively involved in teaching courses at the present time.

There is also another point that should be factored into any analysis of tenure track opportunities, and that is the embedded risk that is connected with any tenure track option. Seemingly a contradictory statement, the obtaining of a tenure track position can actually be considered a higher risk job than a contract faculty position, lecturer, or other type of role. Although tenure track opportunities, if tenure is achieved, do result in a more secure role than other positions, there is no guarantee that tenure will be granted to everyone who applies for it. In fact, there is a very real possibility that tenure will be denied to some individuals, which can create a somewhat awkward situation for those individuals involved. Put simply, if an individual has applied for tenure and that application is denied—for whatever reason—that individual in all likelihood will need to leave the institution. Shocking as this might seem, there is a general practice—although every institution is different—that the application for tenure is a high risk situation due to the fact that an applicant generally only has one opportunity to do so. Risk and reward, just as in the financial markets, tend to move in lockstep and the tenure conversation is no different.

Variety Is Key

As the old saying goes, variety is the spice of life, and that applies equally as much to higher education as it does to anything else. There is no shortage of opinions and perspectives on the different types of roles—from adjunct to tenured full professor—and how these different types of academics should interact within the higher education space. In addition to these opinions, there are also proponents on both sides of the conversation that either celebrate the increased practitioner and adjunct presence in the classroom, or decry the loss of traditional higher education practices and approaches. No matter what side of the debate is analyzed, however, there is one truth that continually returns to the forefront; there is more than enough room for everyone to contribute.

Maintaining a differentiation between colleges and universities and more vocational oriented institutions is critical; there is reason why different types of institutions were established in the first place. Depending on the type of higher education career that you have in mind there might be more or fewer opportunities at these different types of organizations. While there might be a robust debate currently underway with regard to the viability of some academic careers, the market for continuing education continues to grow and expand. To fill this demand, and to do so in a manner that produces a well-rounded graduate, will require the input and expertise from a wide array of educators and subject matter experts. Does this present a challenge to some incumbents and traditional ways of operating? Certainly. Is this also a healthy change and response to an evolving marketplace and mindset? Absolutely, and it's also an opportunity for practitioners to provide real-world expertise as well as subject matter knowledge that all students require.

Wrap Up

As has hopefully been illustrated throughout the conversation in this chapter, there are any number of ways in which a practitioner can successfully transition into a more instructor oriented role and position. While there certainly are merits and opportunities connected to each type of position, there are also certainly drawbacks to each of the kinds of roles that were mentioned within this chapter. Depending on where a specific individual is in their transition from the private sector to higher education it may make more sense to start with an adjunct role, experiment, and see if making this more of a full-time role is a viable option. For other individuals, however, particularly those who may have gone ahead and locked up a terminal degree—or who plan to finish one currently in process—aiming directly for more of a full-time role might make more sense. Regardless of how it plays it, it should be encouraging to know just how many options exist in the higher education space.

Reflection Questions

1. Do you believe that the increasing number of doctoral options and possibilities in the marketplace has helped or hurt the job prospects for recent graduates?
2. In the context of the fast-changing economy and job market, what should the ratio between research, teaching, and service be at most institutions? And, should this ratio change depending on the specific institution in question?
3. Based on your feedback and experience both in the workforce and as a result of reading this text, is there an ideal ratio between tenured

and non-tenured professors, and if so what kinds of classes seem most appropriate for these different individuals.

Additional Readings

1. *The Chronicle of Higher Education*—Negotiating the Non-Tenure Track—https://www.chronicle.com/article/negotiating-the-non-tenure-track/. Inside Higher Ed—The 'Administrative Fiction' of Faulty Workloads—https://www.insidehighered.com/blogs/just-visiting/administrative-fiction-faculty-workloads.
2. *Research Gate*—Internal and External Stakeholders in Higher Education—https://www.researchgate.net/publication/322207362_Internal_and_External_Stakeholders_in_Higher_Education.
3. *Forbes*—The Biggest Myth About College Has Just Been Busted—https://www.forbes.com/sites/brandonbusteed/2019/12/18/the-biggest-myth-about-college-has-just-been-busted/#7bef91e5f022.
4. *The Chronicle of Higher Education*—The 5 Types of Professors: Which One Are You?—https://www.chronicle.com/article/the-5-types-of-professors-which-one-are-you/.

CHAPTER 4

Institutional Options

Introduction

Before diving into the different types of academic careers it is worth noting that there while every institution is different and will come with its own sets of opportunities and challenges, there are a few core elements that seem to be consistent across jurisdictional lines. Generally speaking, and mirroring the type of faculty roles that form a large part of the academic marketplace, institutions tend to fall into two camps. Some institutions, no matter the specific label given to them, will be more focused and oriented toward research. While these types of institutions may normally focus the bulk of research efforts into health and natural sciences, the influence of this research orientation will certainly have an impact on business departments. Conversely, there is another large segment of institutions that are classified as teaching focused or teachers colleges, even if that specific word in not the name of the institute itself. The core takeaway from this distinction takes the form of the teaching workload and expectations of faculty at these array of institutions. For an institution that is teaching focused, and even if an individual is hired as a professor and not a lecturer the expectation may be that between teaching, advising, and office hours that individual will allocate 30+ hours to teaching functions. At an institution that is instead focused on research first and foremost, the expectation for teaching might only end up being

S. Stein Smith, *Shifting from Accounting Practitioner to Academia*, Palgrave Studies in Accounting and Finance Practice,
https://doi.org/10.1007/978-3-030-67546-2_4

between 30 and 40 hours for the entire year. In other words, it is important to assess and understand just what type of institution you are applying to in order to have an accurate idea as to what the expectations will be.

Non-teaching Academic Careers

Building on that distinction this is also an opportune time to conduct a deeper dive into what a non-teaching academic career might actually look like in terms of the two general categories that seem to occur most often. A research-oriented academic career may very well play out similar to how it would be imagined; employment and association with a university that is comprised primarily of publishing articles, books, and research studies. The array of opportunities for research at most institutions is only limited by the creativity of the individual in question. For example, without the obligation of teaching, or only a minimal expectation in terms of time and engagement academics can instead focus on longer-form projects instead of shorter pieces that might be as fulfilling. In addition to the purely academic perspective that should be taken into account, this research orientation also allows the researcher to collaborate in conjunction with private sector and public sectors partners. Depending on the satisfaction that a specific individual can derive from writing and publishing versus teaching and presenting, this type of research-focused career path might make logical sense.

One other type of academic career choice that is not teaching focused or oriented is more or an administrative role, and this can manifest itself in several different ways. As discussed previously, the Ed.D. can prepare an individual for an organizational leadership role at an institution, but that is not the only way in which faculty can participate in more of a governance and management role. Specifically, some of the ways that faculty can transition from a teaching role oriented role to a management-oriented role can be becoming more involved in the corporate governance of the institution. Participation in the faculty senate is a logical first step in this process, as it provides faculty with an opportunity to engage with current leadership as a peer. Transitioning to a role such as campus executive, provost, director of s program of school, or some other leadership position is usually the next advancement step in this process. The upshot of this type of role and position is that, by taking on more of a leadership role the individual is more involved in the actual running of the institution, and will virtually always be relieved of teaching and research obligations.

Granted, this type of career will more closely resemble a traditional 9–5 job than the more relaxed work schedule of most faculty members, but that might be a small price to pay in the big picture.

Types of Qualified Academics

Another point that is worth noting and mentioning as the prospect of different academic careers is discussed and presented is that there are several ways that a candidate can be qualified to have a career in academia. It is true that we had a previous, and comprehensive, conversation around the types of doctoral degrees that are out there in the marketplace, but a doctoral degree is not necessarily a requirement to have a career in higher education. Specifically, there exists, in essence, a parallel structure that is used at many institutions and especially in the business sector, in which an individual can either be considered academically qualified (AQ) or professionally qualified (PQ). Every institution is different, and the specifics as to which individuals fall into which category may vary slightly, but the differentiation does tend to split down the following considerations. First, does the individual have a doctoral or other terminal degree in their field? Second, is this faculty member actively involved in the publication of scholarly works and publications which can include both articles, books, and presentations? Lastly, how the faculty member engage in terms of service, ranging from departmental, to service to the school, and service to the institution. Setting that said for the moment; however, it is perfectly normal for most schools or colleges of business to have individuals that are AQ and others that are PQ, and that usually results in a balanced and realistic approach to how instruct students, develop programs, and develop the institution at large.

Drilling down into what might constitute being academically qualified, and acknowledging that every institution will be different, there are a few key signs that can be used as benchmarks. Perhaps most obviously is whether or not the individual in question has a terminal degree, which can include a doctoral degree, a professional doctoral degree, or something like a J.D. or L.L.M. for a legal oriented professional. Other ways to verify or confirm that an individual is academically qualified can take the following forms. A track record of fellowships, association with research institutions, employment at think tanks, or other type of connection to research institutes might be able to serve as a proxy if a doctoral degree is not present. An addition proxy or type of evidence that might serve as proof of being academically qualified would consist of teaching awards, recognition by national or professional associations, or other types of verifiable recognition. Additionally, substantive publications, an established track record of publications that are widely recognized as either peer reviewed, scholarly publications, academic publications, or complete books might also count as substantial contributions. On top of the criteria and specifications outlined by a certain institution, there are also guidelines that have been published and that are available that have been created by accreditation bodies such as the AACSB.

Professionally qualified criteria, reflecting the varied nature of professional work, is generally speaking more varied and dependent on the institution in question than being academically qualified. In most cases, there is a fair amount of discretion left in the hands of the hiring personnel, other members of the promotion and tenure committee, or other governing body to outline what exactly counts or qualifies as professional experience. Generally speaking, however, there are a few criteria and items that constitute what normally serves as the basis for verifying the professional qualifications of an individual. Having obtained a Master's degree or MBA degree is usually a good indication of being academically qualified, as well as a certain amount of workplace experience normally constitute acceptable professional qualified credentials. Dissimilar to being academically qualified, however, individuals that are seeking to put themselves forward as professionally qualified will need to provide some sort of evidence that they remain in up to date with market trends. This may be for different lengths of time depending on the institution in question, but there is almost always a re-certification or approval process that needs to occur.

At nearly every institute or organization, there is going to be a balance and mix of professionally qualified and academically qualified individuals, and that generally makes institution itself—as well as the quality of the education—more comprehensive and a better fit for the marketplace at large. While the courses taught by certain individuals will vary from place to place, the general rule is that some more niche or timely concepts might be taught by academically qualified individuals that might be more up to speed on certain specific topics or subject matter areas.

The Alternative Academic Perspective

Before diving into, in more detail, some of the more traditional options and opportunities that exist in the marketplace it is worth revisiting the specifics of what non-traditional options may exist for professionals with a blended background of industry and academic knowledge and experience. Corporate training and education is a fast growing and very important aspect of the corporate development process, and is also something that could provide an opportunity for aspiring academics that may not find the idea of teaching on a college campus all that alluring or interesting. Personally, I know that I have developed and led corporate and accounting society training sessions across the United States and have found them engaging and quite enjoyable. This might be an approach and area in which you might find a better fit than pursuing a more traditional academic career especially at the earlier stages of transitioning.

Specifically, corporate training and education in and of itself is a multi-billion dollar business, and is a field that is increasingly important in order to keep pace with emerging technologies that are driving change in the business landscape. That said, there are a few things to understand and take into account when considering working with either a private organization to help develop in-house training programs, or working with professional educational groups, or other organizations.

Every educational association is different, and the accounting and financial services field has no shortage of organizations that are interested in educating and training the future leaders of the profession. Some organizations are privately owned and managed and develop training programs or courses that are then sold off to individual firms on per course or per program basis. This might involve developing not only the PowerPoint or slide decks that will be presented during the training, but might also involve preparing review or other types of test questions that can be included or offered when and if this course is offered on a self-study or self-paced basis. Developing these questions and making sure they are in compliance with various educational standards can be a project in and of itself; there is an educational and financial impact of ensuring that these questions and standards are in compliance and delivered in a manner consistent with other projects.

Something that might also arise during working with different privately owned and managed educational associations is that you might be asked to write an instructional manual or other set of written materials. The length of this written content and pre-packaged material is going to vary and be different depending on the course in general, but every learning organization is also going to have standards and other types of requirements that need to be followed. For example, for a 4-hour course there might be a requirement to produce a slide deck or approximately 100 or so slides as well as an accompanying written manual that might run in excess of 200 pages in length. Without naming specifics, I learned the hard way that sometimes putting together a written instruction manual can quickly spiral into a much larger and time-intensive project than initially anticipated.

Understanding what is expected of you up front, budgeting the necessary time, and managing the workflow process is critically important. Not understanding what the expectations are can lead to frustration and a lack of quality products being produced that might end up causing stress and damage to the professional relationship over time. There is also the opportunity to partner and work with various professional organizations such as the AICPA, the IMA, the ACCA, and numerous other financial services entities that are trying to train and educate the new members of the profession.

Working with an industry association can represent its own unique sets of opportunities and challenges since that does tend to also involve relatively high amount of reputational risk on the side of the association as well as other items. In other words, there needs to be a vetting process before any individual is asked to contribute or collaborate with such an association on producing and disseminating content to other members of the profession. After the vetting process is complete, however, then the work tends to move forward at a relatively brisk pace; a common refrain and saying is that once you are on the inside it is difficult to get yourself out. This is not mean to represent a negative trend or event but rather just to illustrate the fact that there is such a need and opening for educated and objective professionals to deliver high quality and relative content to the marketplace. Building on this connection and point, however, also highlights the importance of bringing an objective and levelheaded perspective to this educational process. What this actually entails is that many of the educational and training services and classes that currently exist and most often produced and led by members of various professional organizations. This is perfectly fine and acceptable, but most of these training and educational sessions usually include some kind of product and service pitch as a part of the training.

New Entrants

Like any other industry, the higher education space has an array of incumbent players and also start-up organizations and new entrants into the space. Framed in the context of disruptive innovation, as highlighted in Chapter 1, this should not come as a surprise at all. Education and the workforce, despite the obvious differences and dissimilarities, do have an integral and broad-based connection that cannot be ignored or relegated to a back burner type of issue. Just like it would be unreasonable to expect accounting, financial, and other professional services to remain stagnant in the face of increasing competition and competitive forces, institutions of higher education will not remain static as the totality of the world continues to shift and evolve around them.

Without purporting to be an all-inclusive listing or compilation of the types of new entrants that can, and have, entered the education space and will continue to enter the space. It is important to remember that for all of the associations and connotations that higher education has with economic empowerment, social mobility, and a traditional liberal arts mindset, that education is a big business. With this scale, and relatively healthy profit margins, comes increased interest by members of the private sector, the development of new types of educational offerings, and entirely new models of educational organizations should not be a surprise.

This is not to mean that there will simply be more offerings, courses, and degrees offered in an online format; that is a manifestation of this change rather than the primary driver itself. Specifically, one of the largest shifts that might actually end up entering the marketplace. Let's take a look at a few of the iterations and applications that could arise in the education space that is increasingly digitized, automated, and increasing remote in nature. The most obvious implication of increased digitization and remote-based education is that this frees the institution from being tethered to any one specific physical location. While seemingly not a big deal overall, it can have a dramatic impact on how an organization is managed, developed, and ultimately lead to several alternative futures for an institution and the employers associated at the institution.

An alternative impact of this increased digital nature of education is the fact that the market for educators will simultaneously increase in scope and also become more competitive in nature. The idea of a traditional university with a physical campus, robust student-oriented activities and services, and a large number of in-person classes and offerings might not be as a prevalent as it currently is. This is not to say that there will be no market or need for a physical college campus or location, but the sheer percentage of college and university offerings linked to what are considered "normal" or "usual" will begin to shift. The most visible manifestation of this higher level change and shift will be a higher percentage of courses, programs, and certificates delivered in an online format.

As has been stated previously, this pivot and shift do not necessarily represent something new or innovative, but the pivot and change toward online education seem situated to only keep accelerating. For example, if an institution is almost entirely online or the vast majority of its offerings and content are online this also means that there are very few restrictions related to where faculty and staff are actually located. Working remotely is nothing new at all, but the distribution and decentralization trends that have manifested in other industries have yet to manifest itself to the same degree in the higher education space. Let's take a look at a scenario that could, in theory, play out that brings together incumbent educational players, private sector and other start up organizations, and a decentralized methodology for operating and managing the institution itself.

Seeking to capitalize on the trend and increasing market demand for flexible learning formats, a new institution of higher education is formed, marketed, and put onto the marketplace. The only physical offices and spaces at this institution are for administrative functions that are legally dependent on, or are required to be, physically located to qualify or otherwise demonstrate eligibility for certain tax or other business advantages. In other words the entire institution operates in an online manner, and actually also operates in a decentralized manner as well. How this might play out in reality is that—since every class is offered online (either in an asynchronous or synchronous manner)—there is no need to limit the applicant pool to any specific area. Students, rather obviously, can attend the institution and be located anywhere in the world, but in this case the faculty and staff can be similarly as global in nature. Operating remotely also allows the institution to charge lower tuition prices and other associated fees, which makes the institution more affordable and attainable for a larger potential student body.

Building on this fact, the reality that the institution operates in an entirely online format also means the percentage of courses offered in a synchronous versus an asynchronous manner can be different than at other more traditional institutions. Even as many colleges and universities continue to offer an increasingly higher percentage of courses in an online format, many of these continue to be offered in a format that is more closely aligned with face-to-face instruction. How this plays out in reality is that many of the courses, even though they are offered in an online or virtual format, may be offered at a specific date and time. What this actually means is that even though these courses are being offered in a virtual format, the flexibility that is so often associated with online learning might not exist at every institution.

For the institution that is being examined here there might be a middle ground, between fully synchronous and fully asynchronous, that would be the best fit for the type of students being pursued by this organization. The appeal of asynchronous learning is derived from several different sources, but a dominant one is the simple matter of convenience; if individuals can take and enroll in courses at any time of day that might be more appealing for working individuals. On the other hand, individuals looking to reskill or upskill might want or need the feeling of live instruction that is delivered via a synchronous online instruction. Developing a middle ground, or having certain courses or instructors available in a live format (such as Q&A answering) to augment pre-recorded courses might be an appropriate midway or halfway point to be considered.

No matter how the specifics of new entrants into the higher education space develop and evolve over time, the fact is that there is more likely to be more competition in the educational space that might have previously existed. The elimination of in-person classes or physical campuses is not assured, but is something that would make sense to form a core component of a new entrant to the sector. That said, online education in and of itself is not a panacea for the issues that continue to impact the higher education sector; it is merely a tool rather than an immediately available solution. Specifically, online education is not a monolithic area or sector and needs to be analyzed both in terms of how the content is delivered, the frequency with which content is delivered, and the type of content delivered in these array of formats. In addition to brand new educational institutions, however, there is also the substantial marketplace for non-academic or non-traditional education providers.

Non-academic Education

The growth and development of non-traditional training and education also provide an important opportunity for professionals that are ready to exit the practitioner realm and enter the realm of higher education. For every college or university course or certificate program that exists that are—without a doubt—a wide array of non-traditional courses, online programs, or courses affiliated in some way with institutions of higher education. Given the fact that the business landscape continues to evolve and change at an accelerating rate, the necessity and expectation that individuals will continuously improve existing skills should not come as a surprise to different individuals. All of these programs and certificates, however, need to be led, developed, and curated by relevant experts in these respective fields: who better to play a role into this then individuals who have both practitioner and research experience and expertise?

Perhaps the first thing to think about and acknowledge when discussing the plethora of options available to aspiring academics is the following truth. Students, generally, are the same no matter where an individual ends up working or teaching at any point during an academic career. In my personal case, for example, I have taught at private universities, public universities, taught online and in-person, and have taught in-person at locations all throughout the country. After these experiences, I can say that without a doubt, students and the people that you will work with, are generally the same regardless no matter where an individual ends up teaching. Students are, after all, people like you and I and generally are dealing with an array of issues both inside and outside of the classroom environment. That said, and before diving into the different categories of institutions that are available for individuals to teach at, it might be beneficial to review some of the stops that I made during my transition from practice and into academia.

As mentioned previously, my journey from practitioner to higher education began with some adjunct work at local institutions that I had some familiarity with anyway. For example, my very first teaching experience was at my alma mater, which was an easy way to start my transition from an accounting professional to an accounting educator. I knew the system, knew many of the people, and understood how the course interacted with each other within the various departments and curricula. Gaining from this experience and on the ground interaction with students and institutions allowed me to (1) build out my CV and resume as it is connected to higher education and further retooling my instructional pedagogy, and (2) allowed me to understand just how my career transition could function and become more developed. Following these experiences, which allowed me to simultaneously dip my toe into the academic pool while continuing to work full time in the corporate sector, also enabled me to conduct one other important aspect of any career transition.

Researching different opportunities, and finding the correct opportunity and opening for you is the first and most important aspect of any academic career development and arc, and here is where I would also emphasize a point of caution. Simply because you have the time to do research, and have taught previously, does not mean that you can go ahead and rest assured that you will always make the correct decision. When I was analyzing the possibilities and options for myself in terms of both an initial transition and future opportunities, I needed to make sure that as I made this transition I did not make a mistake. Even though I had the good fortune to make my transition and pivot relatively early in my career, it was not without any significant risk. Any time a job change in undertaken, there is always going to be an element of risk and reward that needs to be analyzed. That being said, let's take a look at some of the options and opportunities that are available for practitioners seeking to successfully transition to academia and higher education.

It is important to remember that this analysis and examination of various institutions of higher education are just my personal view and perspective, and that depending on who you consult with these topics with there will be different answers and commentary provided. In addition to these institutional options, and as mentioned above, there is any number of non-traditional paths and perspectives that can and should be explored by anyone making a new entrance in the realm of higher education. Education is not a one and done event where a person graduates from some level of college and never returns in the future. Actually, the entire conversation and framing of higher education has changed to encompass far more than just taking certain classes and has instead expanded to include post-collegial education as well.

Community Colleges

Community colleges are often where the educational journey begins for many college students begins, and form an important part of the educational system. If a visualization is easier to understand and frame in the context of this conversation, the community college system can be thought of as the lynchpin as how the US educational system operates. In almost every county or region in the country, there are a number of community colleges that are available for students just starting out in their post-high school education. There are thousands of community colleges in the United States, with a total enrollment in the millions, and so it is rather obvious that this does represent a significant opportunity for practitioners seeking to obtain a toehold in the education landscape.

An alternative way to think of community colleges, and one that is increasingly common thanks to articulation agreements and memos of understanding between institutions, is that many community colleges form the feeder system to other colleges and universities. While this might seem like term or label with a negative connotation, this is actually a very positive connection between community colleges, other institutions of higher education. In addition, this connection creates an opportunity for educators connected between the two. In addition to serving as a pipeline and opportunity for students to enter into the higher education conversation, community colleges can also serve as an excellent point for educators seeking to enter the educational conversation.

With the sheer number of community colleges, courses, and students that are connected through the community college system there are—rather obviously—a large number of openings that open and re-open on a continuous basis. There is some discussion to be had about the percentage of courses, especially at community colleges, covered by adjuncts and other part-time educators, but it still remains true that there a large number of opportunities for educators to enter into. Many colleagues of mine, especially those who have transitioned from industry to higher education, have had an excellent experience teaching at community colleges for a number of reasons. This is due to the fact that, as stated above, the sheer number of opportunities and openings at the community college level at significant, as well as the opportunity to engage with students who are just beginning their journey.

Building on this point, the opportunity to have impact on students and to have an influence of how students interact with both the educational system is also a major driver of why many practitioners enter the educational space in the first place. Giving back, having an impact, and helping the next generation of professionals educate, learn, and develop both from a professional and ethical perspective is a core driving force of many educators regardless of how they got to that point. Community colleges allow both educators and students to participate in the higher educational process in a manner that is flexible, often times convenient, and allows everyone to participate in a manner that best suits them.

Private Universities

Private universities, despite the moniker as a private institution, represent some of the most well-known and publicly recognizable institutions in the country, and can represent a rich opportunity for educators to join the higher education field. The very name recognition that often accompanies many of these institutions is a major draw for aspiring academics since—quite frankly—they are familiar and well known. By the same token, however, the very name recognition and attraction that many aspiring academics (and students) to these institutions also mean that many of the openings at these institutions are highly sought after. Remember that if you are interested in obtaining this position for any number of reasons, there are going to be a multitude of other applicants seeking that very same opportunity. If the connection between institutions and the opportunities for employment could be summarized in one phrase, it could be summarized as follows; higher risk and higher reward.

Starting with the latter, many of the more recognizable of these private institutions and universities are either among some of the older institutions in the nation or the world and/or maybe among the most well established financially. Now, this is not to say—by any stretch—that every private institution is well funded. Out of the institutions that are threatened with financial crisis and potential failure due to lack of financial resources, many of the weakest institutions from a financial perspective tend to be private institutions. That said, the legacy and well-established track record of many private institution make them enviable job opportunities for aspiring academics. Taking this into account is imperative for any proactive or job-seeking academics.

Following this same thread of thought, however, it is equally important to recognize that simply obtaining the job initially is only the first step in this process. Given the fact that some of the private universities, including some of the ones that generate headlines on a nearly daily basis, are so high profile means that the competition and pressure continue even after obtaining the position. These reputations and headlines often associated with these private institutions also mean that there is a certain amount of reputational presence that needs to be maintained and improved upon over time. From a practical perspective this means that, compared and contrasted with other institutions, that it may be more difficult to obtain tenure, promotion, or recognition with such robust and often global competition. This is not to sound discouraging, rather the opposite. A robust and intellectually stimulating work environment can be rewarding in its own right, and also lead to other external opportunities.

Public Universities

Public universities may seem like the complete opposite from private universities in almost every possible way, and while this is certainly true to some extent that is not entirely true. Private universities may, in many cases, be older and have a certain pedigree associated with the name recognition and alumni base, but that does not mean that public universities are subpar in anyway. The institution that I am employed with, the City University of New York, labeled as the Greatest Urban University in the World, is cited, ranked, and applauded for a number of different metrics and benchmarks on a consistent basis. Whether it is connected to economic mobility, percentage of first-generation students attending college, or being able to document and reinforce the benefits of college education the accolades and recognition are not difficult to find. CUNY is one, albeit a large and well known example, is simply one of the large public university systems that have—for decades and even centuries—generated cutting edge research, leadership, and information vital to the economic and societal growth in the United States and abroad.

One of the most recognizable and easily recognizable attributes of many public institutions, be they labeled as colleges or universities is that they tend to be larger and more connected to other public resources than some private institutions might be. This scale can be exemplified by looking at the number of students enrolled at several high profile public institutions of higher education in the United States. CUNY has well over 200,000 students enrolled at the 27 institutions in the network, the California public university system has hundreds of thousands of students enrolled in that system. Individual institutions, such as Michigan State, Ohio State University, the Texas public university system, and other various large public institutions—on an individual basis—can enroll and educate in excess of 60,000 students at any given time. The sheer scale of these institutions and networks can be difficult to comprehend, but a good way to put this into context is to compare the enrollment of public institutions with cities and other communities in the neighboring region.

Another potential impact of public institutions, which is invaluable toward to over dynamism of the higher education marketplace at large, is that many large public institutions often—either directly or indirectly—support or are connected to other institutions in the area. A quick exercise to demonstrate this power and network effect is to look at—geographically—at the number of private or other non-public institutions that have often sprung up around larger public institutions. Be they land grant institutions, colleges and universities originally founded to educate farmers and miners, research institutions, or institutions of higher education established to provide local resources and/or compete with other national institutions (like Western Governors) the overarching goal is the same. The scale and mission of the vast majority of these institutions are to educate and empower the next generation of professionals, educators, doctors, and leaders. This scale, however, has a positive and negative connotation that aspiring academics need to be aware of and factor into a decision as to whether or not a public institution is the best fit for them.

The scale and size of many public institutions can make them attractive employers simply due to the sheer number of openings and opportunities that routinely appear at these institutions, but that does not mean that bigger is always better. While it is true that a large institution may be better equipped to handle new job seeks and candidates this also may mean that it is more difficult to stand out and/or differentiate yourself from other job candidates applicants for these same positions. Additionally, and linking back to a conversation covered in the analysis of private universities, even after obtaining a specific position it may be more difficult to attract positive reviews and reaction to research and service work if there is such substantive competition at the institution. These factors, which can exist at institutions of all sizes and categorization, lead directly to the next topic of discussion; hitting the road and heading out for greener pastures overseas.

There is also something known as the first-generation phenomenon that can negatively impact students who are the first in their families to attend college or university, but it is equally as important to realize that a similar thing can happen to first-generation academics or academics making the transition to higher education. To put this in some context imagine someone who is just learning to drive—manual or automation—versus someone who has been driving for years; all things being equal the individual with more experience will be better at driving than the person who is just learning. A similar analysis can be conducted when attempting to forecast the success or potential failure of an academic transition. This is where public universities can offer an advantage over private or other types of academic institutions due to the size and scope of said college or university. Due to the sheer number of people employed at a public institutions, which can number in the tens of thousands, there is—by default—an advantage for individuals trying to obtain a toehold in the higher education space.

International Work

The concept of traveling for work may, for those reading this with a background of traveling for business in a previous professional life, bring a host of painful memories. Flight delays, flight cancellations, driving and getting lost, and the general unpleasant nature of most travel will—reasonably so—limit the number of practitioners seeking to continue to travel for work after the transition to academia. With all of that said, however, this is certainly a market that could potentially lucrative, fulfilling, and allow a certain individual or practitioner to stand out again other applicants going forward. Given the increasingly global nature of education and higher education at large, it should not come as a much of a surprise that international opportunities continue to expand and develop in nature. Not discussed in too much detail within this text, but a few items that would appear to be worth analyzing further in this conversation include, but are not limited to, the following.

1. Business expertise is always valued, and the reputation of the United States as—generally speaking—a business friendly and oriented marketplace, helps to drive the appetite for US expertise at international institutions. Any analysis of business, taking into account the scale that separates the United States from smaller nations and nation-states such as Hong Kong, Singapore, and Switzerland, routinely see the United States near or at the top of virtually every business ranking. Translating this into actionable business intelligence means that there is almost always interest in former American businesspeople who are willing to relocate abroad to instruct and educate.

2. Teaching overseas can be quite lucrative, building on the first point; institutions are willing to pay for quality talent. This may take the form of an elevated salary, performance bonuses, and other compensation in the form of housing allowances, covering costs of education for children, and other items. A quick Google search and a little digging through from those results will rather quickly reveal an entire sub-culture of business professors and educators that have made a career of periodically moving from one country or region to another.
3. Just like in the corporate world or working in private industry, the willingness to relocate and work in different environments and among different cultures is very valuable. Gaining exposure to different institutions, different ways of conducting business, and working with a variety of different cultural norms and standards is something that is invaluable no matter what the context is for the individual or institution in question. No matter what the ultimate goal or end game of the institution is in question, it is a near certainty that an individual with international exposure and workplace experience can represent a significant upside and benefit to the individuals in question

With all of this said, however, there is one aspect of this conversation and debate that has been lacking—to this date—analysis and conversation surrounding the exact workload and tasks routinely expected of faculty members across institutional lines. Let's do just that in the following section of this text. Work is always going to be work, no matter what specific institution is being analyzed and discussed, but it is important to understand what specific tasks you are going to be expected to complete.

There is also the reality that international teaching and work experience allow you to gain exposure to a global audience and experience a global student audience in a globalized world. Globalization is a fact of both the higher education space and the business environment at large and is something that needs to be addressed and integrated into every course, program, and institutional approach to effectively competing in a globalized and competitive higher education environment. Instructing students to be able to effectively navigate and work within a globally competitive landscape provides a quantitative value and benefit to instructors, students, and institutions alike, as well as providing opportunities for faculty members to work, develop, and learn from other practitioners, academics, and students alike. Given the potential complicated and multi-faceted nature of how geopolitics, economics, and cultural changes can interact and engage with each other this embedded opportunity is something that cannot and should not be overlooked.

A Potential Path Forward

Since this book is written with business professionals in mind, it is not unreasonable to speculate that many of the individuals reading this book may also have an entrepreneurial slant or angle and that is where this section is going to discuss for a few minutes. The institutions that have long dominated the higher education landscape, including the array of institutions discussed within this last section may represent the traditional structure of higher education, but that does not mean that this is the future of the educational landscape. As the forces that are driving change in the business landscape continue to also drive change and innovation in the higher education landscape it is imperative that institutions become aware of the other options available for business professionals to recommend and push forward in the educational conversation.

First and foremost, it is important for the business professionals to understand that one of the most obvious ideas and concepts that business professionals can bring to the table is the idea of spin-off organizations or entities operating the umbrella of the parent organization. An arrangement such as this is very common in the private sector, but has seemingly been slow to emerge in the higher education space. Taking this idea from the conceptual to the practical an idea that could be implemented might take the following structure and form. A liberal arts institution can certainly keep the traditional areas of focus and excellence that it had previously established, but in addition to the traditional offerings it can begin developing additional and/or new types of offerings and courses. These new courses, which may be more trades based, STEM related, or linked to business topics, can either be offered in-person or online. The format of the course is not as important as the structure behind the new ideas.

Framed within the context of corporate venturing, or the creation and support of a new arm of the business by an existing arm, is a business concept that has been adopted and implemented by organizations across an array of industry lines. Higher education institutions can, and should, seek to emulate some of the benefits commonly linked to this concept, and can do so without all that much in terms of initial outlay and investment. Returning back to the idea of a large liberal arts institutions supporting a new business arm, this project can take the form of online courses, a certificate program, or several initial course ideas that are marketed as new offerings. Since these courses are going to be linked—in our case—to business topics and ideas, it would seem logical to seek volunteers from existing business faculty to help develop these new offerings. Obtaining faculty volunteers, while not always a straightforward nor an easy event, is not something that should be thought of as impossible. Offering release time is a way in which faculty can be incentivized to participate in this program without incurring any additional direct financial costs.

Additionally, ways that institutions can incentivize faculty members to become more involved include a few of the following methods. Release time is perhaps the most obvious way in which to do so, but there are other ways in which this can occur. Without touching on the fact that financial incentives always work, there are other ways in which that creative faculty colleagues and managers can do so. One way in which that this can happen is providing opportunities for faculty members to become more engaged in faculty governance, creating venues for faculty to be recognized for their efforts, and encouraging cross-department or even cross-institution collaboration. An example that occurred to me personally during 2020 was the opportunity to be involved with a multi-institution effort to develop new and creative courses. Focusing specifically of personal investing and finance, quantitative analysis, and computer science, this assortment of courses was part of a broader effort to encourage greater intercampus consistency and course offerings at CUNY.

Collaborative Competition

While it is true that the marketplace for college students continues to increase and becomes increasingly competitive, it also seems reasonable to note that this increasing competition also creates opportunities for increased cooperation. Although this might strike some as an unusual side effect of an increasingly competitive environment, taken from a bigger picture perspective, it is not as unusual as it might initially appear. Clearly, there are only so many students that are going to be entering college at any given time, and traditional higher education conversation has centered around acquiring as many students as possible. While this might make sense from a certain perspective, it can also prove counterproductive if all this results in is a scramble for students and other resources. Not every student is as good a fit for every institution, and not every institution is equally as well prepared to handle the needs and expectations of every student. Community college students, for example, might require or expect a higher level of student advising or other support services to help in the navigation of the numerous questions and topics that come up as they make the transition from high school to college.

Traditional aged students, who may or may not even make up the majority of college students in the very short term, are going to have radically different experiences if they are commuting versus living on campus. Commuter and other non-resident students, however, are increasingly forming a plurality—if not a majority—of new college students and students enrolled at college and universities; taking the needs of these students into account is going to be something that is increasingly expected moving forward. Depending on the makeup of staff and other personnel at the institution, having to contend with these varied needs may or may not be something that the institution is interested in handling. Ensuring that expectations are understood on both ends of the conversation, by the students in question as well as the institution itself, is something that practitioners can assist with and should integrate into the planning for certain courses.

The differentiation in terms of student body composition of the student body and students enrolled in certain courses may also be different depending on the type of courses being taught. Undergraduate courses, for example, would seemingly have a higher percentage of "traditional" college students, but that only presents a partial view of the situation. Many students enrolled at the undergraduate level may be people who are either coming to school for the first time, or are returning school following previous efforts. These students, in addition to any work or family obligations, may not as accustomed to the routine of schoolwork and completing assignments as other students might have been. Factoring this into the design of course work and course assessments can be as simple and straightforward and can take the form of simply ensuring that a variety of assessment options are included and built into the classes.

This idea of collaboration and working together with potential competitors might seem like an unusual situation or something that might not make sense given the context of how competitive higher education has become. When viewed from a higher-level perspective, however, this idea of collaborative cooperation with allies and competitors alike is not as strange as it might seem. For example, Netflix—a large multinational organization with billions in revenues and thousands of employees in its own right—was for years hosted on the web hosting services of Amazon. Companies such as telecommunication carriers, search engines, food safety and logistical organizations, and other types of economic segments routinely cooperate and work together to improve services, develop new product lines, and upgrade the end user experience. In other words, the implications of collaborative cooperation should not be as unusual or as bizarre as it would seem to be on the surface.

Reflection Questions

1. Based on some of the current trends in higher education—remote learning, cost pressures, and shrinking college age population—what do you believe the future of the different types of colleges are?
2. Does it seem to you that the increasingly competitive environment will diminish the opportunities for collaborative competition and international work?
3. Given some of the lack of faith and trust in public institutions, what will the role of the alternative academic career evolve into?

Additional Readings

1. InsideHigherEd—A Foreword to “Going Alt-Ac: A Guide to Alternative Academic Careers”—https://www.insidehighered.com/blogs/learning-innovation/foreword-%E2%80%98going-alt-ac-guide-alternative-academic-careers%E2%80%99.
2. CollegeBoard—Types of College: The Basics—https://bigfuture.collegeboard.org/find-colleges/college-101/types-of-colleges-the-basics.
3. InsideHigherEd—More Trustees Fear For The Future—https://www.insidehighered.com/news/2020/01/29/trustees-growing-increasingly-worried-about-future-higher-education-us-polling-shows.

4. Association Forum—FAQs About Working At Associations—https://www.associationforum.org/careers-page/association-faqs.
5. EdSurge—It's Time To Digitally Transform Community College—https://www.edsurge.com/news/2020-08-12-it-s-time-to-digitally-transform-community-college.

CHAPTER 5

The Academic Workload

Introduction

Perhaps the biggest change and shift in the nature of how practitioners engage with the marketplace connected to both industry and academia is the actual nature of the work itself. Industry practitioners, and especially those that are motivated and forward thinking enough to consider a dramatic career change like that from private industry to higher education, certainly have demonstrated work either, ambition, and otherwise proactive characteristics that are critical to success in any professional environment. That said, it is important to do a deep dive into each of the components of faculty workload to help individual seeking to make this transition a successful and—hopefully—less stressful. At a high level or big picture point of view there is an underlying reality and truth that is true about higher education that differentiates itself from other potential roles and responsibilities for practitioners. Something that needs to be outlined upfront is that no matter how collaborative or cooperative an individual wants to be in terms of higher education workload or education, there is the simple fact that a large degree of work performed by academics occurs on a personal or singular basis. In order to succeed and even thrive as a practitioner making the transition there needs to be an acceptance of the reality that you will not be as collaborative or as team based as other types of workplaces.

S. Stein Smith, *Shifting from Accounting Practitioner to Academia*, Palgrave Studies in Accounting and Finance Practice,
https://doi.org/10.1007/978-3-030-67546-2_5

The Big Shift

The biggest difference between industry and higher education workloads and work tasks may be the importance that team-based work and efforts play in the conversation connected to higher education, and succeeding in this manner. Contrasted versus the traditional office environment in which tasks are usually very well regimented and structured, the academic workload is on the one hand, looser and less structured, and on the other hand, very regimented and structured that needs to be followed and organized throughout the employment process. Less structure and deadlines may, for example, seem like a good thing for individuals seeking some breathing room and perhaps a little less stress on the day to day as far as workload is concerned. While this is true, and there do tend to be fewer hard and fast deadlines in the academic environment versus a corporate environment, that does not mean that there are no deadlines or that the deadlines do not count for as a munch in academia.

Linking back to the connection between work, workloads, and the importance of coordination between different faculty members and components of the department and institutional support structure, the differences become clear. Working together, collaborating with colleagues, and being able to have proactive and constructive conversations about both individual and institutional goals and objectives is something that is a responsibility of every faculty member to embrace and do so on a continuous basis. That said, and realizing that every individual will need to approach these conversations in a unique and individualized manner, there do appear to be a few common themes that echo throughout the conversation. Not meant to be an all inclusive or exhaustive in nature, these factors and items should be used as a starting point for further analysis and conversation related to how you evaluate and complete, the transition from the private sector to higher education and academia at large.

Something that needs to be also be incorporated and factored into any analysis of workload considerations for aspiring faculty members is also what the specific institution values the most. Acknowledging that every institution is different is a phrase repeated so often that it risks becoming a cliché, but that is the truth. At some institutions, for example, the importance of service to students versus research will not only be different depending on the specific type of faculty member being assessed, but the relatively weighting of this importance can also shift over time! In other words the goalposts can feel like they are moving on you, and if an individual is not careful and observant these shifting priorities and levels of importance can trip up even the most—otherwise—well prepared and situated academics. Goalposts can shift in every profession, but it is rarely as important as it is in higher education.

An item we will revisit later on in this text, but also seems worth mentioning now, is that the very nature of academic work can be difficult for some individuals to get used, feel comfortable with, or embrace during the transition. Put simply, the academic work environment is very flexible and unstructured versus a corporate or other industry type of environment, and this is something that needs to be incorporated into the analysis of making a transition. Many aspiring academics or professionals seeking to make this transition can struggle quite a bit with this freedom. Although for individuals coming out of private industry, where tasks, deadlines, and meetings are mandated from higher up the food chain it can feel like there is no flexibility for creativity or for working on projects of your own choosing. Given that this is the backdrop for many, if not all, individuals coming out of private industry, the fact that academia and higher education offers a high degree of freedom might seem like a good thing. Too much of a good thing, however, can actually end up being a bad thing or negative; without structure and a framework to operate within many professionals can find themselves struggling to complete tasks and stay on track. Several suggestions and tactics, widely recommended, that can help individuals stay productive and on task even in a low supervision environment include, but are not limited to, the following:

1. Establish and maintain a separate work environment to help ensure that you have place to work and complete tasks on a consistent basis. One potential benefit and upside of the academic lifestyle is that you are often able to work from home or a remote location, but this can also pose a hinderance to completing tasks in a focused manner. Not having a dedicated space that is separated from the rest of your life and habits can lead to increased distraction and less productivity than might be accomplished otherwise.
2. Turning off notifications and otherwise potential social media/technology distractions off when you are "clocking in" for the day. Just because you are working from home or some other non-office location does not mean that you are not working.

In other words it can seem to friends and family that since you are working from home, or otherwise not going into an office or formal work environment that you may be available to help out with errands, take long lunches or otherwise do things that are non-work related. Establishing a set routine and working habits can help keep these well-intentioned but still distracting events from occurring any more than necessary. That is not to say that you should never take a long lunch or otherwise enjoy the flexibility that accompanies working from home, but that should be the exception and not the rule.

3. Holding yourself accountable is something that is easy to say, but can be difficult to execute on a consistent basis especially in an academic environment that consists largely of individual work. No matter what institution is in question, nor what college is being analyzed the underlying reality and expectation is that the individual in question is able to effectively manage not only their time, but their production as well. Academics in general might not might not usually be associated with schedules, deadlines, and hitting production quotas but it is true that these criteria form the basis for how many academics are evaluated and judged. Being able to effectively manage and leverage the flexibility inherent in academic work is something that needs to be worked out, managed, and monitored on a consistent basis.

The importance of being able to work remotely is something that is not unique or only identified with higher education or academia, and this shift and change are both items that are both becoming increasingly mainstream across different industry verticals. Even with that said, however, the often solitary nature of higher education and academic work can come as a bit of shock and surprise to individuals more commonly used to working with colleagues and partners. The most central theme and narrative that is different from remote work in a corporate environment is that even if an employee is tasked on a remote project or small subset of projects there will inevitably be meetings, conference calls, and potentially face-to-face meetings that occur continuously throughout the process. Contrasting this with the remote and solitary nature of academic work is relatively straightforward; the ratio of meetings and contact points are not nearly as frequent.

An example of how this might play out can be summarized as follows. Even for a position that involves a large amount of business travel and working on the road, there will inevitably be a large number of contract points, interactions, and connections between different people. A faculty member, however, may go the entire semester without a face-to-face meeting with certain colleagues. In my current role, for example, although I share an office with an office-mate I often go weeks without seeing them because of the fact that our paths simply do not cross. My current teaching schedule is Monday and Wednesday and their teaching schedule is Tuesday/Thursday. Additionally, outside of departmental meetings I rarely see my colleagues for casual meetings and interaction. While this can cause some to feel some level of anxiety, and justifiably so in some situations, that does not mean that aspiring faculty members have no chance of succeeding. To the contrary, taking advantage of this solitary and often personal nature of the academic workload and lifestyle is something that every academic or recently transitioned academic from the private sector needs to take advantage of and realize.

Specifically, there is something that should be factored into the decision-making process, and that is the flexibility inherent and embedded into the academic work style and process. This flexibility and free-form nature of academic work can, in addition, also create a situation where academics are unfocused and potentially unproductive for long stretches of time. The very nature of academic work is creative in nature, and this is true regardless whether or not the content area is creative or not; creating a written, oral, or other representative content is always going to be a struggle for some people. Content creation and distribution, however, should not be viewed as something to be feared or thought of as unusual or different; it is the core of higher education and academia.

Crafting a Narrative

Building on these topics and key points there is also an idea and concept of importance as an aspiring academic enters the higher education field; the importance of crafting a narrative. This might not seem like an intuitive direction to move in, especially if the professional in question has a background in professional or corporate sectors. In many cases once you are hired for a specific job or role it is difficult to ever differentiate yourself, or become associated with a different type of role, responsibility, or set of tasks. Such an approach certainly does create efficiency and operational gains, but can also lead to frustration, lack of consistent development, and the eventually dissatisfaction of many employees. Higher education, however, does tend to operate differently than most corporations, even those that are known for managerial flexibility, in the sense that the you—in essence—need to create your own position.

A narrative can be a tricky thing to develop in the sense that in order to do so in an enduring and consistent manner requires quite a bit of effort and investment over time. On the one hand in order to have this completed successfully the individual in question must be proactive, engaged, and willing to experiment with different tasks, roles, and topics. Conversely, there is also a risk that by experimenting and engaging with too many different factors that an academic can lose focus, become associated with too many different initiatives, and lose control over how they are perceived at both an individual and institutional level. In other words, there is a responsibility on the side of the individual to be able to stake out a particular position and reputational area that is able to be defined. Linking back to a topic that was discussed earlier and will be revisited again throughout this book is the importance of being able to define the specific area of interest that is in alignment with professional interest, departmental interest, and institutional interest.

Even if this is attempted there is no guarantee that the efforts will be successful or actually result in a position or reputation in alignment with the broader institution. Changing directives and prerogatives, at either an institutional or individual level, can result in previous efforts being rendered less important or secondary given the changing nature of the institution, the profession, or even the individual in question. Simply because things may change over time, however, does not mean it is not worth attempting to so in the first place. Every individual is different, and will have a variety of different interactions with both the institution and their colleagues employed therein. That said, there are a few definitive steps that can, and should, be taken in order to assist with the creation and development of a new professional narrative and reputation.

First, recognize the fact that you are basically starting fresh with this transition from a professional or private sector position to one in higher education. This might seem relatively obvious, but it is tempting to try and either replicate, or continue doing, what you had been doing previously in earlier roles. Academia, as hopefully is stressed throughout this book, does operate differently from corporate or private sector employment. Understanding these differences and incorporating them into your planning and career arc is an essential first step. Building on this first point, it is also worth noting that even though higher education does tend to operate in a cyclical manner—akin to how tax, audit, or quarter end trading periods can be hectic—the overall pace and schedule might be slower than had previously been experienced. This can be a good and bad thing. Good because, quite clearly, this does tend to allow practitioners more time to experiment, develop, and grow than might otherwise have been possible. This same slower pace, though, can also result in some individuals taking too much to time "off," or not realizing that there are still expectations and deliverables.

This extended time, as it connects to crafting and developing a professional narrative, can be quite beneficial for new entrants into higher education. For example, as I was transitioning from private industry to academia, I did sometimes struggle to figure out just how exactly my past experiences and knowledge were going to effectively transition to higher education. I did benefit from just having completed a doctoral program so it was not that I was suffering from a lack of practice or exposure to academia. Rather it was, in fact, a very simple problem but one that did not present an obvious solution. As the saying goes, past performance is not indicative of future success, and this is just as clear in higher education as it is in private industry. Figuring out how to connect your expertise with the requirements of academia is a process that every aspiring or new academic has to complete. The key question to ask, and this is something that I have developed personally and heard others ask as well is; what do you want to spend your time actually doing? Once you are hired in an academic roles, specifically a tenure track or long-term contractual role, there is a large amount of discretion that you have pertaining to how you spend your time, and this is where the importance and underlying meaning behind why academia is creative is imperative to remember.

The Importance of Creativity

Mentioning creativity is, of course, something that is not usually associated with fields like accounting, finance, or business management. In fact, whenever the terms or words creativity or innovative are included in the same sentence or conversation that story usually ends with many of the involved individuals serving jail sentences. All kidding aside, and that is not to minimize the damage that financial wrongdoing can cause, there is usually not a large or well-established track record or connection of accounting and financial services practitioners harnessing or embracing creativity. How this ultimately manifest itself in academia, however, is a bit different than how it usually would do so in other professional settings in such that using some creativity and integrating new ideas into accounting and financial services research are going to be important trends and factors to keep in mind.

When the topic of accounting or finance research comes to mind there are probably a few things that are generally thought of as mainstream. Usually augmented by some financial modeling or other quantitative tools, a few relatively straightforward or basic questions are asked and answered as per the research. Topics that appear to be most popular include, but are not limited to, auditing standards, tax reporting, disclosure requirements, or other somewhat basic or straightforward issues. Now, there is absolutely nothing wrong with furthering existing research or adding to existing analyses that have already been published into the marketplace; in fact that is how many of the findings and studies that have achieved most media coverage are constructed. Specifics will vary from research to research obviously, but that tends to be well-worn path for accounting and financial services professionals seeking to publish research and get points across.

The main problem with this line or research, however, is that over time it can become quite iterative, repetitive, or otherwise not truly interesting or helpful to either practitioner or academic end users. Understanding this fact, in as much as it matters for publication or tenure processes, this leads to several basic points. In a marketplace where the majority of products and options available for review and potential publication are very similar in nature this increases the competition for publication especially in higher quality and higher level journals. This can lead some journals and other publication venues to, for lack of a better word, seeming to have quite a few of the same types of articles and research papers. For aspiring faculty members that might not be employed at top tier institutions, or be without professional contacts in the higher education space, this can lead to a proverbial road block for publication purposes. Adding to this, and here is where the rubber can truly hit the road, is if so many of the articles are so similar in nature that can limit the interest of editorial boards

New Topical Areas

Something that should also be taken into account when attempting to develop and disseminate content is that there are new areas of focus and information that are increasingly important for the financial services space. As digitization and automation, mentioned previously, have impacts that are still trying to be understood, new areas of focus can come to the forefront in terms of what areas can be taught, researched, and published. Specifically, there are a few areas and areas of focus where creativity is of the utmost importance for aspiring academics making the transition from private industry to higher education. Again, it is important to keep in mind that a fine line must always be struck between creativity and accounting research and publications, but that does not mean that there is no room for it. In fact, there are numerous opportunities for expanded research and discussion that can both increase the research reputation of the individual in question, but also possibly create new instructional and course development opportunities.

Cybersecurity, for example, is something that continuously makes headlines and new stories but that misses the larger point as it connects to accounting and financial. Safeguarding financial and other personal information is of top priority to both individuals and institutions from an operational and financial perspective. This is rather indicative of an obviously large role for accounting and other financial services professionals to play a role. Internal controls may be the most obvious place for this dialogue and perspective to start, but that is merely the starting point for a wider ranging conversation. Discussing internal controls may not be the most buzzworthy or hottest topic in the accounting lexicon, but it seems relatively straightforward to see a future where internal controls and other cybersecurity issues will move from the mundane to most important topic for professionals. This topic and associated implications have an array of implications for research, course development, and publications, so let's take a look at some of those possibilities.

1. Conference presentations and other external opportunities, which can include fellowships and fundraising options which can benefit the institution itself as well as the reputation and career of the academic. Cybersecurity is a hot topic for sure, but that does not mean that accounting professionals have no role to play in this

debate and conversation. Actually, the expertise in testing and examining internal control systems to safeguard information creates a valuable opportunity for practitioners seeking to leverage experience to emerging academic and research.

2. Certificates and other courses emphasizing the importance and increasing role of technology in business operations and financial services in general. Given the reality that business managers and professionals are increasingly aware of the how important cyber policies and cyber insurance are to the success of business at large, there is already a demand for these kinds of content and programs out there in the marketplace. Developing programs, building certificates, or even allocating time in existing courses for these topics makes sense
3. Hiring and engaging with different faculty members in different technical subject matters also represents an opportunity to further develop and interdisciplinary team. Constructing and maintaining an interdisciplinary team is something that must be a part of the conversation where practitioners are concerned in terms of what exactly should be covered, taught, and examined in the discourse. What this means in practicality will differ from every institution, clearly, but it is important that different perspectives be brought to bear to asses both content problems and institutional challenges and opportunities that will invariably arise.

Bringing Value in an Interdisciplinary Landscape

The idea of an interdisciplinary team is not something that is usually associated with the business, financial services, and the accounting landscape but that is something that is going to become more important going forward. Whether the focus is spent on workplace practices and trends such as open office plans or some other recent workplace fad, the educational trends and content that needs to be part of the educational discourse in order to prepare students are clear. Drilling down to the core tenet of the idea, an interdisciplinary team is a team that is composed of different subject matter experts, which can be constructed of any array of subject matter experts and areas of focus. Given the traditional nature of interdisciplinary teams, grounded in the liberal arts, political science and humanity realms this might not be something that many practitioners have actually heard of previously. With that background and context let's take a look at what an interdisciplinary team might look like in the sense of a business department or business school in the modern landscape.

Depending on the institution in question there might be a department of business, economics, or an entire business school. There might be slight differences, but there are several general trends that are going to evident and present in the academic conversation. First and foremost there is going to have to be an assessment performed of the current faculty and subject matter experts already in place at the department or school in question. This might take the form of assessing current CVs, certificates, programs and courses, or some alternate developments but the goal needs to be the same. In any team there first step needs to be to understand just what exactly is already present at the team in question, allowing steps to be taken to fill the gaps in current experience or expertise. Second in the debate and conversation is developing a program or plan to fill in the gaps, expertise, and experience that currently exist. Again, this might take several different forms given the particular institution in question but that can be the hiring of additional faculty members, hiring adjunct faculty members, or partnering with different external institutions.

It is worth noting here that not one track, single methodology or tactic is going to have the effect of resolving every potential gap in the current or future content or course offerings. Acknowledging that, it is also worth noting that that there are some common pain points that do seem to arise whenever a new team is assembled that can short circuit even the most well thought out plan or management directives. Leaving for a second a strict academic conversation and even the accounting or financial services conversation, for now it seems more appropriate to factor management decision-making process and concepts that are going to need to be taken into account. Let's take a look at a few of the things that every involved in the process, from the academics involved the management professionals overseeing the changes and transformations underway across the higher education space.

Leading off the conversation there is invariably going to be the issue of dealing with personalities and other individual traits that might not always mesh together perfectly or even all that well. Of course, it is always important to separate the work matters at hand from the individuals involved in the process, but that is always going to occur no matter what work environment is being discussed. Balancing these different personalities and other issues is something that all involved, from the very top down, is something that can be amplified given workplace differences that can manifest in a professional sense. Second on the list is the fact that not every professional is as equally as respectful of other subsets of financial services as other might. For example, some accounting professionals might not the value in hiring individuals with no industry experience; a common question that is asked is "how can these people discuss and actually answer questions connected to workplace and industry issues without having ever completed these issues themselves?" Countering this very argument is an equally as strong statement put forward by individuals who might have completed more traditional PhD programs and training; how can these practitioner focused individual actually teach students without having ever gone through the PhD programming and educational schedule? Balancing these arguments is always a difficult task but can be amplified by the fact that some individuals that only possess practitioner experience might not feel that PhD offer any actual value.

The balancing of practical experience and PhD academic training expertise is perhaps the single most important fact to balance and contend with given the increasing blend of both traditional academics and practitioners that are occupying many of the same classrooms and institutions. Building on this countervailing balance and the associated issues that need to be contended with and counteracted is also the very real issue of keeping all members of the faculty up to date with current trends and information. No matter what path the individuals have taken to join the faculty conversation there will be a need for continuous training and education for all members involved. Partnering with external experts and sources of information is obviously a good place to start, but there is also a role to be played in the context of interdisciplinary teams for leveraging internal talent.

Linking back to the previous point about how important it is to accurately assess and evaluate the current levels of talent and expertise that is already present in the department or at the institution this is also an opportunity to leverage and learn from each other. Coordinating and collaborating with the other experts and individuals is, of course, a goal for individual departmental members but is also something that should be focused on at an institutional level as well. Learning from each other, taking advantage of the information already present and accounted for in the conversation.

Every Institution Is Different

This is arguably the most single most important factor to keep in mind as the workload and responsibilities of the faculty members are examined and discussed both prior to, and after, a job offer has been accepted. As discussed throughout the earlier sections of this text, there are a multitude of institutions out there in the marketplace for potential academic employment. Diving in a little deeper into the differences connected to these institutions is important for a multitude of reasons. One specific reason does seem to be most pertinent if the goal of the individual in question is to obtain and sustain continued employment at the institution. Specifically, the ratio and importance of teaching to other service and workload requirements will vary from institution to institution, and while this may seem rather obvious it is also something that could possibly be overlooked.

For example at an institution, be it a college or university, where research is considered to be the priority of faculty members, this also means that teaching and other types of service may not be classified as equally important, nor weighted as highly in the job evaluation criteria. Interesting from an anecdotal perspective, this may very well also have a significant impact on what occupies the time of faculty and staff members on a day-to-day basis. Conversely, at other institutions—including a few that I have been associated with either via employment or interviews for prospective employment—this ratio and discussion maybe reversed or otherwise altered. There is no hard and fast rule as to which component of faculty engagement should be ranked first, and there are equally as convincing arguments to be made on all sides. No matter what the ultimate result is, the importance of balancing different workload expectations necessitates having a conversation connected to these issues toward the beginning of your employment with any institution. This is a point that I cannot stress enough—both employee and employer need to be on the same page when it comes to what exactly will be the driving forces in how an employee will be evaluated and judged in the near, medium, and long term. Having these conversations up front is something that must be conducted, but this is also something that needs to be revisited on a continuous basis to make sure that all stakeholders are on the same page.

How should this conversation be held, you might ask? Discussing the specifics of a job or criteria for tenure/promotion might not seem like a reasonable thing to be immediately after landing a job, but that is exactly why it is so important. All too often I have seen, as I am sure you have as well, promising individuals and careers become sidetracked or mired in work that does not ultimately add all that much to their reputation or prospects for promotion. Especially since for many individuals the transition to academia also represents an entirely new industry it is arguably even more important to make sure that every effort is focused and allocated to where it will have the maximum impact now and going forward. With that said, let's do a deep dive into how the most common components of promotion and tenure can play out, and the implications that these efforts have on the time and energy allocated by faculty members to these individual areas.

A best practice that I currently employ, and that I wish I had incorporated into my approach to academic conversations sooner, is simply being forward and open about the issues that I wanted to know more about. If a question goes unasked the answer remains unknown, and when these questions are directly connected to how an individual will be evaluated from a jobs perspective, the importance of being able to address this issues in a frank and open matter cannot be overstated. Institutions are different from each other, different departments and schools at different institutions vary, and even specific departments can—and should—evolve and shift over time in terms of what is considered to be the most important.

Teaching and Instruction

Teaching and instruction may be what comes to mind for many people when the topic of college professors and higher education is first mentioned. From Henry Jones to Professor Selvig (from the Indiana Jones and Avengers movies, respectively) the most common connotation of educators is the role played in the classroom. While this is certainly not inaccurate or incorrect in any way, it really is critical to understand that for many academics, this is only one component of the work performed on a day-to-day basis. This may seem incongruous, based on our previous analysis of the duties of adjuncts, lecturers, and contract faculty, but for the moment I am going to approach this question from a different angle. Lecturing and teaching may look the same—an individual presents materials to other individuals for a set period of time—but the two are quite different, and regardless of the specific label used, the emphasis for any academic should remain on the teaching part. Quite frankly, simply reading off of the slide decks or other prepared materials is not a sustainable career arc for anyone entering the higher education field at the current time. With the rise of self-paced courses, online education, and other badging and credentialing programs in the marketplace it is increasingly clear that—in order to remain relevant—simply reading and repeating what had been done in the past will not be sufficient.

Perhaps the first thing that I found most interesting and challenging as I transitioned into higher education on a full-time basis, and even after following my adjunct and contract work in the past, was the effort and lengths I find myself going to in order to keep these courses interesting. For example, and building on both a personal and professional interest that I have, I always go to efforts to try and incorporate headline news stories and other pertinent information into the classroom discussions. Again, this may seem like a relatively straightforward and simple matter, but actually doing so on a continuous basis can be quite challenging if that is something you are not used to. In addition to requiring additional prep time in advance of the course itself, attempting to integrate headlines and other emerging topics into the classroom discussions also means that that the educators themselves must be up to speed and well informed as to what is going on in the blockchain subject matter space. No matter what specific subject matter is being discussed and analyzed within the course itself, it is important to reinforce and support the materials you are using to build the core of your course itself. This conversation, as multifaceted as it can be, also should be expanded upon while taking into account the differences between in-person, online, and hybrid courses.

Teaching in-person is clearly the format that most instructors, educators, and students are most comfortable and familiar with, and that makes sense given the relatively rapid rise of technology both in business at large as well as education. In-person courses, in my personal opinion and experience, can simultaneously be the simplest type of class to teach as well as the most difficult to teach and sustain interest in during a semester. On the one hand, the actual process of instructing in person is relatively straightforward; there are materials that have been prepared and the individual who is the instructor presents these materials, answers questions, and helps students understand specific nuances linked to the content itself. On the other hand, however, it is also important to be sure and maintain the interest levels of students during the semester as the content may be more or less interesting as the course evolves. This is also why myself and many instructors have taken to incorporating headlines and news headlines into the content that links back to the course material itself. Additionally, the level of energy and enthusiasm projected by the instructor can have a dramatic impact on how the class operates, so an in-person course does also place a higher burden on the instructor to drive and shape the narrative direction of the class itself.

Hybrid courses which do appear to have become more popular over the last several decades—augmenting traditional courses with technology—represent a true potential opportunity for instructors seeking to enter the higher education field. The driving force behind hybrid courses can be derived from a number of different underlying sources, and it is important to understand why the course is being taught as a hybrid in the first place. Courses that are part of an MBA program or curriculum may be offered in a hybrid format in order to accommodate the fact that those students may be working full time as well as enrolling this program. For example, I have had the opportunity to teach a specialized course designed as a capstone course at a major public university. This course was broken up into three distinct sections, with each in-person meeting (of 8 hours in length) augmented by discussion posts and other written assignments to keep the conversation and analysis continuing in between class meetings. No matter how the hybrid course is actually designed and instructed, understanding how to maintain interest is imperative. While the specific dynamics of how the course is managed will inevitably vary depending on the institution, instructor, and course in question I believe that a responsibility of the instructor is to make sure that students are engaged throughout all aspects of the course, including the times between the in-person meetings regardless of how those in-person meetings are structured.

Online courses have dramatically increased in popularity during the last decade or so, as the technology tools linked to online classes have finally caught up with the aspirations of educators to teach fully online courses. Entire institutions have sprung up to offer course and degree offerings in entirely online formats, and these offerings mirror the increased interest of students—of all ages—in taking courses that are online. Be it for convenience, remote instruction, or to help juggle the demands of work and education there are numerous reasons why both students and educators would be interested in online course offerings. With all of these course and degree offerings, however, there has also been a corresponding increase in the number of potentially faulty or subpar offerings. Especially prevalent in the lead up to the Great Recession, the specter or diploma mills—or institutions that would basically trade funds for degrees—increased to meet the demand of students as well as providing an acknowledgment that there does seem to be a limit on the number of educators qualified to teach in a fully online environment. Those issues aside, there are a number of factors that educators at every institutions need to keep in mind if and when they are tasked with teaching in an online-based environment either as a part of a program, or in a program that is entirely offered online. The importance of student engagement and interaction cannot be overstated if the class is taking place remotely. All of the tangential conversations and interaction that so often play a critical role during classes that meet in person simply will not occur in a class that happens entirely online. Firstly, this means that—despite some thoughts that suppose that teaching online is easier or simpler—there may actually be more work involved for educators teaching in an online-based class and environment.

Second, and here is where many online courses and program struggle the most, is that the assessment plan schedule need to be modified to reflect that different nature inherent in classes that are taught online. Simply assigning exams or other tests may not be the most appropriate methodology to assess students for any number of reasons. The ability of students to collaborate offline with colleagues, to access resources and answer keys, and to look for previously posted answer keys is all realities that need to be incorporated into the assessment plan. For a fully online class this may include assigning discussion posts, research papers, homework assignments, and only rely on "traditional" assessments as an additional assessment tool rather than the core assessment options. This is something that every instructor that has ever taught online has surely dealt with, but it is also something that needs to be modified and adjusted depending on the course and institution in question.

No matter what the specific format of the course is actually decided upon there does need to be sufficient preparation and resources put into place, and this is something that veteran professionals can be hesitant to invest in given the experience many professionals have. Preparation, taking the steps necessary to gather and present resource does certainly occupy time and energy, but are important for any professionals seeking to successfully transition from private industry to higher education. Different levels of classes, ranging from introductory to advanced courses, need varying levels of preparation and work before the courses themselves are actually launched.

The sheer amount of prep work and maintenance work that goes into a certain course or certain type of course cannot be treated lightly or merely treated as an afterthought. Every single course that is covered by a specific instructor needs to be prepared for and led with an equal level of participation and engagement regardless of the format. Online courses or courses that are taught in a hybrid format may initially seem like easier courses, or item that require less work on the side of the instructor; the opposite is often true. Even if a particular instructor enjoys the online experience and engagement with the student body, it is important to recognize that these types of courses do not operate in a vacuum. For example, many programs and degree programs have a requirement with regard to how many contact hours, i.e., in-person meeting hours, are required to keep the program accredited.

Research

Research is probably the second highest prominent and well-recognized role that academics and professors occupy and are associated with, and that is not without good reason. In many industries and fields, including business, but certainly more commonly linked to the sciences, research, experimentation, and working in various lab and research settings play a critically important role in the academic conversation. Coming from a professional field such as accounting might not bring to mind the same emphasis on research and experimentation that fields like biology and chemistry may bring to mind, but that does not mean that research is unimportant or lower profile in nature. The specific of research will be different from individual to individual or institution to institution, but there are two common areas of research and publications that do tend to dominate the conversation.

Practitioner or industry focused research is something that comes to mind, may be the type of research and information you are most familiar with, and that is because it is the most common and most mainstream type of research and publications. Magazines, trade publications, and other types of publications that are delivered to trade shows, conferences, organizations, and other professional areas and publications. These include many of the most common resources that practitioners are used to working with and referencing to assist with work, research, and providing advice to clients and customers. What this actually means from an academic perspective and is that many of the most familiar resources of information may not carry the same style of weight as lesser known research publications. Magazines such as Accounting Today, Accounting Web, Strategic Finance, the Wall Street Journal, the Economist are clearly high profile, well known, and have an enormous audience, but may not fulfill research requirements and expectations.

Research publications and requirements are going to be different depending on the role acquired by a professional, the goals of the individual in question, and the type of institution that is part of this conversation, so it is important to take a higher level perspective and analysis as to what needs to be examined and analyzed prior to launching this academic conversation. For example, any conversation before, during, and after the entry into higher education needs to be include and answer the following question; what is the expectation at of the institution in terms of both publishing quality and publishing format? Some institutions may be satisfied with a certain ratio of practitioner versus academic publications, but this is important to understand just what the differences are between practitioner and academic publications.

A question that I am asked quite a bit, by colleagues I know who are currently still employed in industry as well as colleagues who are entering into academia is—what exactly does research mean, especially from an accounting perspective? Accounting, at the core of the idea, is both the language of business as well as how internal and external users of an organization can understand and track the performance of a firm over time. Additionally, accounting information allows the end users to compare the performance of the organization to competitors. In this context, and especially if someone is coming from a background in corporate or public accounting, the idea of accounting professionals performing research and analysis in an abstract manner can seem illogical. Depending on the background and work that had been performed and conducted by the individual in question, there are going to be different areas that can be expanded and researched upon by academics. Without purporting to be an exhaustive list, let's take a look at some of the questions and considerations that might help frame the conversion of practical experience to academic research

1. What areas or emerging themes are dominating the specific accounting or financial conversation in the subset of the professional landscape that you have expertise within? This can be a regulatory issue, and accounting standards update, or simply control and

reporting considerations that are being influenced by external forces. Whatever the specific driving nature and trends are, there is always information that you practitioners have that can add value to the marketplace.

2. Are there questions that can be asked and answered connected to accounting themes or topics forming the basis of the research, and this is an important point that professionals need to keep in mind. Simply because there are open items, controversies, or areas of uncertainty connected to accounting work or reporting does not make it appropriate for research purposes. No matter how much or how interesting the topic may be, or how important the resolution is, there has to be a way to frame and address these questions in a logical manner. Diving into the question of how to frame the research, there are also different subsets of research that can be explored and assembled by professionals.

    a. Quantitative research. Perhaps the most logical and straightforward connection between accounting and research purposes, putting together quantitative research questions and publications can be more difficult than it might initially appear. Quantitative information connected to accounting is easy to come by, but it is also important to narrow the scope of research down to something that can be handled in an article format.

        i. Particularly from an accounting or financial services perspective the topic of research almost naturally turns to the subset of quantitative research. Accounting and audit, obviously, tend to focus most of all on the analysis, reporting, and disclosure of various quantitative data. It stands to reason that the majority of research in these fields, academic or practitioner in nature will mirror this reality.

    b. Qualitative research. While not commonly linked to accounting and other quantitative sciences and formats, qualitative research can—and often does—form an invaluable component in the broader analysis and reporting discourse. In most situations, what qualitative research entails is a combination of interviews, summarizing said interviews, and connecting both the interviews themselves as well as the responses to the research questions proposed by the researcher.

c. Exploratory research. This is perhaps the type of research that a plurality—if not a majority of the research—would fall into if it were categorized into predefined categories and areas. The name of the research is perhaps the most self-explanatory and simply to understand of the research types. Given the nature of accounting and financial services, including the many emerging technologies that are driving change and innovation within the different areas of the profession, exploring the effects of these technologies is something that is very much needed. Asking questions, analyzing current trends, themes, and news headlines connected both to the technologies and potential accounting changes are directions and aspects that should be included into any exploratory research.

During the writing of this book I had a very interesting conversation with a colleague of mine that triggered some interesting follow-up thoughts on my end. Following the completion of an article draft that I had reviewed for them, which was very well researched and assembled, there was only one potential issue that was observed. The article, in terms of structure, format, and content, was very well put together and assembled and crafted, but it did not seem to add anything new to the existing literature. An analogy that I had heard repeated during my doctoral studies was that, even if it is just one plank of wood being added onto an existing amount of research (the proverbial deck reaching out to the ocean), there does need to be some kind of additional information added to what already exists. As stated previously this does not mean that, by default, there needs to be necessarily be a creative or innovative approach taken to every aspect of the research itself, but that there does need to be something new added to what already exists. This lack of any new findings was the only potential issue with an otherwise well crafted and assembled piece of academic writing. Bringing this issue to my colleague's attention generated a response that was a partial mix of confusion and curiosity—how exactly could an accounting focused article be put written and submitted by only adding new information to the literature. In other words, didn't the article have to pose, address, and answer questions, instead of just posing potential questions and items.

No matter what type of research is put together and assembled it is important that the research itself adds something, incremental as it may be, to the existing conversation and debate related to the subject at hand. Tax, audit, advisory, or some emerging areas of accounting technology and information systems are not always going to be able to be solved and addressed in a single article. In fact, addressing and resolving an issue connected to emerging areas may take a series of articles, books, or a combination therein of different media sources. Acknowledging this, and realizing that not every article will end up with a positive or even satisfactory resolution or answer, is a fact that every practitioner seeking to successfully transition to academia will need to become more comfortable with. Versus having a definitive problem—tax return, investment thesis, or client request, to document and address, the academic writing and discourse experience can and often is quite ambiguous in nature, requiring that professionals be aware of and comfortable with ambiguity connected to how these issues should be addressed and analyzed. Although explaining this to my colleague in a way that minimized frustration took a few minutes of both of our afternoons it was worth the time. Both for my colleague, who had invested significant time in this research project, and myself, the conversation let us both obtain a better understanding of academic research projects and potential opportunities.

Additional Opportunities

Another opportunity and area for practitioners to apply some of their market knowledge and awareness is to also step into more administrative roles and other areas of higher education and academia that might not be connected specifically to either the classroom or research. One subset of higher education and academia that might be of interest to those practitioners that have recently transitioned is to serve or assist with the leadership of a program or course programs. For example, in the face of declining enrollment at many institutions and the inclusion of non-traditional students into the mix in every larger percentages, there is always the risk that some traditional graduate levels programs will face declining enrollments and lack of student interest moving forward. No matter what the underlying cause may be the reality is that institutions and program cannot survive or exist in the face of declining enrollment without taking proactive action and steps. This is where practitioners and other individuals with market experience can lend a helping hand by bringing some fresh ideas and dynamic thinking to the conversation. Let's take a look at some of the possible applications and instances where this might play out going forward.

1. Developing of new programs and certificates, but especially a CPA prep class. Focusing for a minute on the accounting specific subset of the financial services conversation the development and offering a CPA prep class is something that is routinely cited as something that students, faculty, and administrators are interested in offering. In addition to the desires of students and other faculty members, the CPA pass rate is a metric and benchmark that is used to judge the effectiveness and efficacy of the program. While it is not a guarantee that simply offering the program will lead to increased pass rates or enrollment this is definitely something that students look for.
2. Leading or at least assisting with the management or leadership of a masters program or other type of graduate work. Undergraduate students are certainly one important category of students and mean a lot to institutions of higher education, but that is only one part of the puzzle. Undergraduate students, no matter what college or university is in question, usually do not pay the full sticker price of tuition and all fees, many of them transfer or otherwise leave the institution, and some of them occupy a larger percentage of ancillary costs than might otherwise be incurred. In other words, although a large amount of the debate and conversation around college costs and graduation rates enter on undergraduates, an area of increasing importance and profitability are graduates students and other types of students.
3. Leveraging this understanding and knowledge represents both a challenge and an opportunity for practitioners and institutions alike. What this mean is that practitioners might be able to lend a different perspective and point of view than traditional academics might be able to do so otherwise. Heading up a program as an advisor is a unique way in which someone can add value to current students, future students, and the institution at large.

That said there is only so much time in any given day, semester, or academic year so it is important for academics—especially academics that have only recently joined the higher ed space—make the best use of their time. In addition to weighing the pros and cons of various activities from a promotion or tenure perspective there is also the underlying reality that not everyone is equally as good at everything; it is always important to play to your strengths. Before examining some of the considerations and factors that need to be assessed when deciding which areas are most important, the first thing to decide and realize is that it is always important to discuss these different items with your chairperson, dean, or other applicable individual.

So, What Counts the Most?

There is certainly value that can, and is, derived and connected from both practitioner and academic publications, but one of the major conversations and connections that many practitioners have can be summarized as follows. Practitioner publications, including many of the trade journals and magazines that most practitioners are familiar with, have huge audiences and a large market impact. What this means is that articles, blogs, and podcasts that aspiring academics publish in, or attempt to publish within, may have an outsized or larger impact that other types of publications. Academic journals, contrastingly, often count for quite a bit more than practitioner publications, but have a much smaller audience than other publications. A common joke or comment that is often made among new academics is that there are 3 people that read most articles; the author, the peer reviewer, and the editor that makes the final publication decision. Understanding this, and making sure that the correct and appropriate balance is maintained during the academic process is something that is important for every academic.

Even though many of these academic publications may have a much smaller audience and circulation than practitioner publications, the ranking and impact associated with many of these publications is the subject of debate and discourse within the academic community. There are many scores, rankings, and listings that are published and disseminated throughout the academic community, and that is not even the end of this conversation. Depending on the specific academic subset in question and being analyzed there can be dozens of listings and rankings that can be put together and used at a number of institutions. This is something especially important to discuss and analyze up front when an aspiring academic is discussing the publishing and research requirement that applies to that specific career track. Due to the fact that many of these publications count highly toward promotion or tenure the importance of performing research on the specific listing or journal in question is important. Publishing in academic journals can take several months from submission to ultimate publication, which does need to be incorporated into any promotion timeline.

Basically there is virtually no limit of the side of practitioners seeking to write and distribute as wide an array of research as so desired. There is certainly an audience and market for any format of research, and thought leadership can range from peer reviewed articles to a podcast with an up and coming business commentator. Even though there is such a broad-based appetite for quality accounting research and analysis it is important that researchers focus efforts on quality journals that carry weight at the institution in question. On top of having to analyze the option it is important to figure out what combination of production and content makes the most sense to for you, your role, institution, and career arc. While it is clear that these goals and directions may shift over time there is a fundamentally important factor that needs to be understood and taken into account by any academic. Crafting a narrative is a theme and topic that is reiterated throughout this book, and that is for a specific reason; making logical and objective choices is an imperative given the importance of maximizing time. Let's take a look at some of these factors, including the decision criteria that can be incorporated into how these choices are made, and how to potentially work on these better.

Perhaps the most important criteria that should be taken into account with regard to the type and form of content that you will produce and distribute is the ratio of time investment to outcome. Like any other project or initiative there is always going to be a tradeoff between the time invested into a certain project and the benefits that these projects are going to ultimately deliver. Whether it takes the form of a whitepaper, presentation, or some other form of media it does seem to make sense to focus on topics that you are already familiar with. In my personal experience that has been recently taking the form of blockchain, cryptoassets, and the integration of emerging technologies with cybersecurity, but there is also a significant risk that can accompany such a focus. Given the fact that technologies change so quickly that means that the time invested at a certain time might not seem so important or relevant at some point in the future. Deciding on how to invest ones time and energy is arguably the most important decision that any aspiring faculty member or educator can make, so let's break down what that might look like.

Second, focusing on the correct medium for the content production is something that must be taken into account when attempting to produce and distribute content and other information. Depending on the topic in question, the length of topic that is going to be discussed, and the technical specifics of the content in question it is important to decide what makes the most sense. For a technical topic that contains numerous technical specifics and details it would seem to make more sense to have that topic discussed and analyzed in a longer form written format. News updates and other types of information might be better suited for publication in a shorter form or online format. Blog posts, practitioner articles, or other online formats and media outlets might be a better fit for topic such as market updates, news items, or industry headlines. Deciding how long a written piece of content should be is almost as equally as important as the topic to be covered itself; longer form publications might not attract as many readers or social media impressions, but simply might make more sense.

Taking into account the entire process of editing, reviewing, and eventually publishing content a good approach and mindset to take might be to attempt to find a balanced approach of practitioner and academic content. Certain forms of content and information may be more or less appropriate for different publication venues, but the overarching theme is that there should always be a blend and mix of content and information for every topic that is discussed. Even if initially it is difficult to compose and author a full-length academic article it is important to start writing and composing research and other types of information into a written format. No matter what type of content is being discussed and analyzed, written content is the gold standard from an academic perspective. Writing and publishing written content is going to be something that is going to have to be done anyway, so it is essential that a writing routine and consistency be established.

The Review and Editorial Process

Before discussing the ins and outs of how the editorial process might actually play out, there is something else that needs to be mentioned first; you need to have proof and evidence for everything that you claim as an output. In some instances the evidence or proof related to your work will be pretty straightforward and simple to get the backup or supporting documentation that you need. For example, a peer reviewed journal article will either have a physical print issue, or at the very least have a PDF version that is available to be downloaded, shared, or otherwise distribute. Even for newer journals or journals that might be as well established or as prestigious as some of the other journals out there and available for publishing with there will be some sort of output that results from the writing and publishing of the piece. Books are even easier to have evidence or proof for—the very end result of the efforts (be it a solo book or a collaborative effort) is the proof or evidence that would be requested anyway. Where this can be a little bit tricky, however, is if you are undertaking work and projects that might not have a tangible end result or product. Let's take a look at how this might play out for many aspiring or even newly established academics.

Many of the most widely known and read practitioner publications in the accounting and finance space might have not a physical or print edition, or even if there had been a print version previously it may have been superseded by an online or otherwise digital version. This might not seem like an issue—after all virtually everything is online in the current environment—but this can trip up some people who do not think this through all the way. Let's take a look at some of the issues that can arise for articles and other published works that are only in place in a virtual or digital format.

1. What if the hyperlink to that article breaks or otherwise becomes unavailable? We have all experienced an issue where a Web site or hyperlink that had been fully functional previously is, at some future point, unavailable. In most cases this can be chalked up to being an inconvenience, but in the realm of publishing this can not only qualify as an inconvenience, but a serious negative impact to the publishing track record of the aspiring academic.
2. What happens if the article, which may have been freely available previously, gets placed behind a paywall or otherwise becomes restricted? As more and more content of all kinds moves behind paywalls or other restrictions this is not an idle concern, and there is little that independent authors can do about this.
3. In the context of publishing and content production there is also something that can easily happen; the work and editorial slant of the publishing house and Web site can always change in between the time of an initial article submission as well as your own opinion evolving over time.

The importance of having proof or evidence might seem like an extraneous piece of information, or something that is not terribly important, but that could not be further from the truth. Basically, the only way that an aspiring academic or someone that has recently moved from private industry to higher education can prove that these events have happened, occurred, or have actually been published is with evidence. Establishing and maintaining a consistent recording keeping policy might sound like a topic covered in every introductory accounting course, but can be something that is very often overlooked or ignored during the early transition to higher education. Let's take a look at a few tips and ideas that I have developed—through trial and error—that might be of assistance for any former practitioner seeking to make a smooth transition to higher education. No matter what specific type of academic position is sought after or obtained it is critically important to make sure that everything that you are going to claim as something that you have done has proof to that be independently verified.

1. Immediately after an event, presentation, article, or book happens or is published you should document the where, when, how, and why this event or publication happened. This might take the form of obtaining a physical copy of a book or other paperwork, taking a screenshot of an article that is only available in an online format, or even saving pictures of an event program, or your session that occurred on site.
    a. This is just like the importance of documenting receipts or expenses immediately after a business trip or other type of business event; something that might not be super fun or enjoyable but something that is absolutely necessary.
2. Save this evidence as soon as possible in whatever platform, portal, or format in which your institution provides or prefers. In my case this has taken two forms; at one institution it took the form of a physical record, and at Lehman it has emerged and taken the form of a digital record. No matter what the preferred methodology is, it is important to make sure that you make every effort that you monitor, update, and maintain these records on a continuous basis. Doing so helps enables that you will not find yourself following behind on documentation, which can negatively impact your likelihood of obtaining promotion or other benefits.
3. Establish and maintain a record keeping process that you can actually maintain, which sounds like a simple and straightforward process, but can be more complicated than it might otherwise appear. Like

any other habit or process there needs to be consistency—working out, establishing a financial plan or trying to complete a home improvement project—there needs to be a balance between your goals and ambitions and the reality on the ground. It can be tempting to construct a complicated and multifaceted plan, but the plan needs to be balanced out by the fact that some weeks will be busier and more active than others.

Let me drop in a personal story that might illustrate just how important establishing and maintaining appropriate documentation policies can be. During my time on the tenure track I was doing all of the right things—presenting, writing, and providing service to the institution. That said, and because I was so occupied in doing things rather than also tracking them, I ended up having to spend the equivalent of an entire week putting together the supporting documentation and support for all of my activities. Fortunately I had the time and bandwidth to go ahead and do so, but this was a pointed remember to me of just how important documenting what you are doing is. In fact, the argument could be made that documenting and reporting what you are doing in full, rather than putting these process off until a future date, might be important than any single event you are a part of. This might sound strange, or outright unfair, and I fully understand that perspective, but it's also important to understand this from the perspective of your department chair or administration team. You certainly know what you have been up to and doing over the last year or several years, well, because you were there. These individuals, no matter how well you try to keep them informed, are simply not going to have the same memories or experiences as you. This is through absolutely no fault on the part of these individuals; it is up to you to help and try and ensure that all of your accomplishments are well documented and presented in the most favorable manner to you. Acknowledging how important these factors are also raises one last consideration that I would highly recommend to anyone seeking to successfully transition from the private sector or practitioner sector to higher education—backing up your information!

As anyone who has ever written an scholarly article or, even more so, an entire book can attest to this process can take months, if not years (in the case of some books) to actually go from idea, to draft, to final draft, to final publication. While in and of itself this is not something that is necessarily a bad thing this can open you up to a significant potential risk;

the potential loss of your information. Practitioners might scoff at this being presented since we all know the importance of backing up information, but in most corporate or private sector environments this is normally handled by either an internal IT team or an authorized third party. As an academic or potential academic it is entirely upon you to make sure that all of your information is backed up on a continuous basis. We are going to revisit some strategies and tips to assist with this, but for now let's pivot back to the deeper conversation around editorial processes and the specifics of how these processes work. With all of that said, let's dive into some of the mechanics and specifics that drive the editorial process forward for all academics.

One cannot have a discussion, much less a robust discussion about the academic publishing landscape without taking a quick stop to discus and examine the important role that editors and peer reviewers play in the process. This may come as something of a shock for practitioners that have published in magazines or web portals previously, and might seem completely alien to practitioners without a history of publishing an array of written content. Especially for peer reviewed articles the process that every article much undergo prior to publication is known as peer review, and can take large amounts of time and energy. For example, it is not unusual for an article be submitted and for the author to not hear as to the status of the article for months. Even after the author hears back, a common response is known as "R & R," or revise and resubmit; depending on the scope of requested revisions this process itself can take a month or so to do comprehensively. What can be the most frustrating of all, however, is that after this initial review and subsequent revision there is no guarantee that the article will be accepted for publication. Given the amount of effort, time, and sometimes financial resources (in the form of review or publication fees) that had been invested into this project this can be an extremely frustrating outcome. Understanding how this process works from the beginning, and trying to not become frustrated if items do not work out exactly as planned is an important mental adjustment that many authors—including this author—had to make.

Although usually the editorial process is normally associated with peer reviewed articles in academic journals that may be more or less interesting and widely spread, there is also a peer review and/or editorial process that is associated with non-academic journals. There is also something to be said about the fact that not every journal is going to be classified the same, or even close to the same, by every college or university; figuring out how certain journals are classified and reported is an important part of the writing publication process. Like everything else in the marketplace, not every single product or deliverable is going to be ranked or considered as legitimate, high profile, or worthy of inclusion as other journals or publications. A quick Google search will reveal the sheer number of options that are available for academics to rank and assess different publishing venue. For example, some journals and publications might be ranked as an A, or top level journal, and other journals might be ranked as a B or C, which indicates that while these journals are included on the listing and are going to be considered as part of the peer reviewed journal process they will not count for as much. In practice this might play out that every 1 "A" level article or publication counts for multiple articles or publications included in lower-tier journals.

Adding on to this implication and implementation there are journals that might be considered peer reviewed by some institutions that are not peer reviewed by other colleges or universities. In my personal experience there are two journals in particular that, while not listed or included on the list or peer reviewed journals, do go through a peer review process and are included as a peer reviewed publication venue at some other places. The review or editorial process varies from publication to publication, clearly, but virtually every article goes through some sort of review and editorial process. While this might take different forms, and may include only a review by the editor and in-house experts versus being sent out to external reviewers, there is almost always going to be edits, comments, and suggestions that are included in different drafts of the article. This might seem like a nuance or relatively unimportant clarification or part of the article publishing process, but can make all the difference in the world when deciding what journal or venue to publish articles in or associate with going forward.

This is not to say that the review process is always going to be the same or even be consistent across different journals or magazines, but it is important to understand that there are going to be differences involving what is associated with publishing in different magazines, journals, or articles. In fact, it might even be in your best interest and of better interest for your academic career and progression to spend the time developing what might be considered to be a multi-prong approach to publishing and information production. While this does sound good on paper, quite clearly, it can be more difficult to implement in reality than simply on paper, and requires that the author understand what is going to be expected in the article and conversation around these articles. Specifically, this might understanding and developing, in essence, two types of writing styles and voices depending on the audience, so let's dive into what that might entail from a practical sense.

1. Academic journals and publications are normally less interested in the opinion or perspective of the individual contributor or author than the quantitative data that can support the claims and information stated within the article. This approach makes logical sense from the point of view of academic reviewers and editors who are tasked with safeguarding the reputation and rigor of the journal itself. By that same token, however, it can also make the submission and publication of articles in the journal seem to resemble themselves over and over again. One phrase and piece of advice that I received during my doctoral process is that academic research and studies are not meant to shake the world or discover new pieces of information, but to rather build on existing research. A mental example that might make this proverb make more sense is the concept of—instead of constructing an entirely new deck—that authors and researchers should focus on adding additional planks to the existing structure
2. Practitioner journals and publications are, conversely, focused on the opinion and technical expertise of the contributors and authors which is often why they are invited to contribute in the first place. Usually shorter in nature and more focused on the opinion and current interpretation of marketplace trends, these types of articles can also be focused on offering advice, guidance, or perspective as to how this information, trends, or data should be analyzed and dealt with by the profession. From a practical manner it is also worth noting that there are many more non-academic venues and places for publication than academic sources. Framed in the context of the number of practitioners versus faculty members it should be readily clear that there are many more practitioner journals than academic publications.

How to Approach Editors

Approaching editors is always a tricky business, and can even be more complicated than other contact and engagement with different members of the publication and media landscape. As outlined in other places throughout this text the power that editors and editorial board have over what articles are published, what types of articles are featured, and how this entire process tends to evolve and work is difficult to understate. Making sure that the editorial format and take of your article are in alignment with the goals and objectives of the journal at large is something that should definitely form the first base and foundation of how any editorial process is started and further developed. In addition to making sure that the framing of your article fits the narrative of the journal or other publication in question, it is also worth noting that editors and other editorial personnel are people as well. This might seem like a clear cut and obvious statement, but it is worth repeating simply because it is tempting to treat these individuals as faceless and emotionless people. Conferences may often be derided as simply an opportunity for certain individuals and organizations to enjoy themselves on the company tab, but they also do present a unique opportunity for aspiring authors and early career academics to meet and speak with editors and other editorial minded individuals.

That said, approaching an editor—either via an email or in-person conversation—should be constructed and handled as if you were meeting anyone else for the first time. People are people after all, and it is important to not just launch directly into your elevator pitch the second you make eye contact with someone. Elevator pitches are things that are often rehearsed in business schools and classrooms, but in actuality they often serve to put people off and cut off any natural flow of conversation. It is important to always have a summary and other sort way to explain and categorize your research—of course—but it is also important to only play that hand if the opportunity presents itself. For example you might run into an editor or someone who you might want to work with at a conference or other type of engagement, and after that initial meeting and/or conversation it might be worthwhile to follow up with an email or other type of message. This approach, rather than pouncing on them the instant you make contact, is a great opportunity to outline some of the ideas and topics you might want to pursue in more detail moving forward.

Non-academic Editing and Reviews

Although the review process and procedures that are normally associated with the publishing and editorial process are normally associated with academic journals that does not mean that there is no review process or component when publishing in practitioner journals. In fact, the review and editorial process associated with some of the higher profile practitioner publications and magazines can be equal to, if not more, rigorous and comprehensive than some academic journals. While there is a review and editorial process embedded in the publication of any article this also means that it is important to understand what precisely this might entail. Not meant to be an exhaustive listing or chronicling of how this process will work, these considerations should rather serve as a reminder and listing of what to expect when you are dealing with a practitioner journal.

1. First and foremost is the fact that the editorial review process will invariably take time regardless of whether or not it is associated with an academic or practitioner journal. Taking a peek behind the curtain, let's see just what reviews can take what can feel like an inappropriately long amount of time for a review product that might actually be quite short and uninformative.
   a. Reviewers are almost without exception volunteering their time to conduct these reviews and are most commonly either fellow academics or practitioners with significant experience in the field being analyzed within the article itself. Volunteer efforts and work can, at the end of the day, only be expected to produce and provide so much in terms of timelines and work product. In addition to this underlying reality there is also the simple fact that these individuals are also trying to juggle the demands of regular jobs, social lives, and what other professional endeavors they are participating in.
2. The review will be by practitioners so it is important to remember that these individuals are not likely going to be as concerned with the academic integrity and informational clarify as academic individuals, but will rather focus and pay attention to the practicality and applicability of this information and articles for practitioners employed in the workforce. To that end the implications and areas of focus for these individuals are less likely to be concerned with the ability of this information to add to existing research, and instead will be focused on what practitioners can use this research for in the workforce.

3. While it is true that the areas of focus for practitioner reviewers and other individuals will not be the same as academic reviews and articles this is no excuse to do less than expected with regard to how the research is constructed and put together. Specifically, there are some practitioner journals—labeled as such—that are going to still expect academic citations and other references in order to consider this research for inclusion in their publication.

Clearly the conversation around the editorial process is something that is usually focused around the peer reviewed and academic journal conversation and dialogue, but it is also something that needs to be taken into account for practitioner or other non-academic journals. Even if it does not purport or present itself as a peer reviewed journal or publication you can certainly rest assured that someone will be reviewing and examining your submission for accuracy and other factors.

It is also important to take into account the fact that even in the face of edits and reviews there is going to be the need for individuals to be able to incorporate these reviews and comments into the working document. Receiving feedback and commentary on your articles and intellectual property, especially if that feedback and commentary is not positive in nature, might not always be an enjoyable process. That said, there are a few ways in which this feedback can be received, incorporated in updated drafts, and used to improve the overall quality of the product. Let's take a look at a few of ways in which you (1) receive feedback and other commentary, and (2) some steps and tactics that can be taken in order to effectively incorporate this feedback into your working product/paper. Not meant to be an all inclusive or exhaustive listing, this should be taken as a listing of suggestions and considerations that might assist you as you content and work with the feedback that invariable comes from submitting articles.

1. Don't take it personally. This might be easier said than done, but it is important to not take the commentary and feedback related to your article or submission personally. While it might seem difficult to not incorporate these feedbacks and other components of the commentary that is an important part of the feedback process. In other words, as you are receiving your feedback and other comments

on your submission it is important to retain a level head and be able to contextualize this information as it occurs.

2. Be willing to incorporate the feedback and comments into your pieces and submissions that are going to be reviewed as a result of the editorial process. It is never easy to receive feedback and commentary as it relates to your submissions, but it is especially important to be able to leverage this mindset into your feedback and revisions going forward. Being able to take the feedback that you will need to integrate into your paper is important, but if you are unable to do so in person there is the need for you to take the feedback into account.
3. You have to be able and willing to incorporate the feedback that is provided to you within the context of both your article and the broader economic landscape at large. What this means will vary from article to article, clearly, but will otherwise be important from the point of view with regard to your article. What this means, from article to article, is that you will need to be able to incorporate these insights and feedback into your piece on a case by case basis.
4. If you need to review and revise your article on a case by case basis there might be a need to institute some sort of rewrite and revise policy that might indicate the significant revision of your article at a certain point in time. Rewriting the article and adding some additional content to the piece and written may be a frustrating process, but it is something that every author or contributor to any academic or established publication needs to be aware of, and accepting of, as a part of the publishing process.

The Review Process

The review process itself is a rather interesting quirk of the academic publishing field and process that is conducted in virtually every corner of academia. No matter how prestigious or well known an individual or team of individuals may be, or how unknown and new to the field they are, the person must undergo the exact same review process for every academic article that is published. Every journal or journal association will have its own quirks and unique way of conducting itself, but the following steps are most likely going to be a part of how the article production, approval, and publication process are assembled. Before diving into the specifics of academic publishing—always a riveting topic at cocktail parties—it does make sense to point out one important piece of information that does need to be understood; any potential article needs to be pitched and aligned to the aims, scope, and interests of the journal itself. It is all too common for an author to develop an article concept, idea, or pitch and complete an entire first draft before even having reviewed the publishing track record of the journal or institution that sponsors the journal. Doing this is not only frustrating, but can lead to a long and drawn out review process that results in the rejection of the article in any case. That said, let's break down how exactly the peer review process usually works in academic publishing, and some key points to consider during this process.

1. The first step in any article submission is to usually create some sort of account with the journal or institution that is sponsoring the journal that requires you to submit profile information and other meta-data. Seemingly a straightforward task, it is worth taking the time necessary to make sure that are completing this section and aspect of the publishing process correctly. For example, if you are working on a project that might take a several months or even a year to complete, be sure that you have the ability to edit or otherwise update the information being incorporated at this stage. There are few things more frustrating than having to assemble a new profile every time you wish to submit a new draft or manuscript.
2. Secondly, and here is the where the proverbial rubber can hit the road, is that you must also be able to construct and write a manuscript that can—for lack of a better word—stand the test of time. By that I mean that if you are working on a manuscript for an academic journal or other type of publication it can easily take several months for this article to move through the publication process. Topics and updates that might have been relevant at the time of publication may not be nearly as relevant, or might even be out as date. Such an occurrence actually happened to an article I co-authored with a colleague, with a (very) slight edit needing to be made to several words. This was not due to any definitive change to the source material that had been utilized, but was due to a determined individual of the firm insisting the meaning was different than what was in the writing. Deciding whether or not to make changes or adjustments going in an already published text is

a separate conversation entirely, but is something that does occur from time to time.

3. Every so often you are also asked to compile and put together a list of proposed reviewers for your work as you are submitting a journal article for potential publication. While this might seem like an unusual request—some might think it akin to stacking the deck in your favor—many journals make an explicit point of stating that the individuals recommended or suggested may not take part in the review of your submission. In other words, the individuals that you recommend will most likely just be added to the potential reviewer pool for other submissions going forward. There is, of course, the possibility that an individual that you know will receive a submission you put forward to a journal, and this is where the double-blind portion of the peer review process serves the most important role.
4. The term double blind might initially bring to mind some kind of school yard game, but the idea underlying this concept is actually relatively basic in nature. When submitting an academic article for review and potential publication in an academic journal it is important that this process be as unbiased as possible. Compared to publication in a magazine or trade journal the importance of publishing peer reviewed journals the weight and importance of peer reviewed articles is difficult to overstate. In virtually every case the number and quality of peer reviewed articles that have been published in academic journals plays a large role in the promotion and tenure conversation.

    a. How the double-blind process works in practice is that even though identifying information (name, institution, etc.) is included in the submission portal or meta-data none of this information is included in the submission sent out to reviewers. This, combined with the anonymous nature of the reviewers—the submitter does not know who exactly is reviewing their submission—helps remove any potential bias from the process.

5. Following the completion of the review process in general the submitting author will receive feedback that can take several different forms. In any event there is usually a summary or letter from the editor that provides commentary and/or the opinion of the editor on the reviewer feedback that has been received. On top of that summarization that will be provided there will also be

the individual feedback and commentary that is provided by the reviewers themselves. Said feedback can take several different forms but will normally include what the reviewer considered to be the positive attributes of the work as well as any negative attributes of the work as well. Depending on the scope and tone of the feedback that has been received by the author individual the author may have to revise and resubmit the proposed article.

a. Assuming that the article does eventually get approved for publication it is also important to remember and keep in mind that the time between acceptance, approval, and publication can be several months. In fact, and if the research itself requires the surveying of information and other data, the publishing process can end up taking over a year. In terms of keeping data and the associated findings relevant this is something that needs to be incorporated throughout the research and publication process.

The review process can be controversial in nature, can lead to hard feelings, and might even be construed as unfair by some individuals. Given the high stakes nature of peer reviewed publications for the tenure process the importance of selecting a journal that is appropriate for your publication or content ideas is extremely important. Peer review processes can stretch through months if not even years, and an unsuccessful publication attempt can result in extreme frustration and aggravation if that is not taken into account and acknowledged. What this means, for example, is that you must take that time factor into account when selecting journals for publication, and while this listing is not all inclusive nor exhaustive it should at least be used as a starting point for your own individual conversation and debate.

First and foremost, it is an important step to review prior published articles that have already been reviewed, selected, and published by the journal itself. Not a perfect way to judge whether any new article is appropriate in a journal, but reviewing the articles that have previously been published might give you an idea as to whether or not your piece is acceptable. Given that each journal is different and can focus on different types of research (qualitative, quantitative, or a mix of both) even if other articles have been accepted that does not mean that your specific article will be accepted. Second, review the editorial boards of any journal that you are considering to submit an article too and, if possible, try and glean any insights or other information that you can from that personal track record. Something else that might be worth doing or considering is to track and review the citation and publication history of the individuals included in the review and editorial process. There are many different sources and places where this information can be gathered and reviewed from so it is a good idea to cross reference and review just what exactly these grades and review scores can indicate.

Third, and only after you are relatively sure that this journal is indeed a good fit for you and your article should you take into account the formatting and guidelines that the journal seems to prefer and request. Every journal is different and will have varied guidelines in terms of what they request and would like to see in submitted articles, so trying your best to follow directions is an important part of the article submission process. Taking the time to format and organize your article submission before you sent it for review and potential publication is a step in the process that might seem tedious and optional but that is a mistake that can delay or even permanently hinder the potential publication process. If I could do back and do one thing over again as far as my early article submissions were concerned it would be to take more care and time to correctly format and organize my articles in the templates and guidelines.

Attempting to format and compose an article that is in close alignment with editorial and publishing guidelines at any one specific journal, however, also can cause several different issues along the way. For example, there is something that should be taken into account; even if you take the time and effort to format and integrate the specific formatting and editorial phrasing and other associated information that is no guarantee that the article will be accepted. An approach that I have had significant success with in the more recent past is comprised of the following steps and processes. Composing an article, first and foremost, is based on deciding on an idea, research methodology and research questions that has academic validity and robustness that makes a contribution to the existing research field and academic discourse.

Next, there needs to be an appropriate literature review comprised of both practitioner and academic sources that both support and reinforce the arguments and hypothesis being presented in the article itself. After creating an approach, research question and research methodology, as well as getting appropriate sources that are current and relevant in nature, there should also be some kind of conclusion, wrap up, or other concluding thoughts. These core components and information should always be present in every article, but there are a few different forms that these components can ultimately take. Depending on the specific research question and research topic that is being proposed the outcomes and end result of the research itself have potential to vary widely. Drilling down specifically to the some of the examples, research results can include, but are not limited to the following.

1. Expansion and reaffirmation of existing research
2. A repudiation of existing and previous research that had previously established facts and norms
3. Open-ended questions that leave the door open for future research, examination, and discussion
4. An exploratory framework that can, in theory, be used by future researchers to complete or augment that the research in question has raised
5. The disproval of specific hypotheses or research questions that were posed at the beginning of the research, and the reality of where the research ends up.

It should be obvious by this point that the array of research possibilities and opportunities is widespread for any accounting or financial services faculty member. These very possibilities, however, can also result in some confusion and misunderstanding as to what exactly is going to be expected in terms of content. If I had to offer one piece of advice that has served me well it would be to focus less on the specific output in mind, and to instead focus on putting together good research idea and concept. As long as the idea and research is comprehensive and robust, the end result and format does not matter as much as one might initially think.

Trends in Editorial Processes and Content Production

Like any other industry or segment of the economy there are inevitably going to be changing trends and directions that influence the direction of the academic publishing sector. While the initial analysis of this sector might lead some to believe that it stands apart from others due to its academic affiliation, the exact same pressures that influence other economic sectors have also impacted the academic publishing circuit. Cost pressures, competitive pressures, and the growing threat of open source alternatives are core to the changing dynamics in this academic publishing sector. Taking a look at a few of them, the following section seeks to document, present, and examine some of these fundamental trends.

Commercial Versus Open Source

Academia and academic publishing might not seem like a place where debate and change would be occurring on a continuous basis, but in fact that is exactly what is happening in virtually every aspect of the publications landscape. Alongside the increasing cost of college education at large, there is an increasing focus on the cost of text and other educational materials. Drilling down into what this might exactly mean it is relevant to first point out that this focus on the cost of educational materials is neither a new occurrence nor should it be something that should come as a surprise to anyone familiar with the educational space. Textbooks, particularly texts books for focused or more niche subject areas such as accounting or finance, can routinely cost in excess of $200 for a single course. High costs can be frustrating for any number of reasons, but can be especially frustrating in the instances where these textbooks are only usable or applicable for a single course and cannot be reused or even used for a one year. This growing area of frustration has eventually manifested itself into the current criticism and feedback linked to textbook and other educational material costs. The end result of this pressure and increased focus on costs has been the proliferation of focus on the creation and distribution of open educational resources.

Open educational resources, or OER, as they are commonly referred to in conversation, have taken the conversation by storm during the last several years as a direct result of the continued cost pressure and feedback loop as a part of the broader critique on higher education at large. In essence the focus of this OER conversation is the question whether or not quality educational content and materials can be created and distributed at low or no cost for students. From a high-level perspective, it seems to make sense that higher education would eventually begin to leverage the trends toward crowdsourcing and open source product development that continues to permeate other aspects of the economy. Producing content for free, however, does lead to the rather obvious question; if the content is going to be provided for free to students how are the content creators and publishers going to be compensated for their efforts? The appeal of OER is that it, on paper, creates a situation in which the students obtain access to the same quality of materials without the expenditures that are currently necessary. With every potential benefit, however, there are always going to be drawbacks and negatives as well.

Taking a look at the ongoing debate and conversation surrounding the commercial versus OER content and information there are several areas and instances in which there are merits to both sides of the issue. Without purporting to represent an all-inclusive representation of the issues, these items listed below should instead form the basis for a more comprehensive and robust conversation moving forward.

1. Students and other individuals are being increasingly accustomed to accessing information and content either for free, or on a low-cost/streaming basis with services such as Uber, Netflix, and others providing on-demand, customizable, and real-time value. This convenience and lower costs have led to explosive growth—if not profitability—in the streaming and on-demand sectors of the economy.
    a. On the flip side, however, it is worth pointing out that examples of streaming services are—in essence—charging for access to content that has already been produced versus providing this content for free or at extremely low cost. For text book manufacturers and other content producers it is logical for them to expect compensation in some way, shape, or form at some point.
2. There is a growing level of discontent with the status quo as it is related to the current academic publishing environment. A brief Internet search reveals dozens, if not hundreds, or articles, podcasts, and other such issues connected to the dissatisfaction that many academics have with the current state of affairs. In any other industry a concentration of market and pricing power in the hands of a small handful of organizations would lead—rightly so—to charges of oligopoly, price manipulation, and other non-competitive actions. Anti-trust regulations would be brushed out and brought to the conversation, but in the academic space these calls to action have yet to materialize.
    a. It is true that the scale, scope, and complexity of academic publishing may seem to lend itself to economies of scale and the greater efficiency that can be generated through a larger team of

experts and reviewers. That said, there is a limit to how much—in terms of accrued benefits—can reasonably be expected from such a situation.

3. Higher education should encourage the sharing and collaboration of information, views, and the resources associated with these different initiatives. The core concept of education and learning at large is dependent on market participants—institutions, authors, and publishing houses in this case—being willing and able to share information and insights on a continuous basis. Many of the most significant breakthroughs that have occurred in recent history are a direct result of benefits derived from sharing information between different parties. At first glance there is no reason that higher education cannot also benefit from such an outlook and mindset.

    a. Sharing information and insights is an important part of the academic discourse, but that does need to be tempered against the reasonable expectations of content creators to be compensated for their creations. From YouTube channels and social media content producers to the OER movement, there needs to be some kind of mechanism established and put in place to help ensure that those individuals tasked with creating and maintain said open source content are able to obtain compensation commensurate with the value added to the academic conversation.

The dialogue and debate surrounding the future of educational resources, and what role OER content will play in this conversation moving forward seems to be reaching a fever pitch as of the writing of this text. During the fall of 2019 an established conference meant to bring together commercial publishers and OER content, producers found itself in the middle of controversy when a panel designed to include participants from both sides of the conversation was canceled. It may strike some observers as ironic that a conference built around the production of open source and freely available information and debate canceled a panel designed to spur constructive debate, but nevertheless that is what occurred. While the specific conference and panel cancellation will invariably fade from the headlines over time, it does point to be a much broader and potentially existential question for higher education at large. Do OER resources have a legitimate future in the educational conversation, and if the answer is yes, what does that future actually look like? Drilling down into several of the core issues and considerations that need to be factored into this conversation, several common themes do seem to be emerging and moving to the forefront of this sometimes contentious debate.

Benefits associated with OER may be relatively easy to list in a narrative format but do tend to ignore an important part of any publishing process; quality control and ensuring materials are updated over time. Assuming that an individual or team of individuals is/are willing to produce a textbook for free (a tall order to assume) there needs to be some kind of process or protocol in place to ensure that the content is updated as necessary in response to changing market forces. Particularly in the fast moving business sector which is changing and being influenced by any number of internal and external forces the reality is that any content produced will need to be updated and modified over time. Even if an individual is willing to produce content initially without direct compensation it seems unreasonable to assume that this generosity will continue and extend beyond the first edition or version of this content. In any case, and even for freely produced content there need to be checks and controls in place to help ensure that only quality information is produced and distributed to the marketplace. In other words, someone or something has to be made available to check and review the work submitted as an OER option for various courses. Building on this, there are also the costs and resources necessary to actually support the back end support and logistic components of publishing a textbook. To put these costs and processes into context, let's take a look at a few of the components of requirements necessary to successfully write, edit, and market a text or other core educational materials.

Kicking off this conversation is the most obvious cost, the hiring and paying off authors, editors, and other subject matter experts to create and curate the materials that are going to form the basis of the open educational resources. This can vary from publisher to publisher, but is not something that can be ignored or relegated to the back burner; individuals that are providing services expect (rightly so) compensation for their expertise. Additionally there are costs that are routinely associated with the editing, publishing, formatting of the content and educational products, as well as the time that is involved in this process. Lastly, there are time and costs that come with the marketing and distribution of these products and content; institutions and individuals need to know what exactly the product is, who it is for, and what the information included therein will include. This is a topic that will be revisited later, but is not something that can be ignored or relegated to a back burner issue.

Open educational resources are certainly something that does tend to represent a trend that is not going to be going away anytime soon. What this actually means in terms of context and how it plays out in terms of the development of resources and other content that will be produced is still uncertain at this point. Regardless of how this will ultimately play out it remains a constant and a fact of the economic conversation that is connected to the higher educational landscape. Let's take a look at how some of the trends and directions that are already emerging from an OER perspective that might otherwise:

1. Costs related to higher education will continue to be a conversation point going forward no matter what the form of these educational offerings take. This is an important point to take into consideration, especially from a practitioner moving or transitioning into higher education. The costs associated with higher education will need to be taken into account at both the individual and institutional basis, but no matter what lens this is viewed through this means that this topic and type of conversation will need to evolve and develop.
2. Faculty will have to evolve and adapt to the changing business landscape, and this is true no matter what specific segment of the economy or educational field is being discussed. Clearly the focus of this book is on accounting and business faculty at large, but this is going to be a trend and direction that is not going to go away. Accounting and business faculty, for example, might not be usually associated with innovative thinking and emerging technologies and thinking, but this is going to be something that needs to be factored into the product and educational development process going forward.
3. Students will be a part of the product and education process in a more interactive and engaging way as a result of the shift toward OER technologies and platforms. This might strike some more established faculty as something that seems erroneous or inconsistent with the traditional student-faculty model, but that is also an indication of how higher education is changing at large. The percentage of college and university students that are "traditional age" will continue to shrink going forward; as an ever increasing number of students are coming to the classroom with real world

or boots on the ground experience it is going to be required and expected that the learning experience will become more iterative and interactive going forward.

4. Practitioner and industry best practices will need to be leveraged and brought to bear on the educational conversation, specifically due to the fact that these issues and trends associated with business need to be updated on a fairly frequent and continuous basis. This might be a challenge for some institutions, but also represents an opportunity for motivated and proactive individuals.

Text Production Process

The first and perhaps most obvious component that is required to assemble and market a textbook, or other educational materials is the solicitation of a primary author to work on the manuscript itself, which can be easier or more difficult depending on any number of external factors. Some faculty members, even those that are tenured or near tenure, may balk at the prospect of putting together a textbook due to the sheer amount of work that is necessary to put a textbook together. Assembling a textbook that is going to be usable and practical in nature as well as affordable is a fine line to walk for a few reasons. First, writing a textbook or any educational material will take months, if not years, to get some the drawing board to the marketplace. Especially with the fast moving and rapidly changing nature of accounting and finance there is a risk that if the materials of references are too specific that the materials will seem out of date relatively quickly.

Secondly, textbooks need to be of a certain size to fulfill the expectations of students and faculty members that are the potential customer groups. Intermediate accounting materials, for example, often can have in excess of 20 chapters contained between the covers. These chapters have written content, slide decks to assist with classroom presentation, and links to additional resources to assist with assigning homework and exams. At the risk of sounding repetitive, in order for all of this content to be produced and maintained, the first step is to get someone to actually create it. On top of the initial creation of these materials there needs to be either an individual or team tasked with reviewing the editing all of this content before it is released to the market. Even after all of the content-focused areas and work is completed there remains the marketing, advertising, and customer cultivation aspect of selling text materials.

Taking a step back it should be readily apparent that the traditional process of creating and marketing text and other educational materials necessitates a team of individuals spread across various expert verticals. Attempting to replicate such a team of experts and resources in an OER environment inevitably runs up against the underlying truth of why any person or institution creates content; the monetization and compensation tied to this content. In other words, how will the individuals and institutions involved in this process actually be able to be compensated for the efforts and time invested in this process? Much conversation and debate has occurred in this space with no definitive end in sight, but there does appear to be an option that has—to date—remained undiscussed.

One option that has been used for decades in other forms of media and communication to subsidize and support the creation of content is the inclusion of advertiser or other commercial support within content. Television, radio, social media, and virtually every other form of communication is usually supported at least to some extent by the inclusion of advertiser content and support. Such an approach and idea may strike some more traditional or established members of the educational landscape as very unusual, but it seems worth discussing for the simple fact that it provides a logical solution to the following conundrum. Even as OER resources and the idea of OER gains popularity in academic circles, and as the current and future generations of students are used to accessing online content for low or no cost, established commercial publishers and content producers remain entrenched players in the space. Simple market economics, including the supply and demand for content as well as the perfectly reasonable expectation to be compensated for services rendered, are an unspoken truth of the marketplace.

In order for OER to succeed in the long term, and be a sustainable alternative to more traditional forms of educational content and text production there must be a mechanism or policy in place to compensate the producers, editors, and distributors of OER content. Advertising as mentioned above seems like a realistic option, but will really only work under the following two situations. First, the OER content could be entirely digital in nature, which in addition to appealing to the needs of current and future students, would also provide the advertisers that support the content itself real-time insights into how specific ads are performing. Now it is true that a conversation needs to be held to help ensure that advertisers do not exercise too much control over the content being produced, but that does not seem to be as large an issue as some might suggest. Put simply there is a general awareness of what should be included in various business courses no matter what institution is being analyzed; having to contend with potential influence of outside financial interests is no different than dealing with current commercial publishers. This may lay at the center at some arguments as to why including advertising in OER content—why bother if it replicates many of the same issues that currently exist—but acting like it is unreasonable to compensate content creators is unreasonable and a surefire way to doom the movement before it starts.

Linking back to an earlier point it also seems to make more sense to prioritize online or digital content in an OER environment rather than print materials. This is not to say that print materials have no place in an OER environment, but that the majority of content should take the form of online or virtual forms. This makes sense not only because virtual or digital content eliminates some of the costs associated with traditional print content production, but it also allows the content to be updated more consistently and on a near real-time basis.

OER resources have taken the higher education field by storm for several core reasons, but the overarching themes and driving force do appear to coalesce around the cost of higher education, as well as the fact that there are routine complaints that students are graduating from college without necessary skill sets. Especially from the perspective of practitioners making the transition into higher education and academia, this is a valuable opportunity to bring some real-world issues and considerations into the classroom and conversations. One area in particular, the so-called soft skills that can bring to mind items and issues that are less important, is actually of increasing importance. Integrating these skills with traditional text materials can be a bit difficult depending on the course and source materials in question, but that does not mean that it is impossible. Assessment is also going to be a part of how these new skills and areas are incorporated; this is also an area for professionals to be a little creative with how these topics can be built into the conversation.

For example, and specifically focusing on the conversation connected to assessment, it is reasonable to assume that assessment will need to evolve and change over time to include the OER materials. Drilling down to the core of the idea is the fact that as OER materials continue to develop and permeate the marketplace the possibility and risk of subpar materials being introduced will also increase as well. Assessment procedures, in other words, will not only have to focus on courses, instructors, and other employees but also will need to expand to include the materials used at the institution. Framed in a practitioner context a similar idea and concept can be found as underpinning the audit and attestation process. An audit includes and audit and examination of both the financial statements and the internal control system in place at the organization. Assessments, in essence, are the higher education equivalent of an audit and so it stands to reason that as higher education changes and evolves, the process by which this information and results are reviewed will also need to change.

Can Publishing Be a Service?

A question that I have been asked, and have in turn asked myself, is what exactly does the service component of the tenure requirement package actually mean? Teaching and research, although they may vary from institution to institution, are generally relatively straightforward to understand and discuss from the point of view of aspiring academics. Service, on the other hand, can be an amorphous concept that can confuse even the most diligent and hardworking member of the academic community. There are several different categories of service that are generally analyzed, and while this will not cover or include every possibility, it should provide a reasonable basis for further discussion and analysis.

First, service to the university or college, which may include something as simple as serving on a university or college-wide committee, or serving in the faculty senate to some extent, is almost always encouraged and is additive to the tenure or promotion portfolio. Some roles are more time consuming and challenging than others, so be sure to check both your department and the committee chair themselves to ensure that the time and effort that you are investing will be evaluated and awarded appropriately. Second, service to the department or school is usually not only encouraged, but considered part of the responsibilities of all full-time faculty. Depending on the institution in question this may also serve as a dividing line between individuals that are tenure track or tenured versus those individuals that are lecturer track or otherwise not on track for a tenure position. Third, and perhaps the most abstract idea is the concept of service to the profession, which many practitioners have been actively doing for years in any case. Serving on local or regional boards of professional organizations, presenting or volunteering at conferences and other events, and even presenting at industry conferences and trade shows can all qualify as service to the profession to some extent.

No matter what specific activities and events are presented in satisfaction of the service requirement it is especially important that all activities, events, and participation are properly documented. What that means is going to be different depending on the activities being cited as well as the intent of having the service requirement as part of the tenure process. Some institutions intend that, as a result of providing these services to the institution, that faculty members are active participants in the corporate governance process of the institution. Others encourage faculty and scholars to strive for more of a public intellectual approach, where the ability to bridge the gap between practice and academic is especially important. Lastly, there are institutions that do exist that consider service to be linked to how well a faculty member services the students of the department in question. Be it via office hours, increased online resources, or making effective use of grant funding to secure various tutors for particularly classes the importance of documenting and updating the record of these activities is of paramount importance. In any event, and echoing earlier comments, ensuring that everything that should or could be counted as service needs to be properly documented and recorded is of the utmost importance.

Grant Writing and Fundraising

Fundraising is a component of any entity, and this is increasingly an important part of the higher education conversation. This may seem unusual given the headlines and articles documenting the size of both some institutional endowments as well as the size and scope of higher education at large, but upon further analysis this reveals only a partial and incomplete view. Private institutions, given the moniker of a private institution, do not (in general) usually receive nor have traditionally received much in the way of state or federal funding for educational programs. One on the hand this has traditionally granted additional leeway to these institutions to develop specialized programs and reputations, but has also made these types of institutions more dependent on tuition revenues. As tuition prices continue to come under pressure, the dependency and pricing focus continues to increase on institutions dependent on prices.

Given that context, the focus on fundraising and capital raising at private institutions does tend to make sense, but that is not the entire picture.

Public universities and community colleges, which by the very nature and mission of many of these institutions are more closely aligned to state and federal funding, are also beginning to realize the importance of fundraising and capital raising. Federal support and funding for higher education continues to drop, following the rise of for-profit institutions and subsequent crackdown on those institutions, and so is increasing the pressure and financial strain on institutions across the board. Community colleges are often heralded as an important link and factor in the higher education pipeline, but in order for these institutions to operate as advertised it is important for them to have funding to meet the influx and growth of student populations. This growth, however, is not taking place in a vacuum but conversely can be seen as a direct result and implication of increasing price pressure on traditional four year colleges and universities.

In the higher education space the specific label used to characterize and classify fundraising and capital raising is frequently labeled as grant writing. Writing, as is often the case with educational projects, lies at the core of what academics and institutions are expected to deliver. Simply characterizing grant writing as just another writing project or obligation, however, misses the point as connecting the writing process to the fundraising and capital acquisition that occupies ever increasing amounts of management time and energy and different institutions. Grant writing can take many forms, but regardless of the specific grant or fundraising source that is sought out there are a few common themes and core threads that dominate the conversation around the grant conversation. Prior to drilling into the specific steps and implications of a grant process, however, it does seem reasonable to review and analyze just why grants have become so important. As documented and explained above the federal and state support for higher education programs has continued to decline over the last several decades. Underlying causes for this have been debated in numerous formats and places, but that is not as important as the fact that this pattern does not seem to be a blip, but rather a representation of a longer term trend.

Grant writing, by its very title, does seem to be rather straightforward and descriptive in nature, but the details of this process can be a bit more complicated than initially thought. The grant writing process can be summarized as follows, but this should not be used as the definitive terminology of the entire grant writing process. Rather these key points should help aspiring academics, or even seasoned academics looking to facilitate the grant writing process get a better handle on just what the potentially mysterious process actually entails.

1. The first item and piece of information that needs to be taken into account is the type of grant and financial assistance is being sought out during this process. What this means will be different in different situations, but the ultimate goal of most grants is to obtain some sort of financial support or capital. A wide array of organizations and associations offer grants and other financial incentives to institutions seeking to leverage research and other external resources to further the goals of the association. The array of organizations offering such support, however, also presents a potential hinderance to the ability of academics to obtain this funding.
2. Simply being affiliated or interested in the same general area as the area being supported by the granting institution, however, is insufficient for a successful obtainment of grant funds. In order to "win" the often highly competitive grant writing and publication process it is necessary for the submitted proposal or idea to be narrow enough in nature to be of interest to the granting institution. Developing an effective and viable problem statement and research area are critically important first steps to actually unlock the funding being offered
3. Building on this first point it is important that as the grant writing process is undertaken and submitted that the focus of this research and information are not overly focused or restrictive in nature. Rather the research problem or statement should be broad enough that it can be applied and viable across a number of industry verticals while also remaining narrow enough to be of interest to the specific granting organization or institution. In other words there needs to be a balance struck between following the criteria listed on the Web site or other source of information while also being interesting and differentiated enough so that it is of interest to the individuals in charge or approving grants.

This is also a good opportunity to discuss and present one of the dirty little secrets of most academic processes and functions, from everything to completing a doctoral degree to grant writing, assessment, and other important academic tasks. Something that can often get lost, overlooked, or simply overshadowed in the jargon and inherent complexity that accompanies adapting to new processes and ways of doing business is the fact that many of these tasks are not as inherently difficult or complicated as might initially appear. Comparing the CPA exam to my doctoral journey, I think, illustrates this interesting topic in an understandable manner. The CPA exam to this day remains—to my mind—the single most difficult academic task that I have ever had to complete. Comparatively speaking, and fully recognizing that completing my doctorate was also a time consuming and mentally intense process, the doctoral process more closely resembled a recipe rather than an academic challenge. Every doctoral program, or any degree for that matter, consists of certain steps that need to be followed in a certain order, and that need to also be completed or assessed alongside other actions taken by the student/learner.

Many of the topics identified in this text including but not limited to the tenure process, grant writing and other forms of fundraising, or even trying to understand and identify opportunities for service at the institution more closely resemble steps in a recipe rather than an inherently difficult academic task. This is not meant to understate the difficult or challenges that can—and often do—arise over time but should rather serve as a reminder that these activities are never as nebulous or as amorphous as they might initially appear. Analyzing the process from start to finish and building the requirements into how you approach the end task do tend to make these items simpler to complete on time.

Taking this into account there are a few steps and components in the doctoral process that need to a part of assessing what will be a component of the higher education process. No matter what type of program or courses are going to be covered in the program itself, there is going to need to be a few factors that will need to be highlighted. First things first is the organizing and time management skills that are going to have to be developed, refined, and implemented across the board. Time management, I would argue, is the most underrated skill and competency that anyone seeking to complete a doctoral journey or transition to higher education will have to develop. Second, it is equally as important to make sure that you are aware of how the various obligations and duties associated with the program will intersect and impact your personal and professional life. Any rigorous academic program will have multiple levels or tiers of content that you have to produce; making sure to properly pace and manage your efforts and content production schedule accordingly. Lastly, and this might be something that is difficult for some individuals to deal with is the fact that not everything is going to work smoothly from the very start. Personally, this is something that I had to deal with; when I first got a grade below an 80 on an assignment I was not only stressed, but also surprised! Clearly there was work I am going to have to do, and I was going to exert extra effort if I wanted this endeavor to succeed. Making any transition, or starting a new project or educational process is always going to be result in some obstacles and struggles at first. That is perfectly fine, but the core important step is to continuously invest in the time, effort, and energy necessary to improve the output and increase the likelihood of your success.

Building a Balanced Brand

An item that is discussed quite often in the business press, but usually only in the context of organizations is the importance of building, developing, and maintaining a brand position and brand equity. Organizations that include, but are certainly not limited to, Apple, Microsoft, Tesla, Coca-Cola, and Disney are able to charge above market prices for products and services that are similar to competitors, and have done so for decades. Now it is clear that all of the aforementioned organizations have, and continue to, invest billions of dollars in product development as well as researching the future of certain industry verticals. That, however, in and of itself, is not an indication or leading indicator of future success, or pricing power in the marketplace; customers and consumers do not usually care or even notice how much is invested into the operations of an organization. Brand power, and the awareness that consumers have connected to brands as well as the quality and consistency of these brands, can make a significant difference in terms of the prices consumers are willing to pay for certain goods or services.

Building a brand from a personal perspective should not be thought of differently from the construction and maintenance of how this is from an organizational perspective. While it is true that the individual institution and the individual employed therein will have to focus on and analyze any number of factors and work-related items, all of the efforts employed therein should have a unifying end goal in mind. Positioning oneself as a certain expert, or to become associated or known for a certain set of competencies should not come as a surprise or shock to anyone; this is what employees attempt to do no matter what sector of the workforce they are employed within. In academia and higher education, however, the stakes for doing so successfully can be quite a bit higher than in other subsets of the professional landscape

Establishing a track record of service, consistently producing work products and other type of output that can be reviewed, discussed, and examined by peers both inside and outside of the organization are the foundations on which an academic reputation and brand can—and should—be constructed. Specifically, as it links to higher education, the ability to construct and develop a successful and consistent brand not only depends on the successfully production of work products, but to also balance the sometimes competing requirements associated with promotion or tenure applications. In order to do this, there are a few items that need to be factored into this brand building initiative. First, the level of importance connected to certain sub-categories of information should be understood and discussed up front. Second, and based explicitly on that conversation, a plan for the faculty person should be assembled that reflects both the relative importance of different classes of output but also the strengths of the faculty member. Third, and arguably most importantly, there need to be steps taken to actively close the loop.

What this closing the loops will look like will vary depending on the individual in question as well as the institution in question at large, but there are several traits and characteristics that can and should be taken into account on a consistent basis. Every class is different, rather obviously, and this can manifest itself in any number of ways but regardless it is important for professors to build these differences into the development of certain courses. Assessment, class engagement, and the interactions that take place both inside and outside of the classroom represent important touch points that should be leveraged to improve the student experience and outcomes. Now there does also need to be a balance struck between the time dedicated to instruction versus time and effort allocated to student support and guidance.

Regardless of the specific topic or area that is going to be used to build and develop the brand of the individual, the importance of consistency cannot be overstated. Much like the organizations mentioned previously in this section are well known and have consistent branding, individuals seeking to develop brands must be consistent. That is not to say that everything always have to be on brand, or that there is no room for creativity or other types of activities, but to build a brand it is important to be consistent in the activities and events participated within.

The Importance of a Backup Strategy

Building and linking back to an earlier point that we have raised throughout this text, the importance of maintaining records and information connected to your intellectual contributions cannot be overstated. Without seeming to over emphasize the matter, if you do not have appropriate levels of documentation and record keeping it is going to be awfully difficult for anyone to grant your credit for these accomplishments. Depending on the asset and information in question, the specific approach and tactics will vary from backup to backup, but a few core considerations seem pertinent to keep in mind:

1. Will you be using a physical backup or a virtual backup such as an online storage platform or other online accessibly tool? Both of these options have advantages and disadvantages, but can be distilled down to the following. Physical backups such as external hard drive have the benefit of being in you physical possession, but that also means that they can be damaged, lost, or other rendered not useful. Virtual backups eliminate the risk of physical damage, but can also expose your information to the potential of hacks, breaches, or other online attacks.
    a. One approach that I have taken to using is to share and collaborate content with colleagues via an online data sharing platform like Google Drive, but to store final copies or records of information in a physical format. This seems to present the best of both worlds; the convenience of online access for day-to-day, and a final copy that is stored in a version that is able to be self-custodied.
2. The frequency of the backups also matters quite a bit—sometimes even more so than the physical backup location at large. You can have the best laid backup plans and strategy in mind, but if the backups are not conducted on a continuous or frequent basis the benefit of these plans will decrease every time. Depending on what you are working on, and who you are working with, you might want to conduct backing up on a more or less frequent basis, but in

any case you are going to need to establish and enact some sort of consistent schedule and calendar.

a. To my mind I try to back up my information that is physically stored at least once every week or two; that way even if something disastrous happens to my physical computer or storage device I will not have lost too much in the way of information or data.
b. Online backups are a bit of trickier scenario, but that does not mean that it is impossible to do—just requires a little bit on creativity. One tactic that might make sense in your situation would be to occasionally back up information that is even store in an online format into a physical format. Google Drive documents, for example, might be copied and pasted into MS word file which can then be backed up.

Wrapping up this chapter is a complicated task, as this chapter did cover quite a bit of area and quite a few topics and ideas. In that sense, the simplest way to do so would be as follows. The academic workload and tasks that are expected of individuals are certainly different from the tasks and workload for practitioners, but that does not mean they are different or similar. What this does mean, however, is that in order to successfully navigate these differentiated workloads there will need to be a plan and approach to do so, which might be something new or unexpected, but is certainly something that anyone aspiring academic can certainly accomplish.

Reflection Questions

1. In terms of an academic workload and how it differentiates from the corporate workload, what would appear to be the largest single difference in the expectations of new hires?
2. Publishing content is increasingly a core component of the academic conversation and dialogue, but is not immune from profit and cost considerations. Given these facts, what does the future of OER resources have for academic publishers and publications?
3. Since costs and costs pressures are going to be part of the higher education conversation, how important does it appear that grant writing and fundraising will be for faculty members moving forward?

Additional Readings

1. The Chronicle of Higher Education—"Can Faulty Workload Be Captured In A Database?"—https://www.chronicle.com/article/can-faculty-workload-be-captured-in-a-database/.
2. The Chronicle of Higher Education—"10 Tips For Successful Grant Writing"—https://www.chronicle.com/article/10-tips-for-successful-grant-writing/.
3. Academia.edu—"Open Educational Resources"—http://www.academia.edu/Documents/in/Open_Educational_Resources_OER_.
4. The Times of Higher Education—"Five myths about academic editing"—https://www.timeshighereducation.com/blog/five-myths-about-academic-editing.
5. Educause—"The Future of Education Is Open"—https://er.educause.edu/articles/2017/8/oer-the-future-of-education-is-open.

CHAPTER 6

My Personal Transition

Introduction

At this point in the book, I thought it reasonable to introduce some additional context as far as how my story and transition evolved and changed over time. It is important to note, and this is something emphasized throughout the chapter, that everyone's story and career transition will be different depending on the specifics of just what exactly is being attempted. Some of the items that will be discussed is just why I decided the move from private industry from higher education was appropriate for me, what changes in work and personal lifestyles resulted from this transition, and what I would do differently if I had a chance to do it over again. Without further preamble, let's get into it.

The Why?

A question that I used to get asked quite a bit, and something that I still get asked from time to time is why I ultimately decided to make the shift and transition from private industry to academia and higher education. On the surface it surely did seem like an odd choice; I had held several accounting and finance roles of increasing seniority at a couple of firms and my career seemed to be moving in the right direction. I have earned my MBA, passed the CPA (still think that might be the single hardest

S. Stein Smith, *Shifting from Accounting Practitioner to Academia*, Palgrave Studies in Accounting and Finance Practice,
https://doi.org/10.1007/978-3-030-67546-2_6

academic exercise I have done), and was held in positive esteem by virtually everyone I had worked with so far. What I could not quite articulate at the time was this feeling of restlessness with where my career had moved to. I would not say that I was ever bored or truly dissatisfied with my work; generally I liked what I did and enjoyed the new opportunities to try new things and learn from other people. As mentioned throughout this text, however, at the same time that had been working full time at my corporate positions I had been adjuncting at several institutions in the area. Teaching these multiple courses at multiple institutions as an adjunct have given me the following idea.

I really like talking about accounting, financial topics, and how they influence business decision making; is there a way I could do that more often?

That really is the truth of how I first started dabbling with the idea of returning, once again, to school for a terminal degree. I truly did enjoy talking accounting and finance, especially accounting technology trends, but knew that in order to make a career out of doing that, my current credentials simply would not be enough. After doing some research, talking to my family, friends, and colleagues who knew more about this than I certainly did, I did decide to go ahead and give the doctoral process a try. To be perfectly honest there was a bit of uncertainty (in my mind), as to whether or not I would actually be able to pull this off. The only people I had really every seen with doctorates were PhDs that had been teaching in universities for longer than I had been alive, so I was a bit hesitant to imagine myself completing or even attempting the same level of work that they had completed. Once I had jumped over that mental hurdle, which was easier said than done, then I began putting together a listing of the pros and cons of attempting what I was setting out to do, because every business decision has pros and cons that need to be assessed and ranked.

Something else that does have to be acknowledged, and should be a part of any analysis of changing careers in any case, is that the different type and level or workload can open the door to other opportunities. For example, if an individual is working 70–80 hours a week (not uncommon during audit season, tax season or during a busy time of year for individuals working in business and industry) it can be very difficult to find time for other intellectual pursuits. I am not talking about picking up a new hobby or arts and crafts activity—although those are certainly worthy pursuits—but instead am focusing on strictly intellectual activities. Specifically it can be difficult for individuals below the C-suite or upper management level to speak publicly on issues, present at different conferences, or produce intellectual content and property.

While that might not be an issue or potential issue for many individuals working in the accounting and financial services area, it was something that always was a bit frustrating for me working in industry. In order to truly be able to explore intellectual pursuits and topics, both in terms of having the time to do so, but also having the ability and flexibility to do so, might mean a career pivot or shift is in the cards. To that end, and after looking at the different possibilities out in the marketplace I decided that—in my case—that a transitions and shift to an educational role made practical sense. Hopefully after taking a peek behind the curtain at what exactly went into my career transition and shift, you will have a better idea as to what exactly this shift entails.

Because the intent of this text was to hopefully educate and to also share my own personal experience and insights, I do think it is realistic to also mention the fact that a transition from private industry or a more corporate role to one less structured makes sense for some people more than for others. Especially for some individuals seeking more flexibility, potentially a lower stress environment, and the opportunity to conduct a different kind of work is appealing from any number of angles. The lower stress levels that are often accompanied with higher education, the idea that the amount of work required is less (although this may not be as accurate as initially thought), and the concept of flexibility inherent in academia can sound awfully good to someone more accustomed to a structure corporate environment. Although this may come off as a positive, and may very well be one of the most commonly associated positives of moving into higher education, there are negatives that also need to be assessed.

Every career transition or career arc will have both negatives and positives associated with it, and it is alluring to imagine that—as the saying goes—that the grass is always greener on the other side. This may or not may be as true as it might initially appear, but it is important to take into account that balancing these pros and cons is equally as—if not more—important than the specifics of any subject or specific institution. Being able to objectively analyze these things objectively is an essential component of any career transition, especially one as dramatic as the shift from practitioner to academic.

Starting with positives, because I tend to be a positive and upbeat kind of guy, there was a bit of excitement and anticipation as I began my doctoral journey and got this proverbial ball rolling. Specifically I was interested in learning and figuring out just what my doctoral research would be on, because with the exception of some papers that I had written throughout college, I had not really had to do much in the way of research and paper writing during my educational journey up until this point. Additionally, since I had chosen to do a doctorate in a different area than the rest of my education, strategy, and innovation versus accounting, this was going to be a new area for me to explore and get into. Of course, with every bit of excitement and anticipation I had in the process there were also quite a few negatives or concerns that I had as I began to take this from concept to reality. Without diving too much into any specific one, some of the areas in which I was facing challenges and some doubts were.

Will I be able to juggle the demands of work and school, given that my workload responsibilities had been continuously increasing? This is not an abstract or theoretical problem, as most people who are making this transition and career change might not have the luxury of being able to leave a current position during this process. A doctoral degree of any kind is going to have certain expectations and workloads that students have to be able to complete in a timely and complete manner.

Am I going to be able to create and complete an academically relevant piece of research? While it is true that most individuals that are pursuing a doctoral degree are intelligent, motivated, and well informed individuals, that does not automatically translate in the ability to create an academically relevant and applicable piece of research. Academic research and data analysis is different from practitioner or industry research, and understanding these differences is critical when this pivot is attempted.

How is this research actually going to connect to anything that I was actually in my day-to-day roles? Something that often goes undiscussed or underdiscussed is the possibility that in order to produce a relevant piece of research and information might mean embarking on an analysis of topics and areas that are not in the same areas that were the focus of your practitioner career. Interesting and exciting to be sure, it can be also be a bit of slog since there is learning and content production occurring simultaneously.

Do I really know how long this process is going to take, and by extension, how much it is going to cost me in the long run? This is the question that can be the most difficult to answer, and not only because the different doctoral programs can take different lengths of time depending on the program selected. If, for example, there is a need to take a semester or two off from a program—for any reason—that will set you behind but that specified amount of time, but might also have other impacts. After these off semesters, the initial cohort that you began the doctoral process with, and may have very well become friendly with, may have either finished the program entirely or at the least be at a different stage in the doctoral journey.

Can I *really* do this? This is the question that inevitably arises in the mind of anyone attempting a career change, and the transition from practitioner to higher education is no exception to this rule. Some level of apprehension and perhaps even self-doubt are going to be a part of any dramatic career change or pivot, but the most important piece of advice is this; have a plan and have a plan to execute on that plan. Without those two components—the plan itself and the ability to consistently execute on that plan—very little else will make a significant difference.

This is not to say that I have all of the answers, or that how I approached this conversation and debate is the only way, or the best to do so, but I did eventually—after some trial and error earlier on—manage to get my time allocated and organized in such a way that did indeed allow me to successfully complete this endeavor. Something that we are going to be getting into in the coming section is the importance of effective time management; an often overlooked or underdiscussed skill that should instead be at the forefront of every individual making any career change or even trying to maximize their current working situation. Not meant to toot my own horn, but to rather illustrate how practitioners can start to replicate this process, the following represent some of the items and strategies that I employed.

Time management is perhaps the most important skill that I supercharged during this doctoral process. Obviously, everyone who has managed to advance in their career, and obtain advanced degrees possess excellent time management skills, but the doctoral process truly does force you to become even better at allocating your time effectively. To put it bluntly this was a skillset and competency that had to improve if there was ever going to be a chance that I could juggle both a demanding professional role, the doctoral process, and subsequent job search that almost always following the completion of a terminal degree. Drafting up a weekly schedule, making lists of specific tasks to be accomplished on specific days, and allocating certain amounts of time (or output results) to different projects were a few of my favorite techniques for doing so effectively.

Picking a topic and research area that I was interested in. This is something that might seem to be relatively obvious and barely worth mentioning, but it is surprising how often this either goes undiscussed or is seemingly relegated to the backburner of analysis. If this has not been communicated effectively throughout this text, the doctoral process is very long and takes a very long time to complete. Maintaining interest in anything, especially something as academically challenging and intensive as a doctoral research project, can be challenging even for the most invested academic. Remember the topic that your research study will focus on is a topic and subject area that will be a part of your life for years, and in all likelihood is something you will be asked to discuss and talk about on job interviews, conferences, and even other events early in your academic career. Ensuring that you are interested and motivated to continue with your subject matter focus is not something that should be casually forgotten about.

Working with a cohort. This is not something that I had to actually to or launch on my own, but was rather something that Capella (where I completed my doctoral research) actively encourage. Building on point #2, it can get relatively discouraging if you are slogging through the doctoral process without anyone to confide in, talk to, or even just complain with along the way. Having a peer group of colleagues that is going through the same process you are is invaluable in the sense that it is a built in support network that can you deal with inevitable challenges and headwinds that will come up along the way.

There are any number of articles, podcasts, and books (but none as good as this one) dedicated to assisting practitioners making transitions at various points in their career to new roles or engaging with new responsibilities. Underpinning any of the advice embedded within these texts, however, is a common message and theme; in order to make this transition work there are going to have to be new tactics deployed than what had worked in the past. Realizing this from an intellectual perspective is one thing, but sometimes integrating these new ideas and concepts into practice I something that is entirely different as well as being difficult to actually articulate and implement.

Adopting to a new paradigm of work and work-life balance is definitely something that needs to be considered and factored into any career planning arc or career strategy; this might not be as easy or as simple as it initially appears. It is not as simple a manner as immediately transitioning from working in a corporate office environment to transforming into a stereotype of a tweed wearing academic. The very flexibility and freedom that can come from higher education can simultaneously be a frustrating and confusing new way of managing time, workloads, and expectations.

What Practitioners Need to Consider

On top of those few items that I listed as critical to my mission there are a few other items that practitioners need to consider, especially if attempting this transition is being done while otherwise still employed. Employers, quite fairly, are not usually pleased to hear an employee, and even more so if it is a productive and engaged employee, is looking to make a transition to another firm, industry, or some other venue. In other words, this transition and doctoral journey—be they happening at the same time or one after the other—may not be the best thing to be discussing at the water cooler in the office. On top of the logistical problems of trying to complete assignments, write papers, think of a dissertation topic, and balance work obligations, this may also have to a process that is conducted primarily under the radar. That is not to say that it is impossible to share anything about your process; quite the contrary. Everyone that I worked with knew I had gone back to school for my doctoral degree and was kept in the loop as far as that was concerned. Clearly, what might be unsaid or not shared between co-workers is the fact that a change in employer is also a part of this academic transition. Assuming this all goes well, however, there are also items that need to be considered even after you get the position you have applied for at a different institution. Without rehashing too much some of the previous topics that we have discussed previously in this book, let's take a dive into some of the items that were particularly interesting and challenging for me.

This is also something that reflects and presents an opportunity to preview and give a taste of what of academia might very well be like for aspiring academics. Working alone, or only having periodic contact with colleagues, peers, or a supervisor is the norm and not the exception for academic work, and being able to keep to navigate the vagaries of this academic transition is imperative in order for it to ultimately work and complete work processes on a solo basis. Translating this concept into practice and actually implementing such an approach is going to be more or less difficult depending on the background of the individual, but that is no reason to simply put this consideration on the back burner. This is not to say that will never be an area or opportunity to collaborate and coordinate with colleagues and co-workers, but there is something unique about the type of work and outputs connected to higher education and academia at large. And, to be sure, the nature of the work you might be involved in is going to change and evolve over time as your position and role in your department and institution develops and matures. A large issue that is brought to the forefront on a consistent basis is the reality that much of work and efforts invested by academics and recently transitioned practitioners does seem to occur and happen independent of other individuals.

Another piece of advice or insights that I would add to this conversation here is the reality that your dissertation may have to change over time, and that it might actually take you in directions that you did not initially expect. This is actually what happened to my research topics, which originally was focused on the concept of strategic management accounting but ultimately evolved into something more technology related. At the end of the day that shift and evolution actually made sense, as the profession at large was moving and evolving to more of a technologically focused arena anyway, but the specifics of what actually became the main topic were interesting.

Instead of focusing on the concepts or ideas connected to an accounting theory or concept my research topics instead pivoted to an analysis of certain financial reporting frameworks, the implications of those frameworks, and what these different frameworks meant for the profession moving forward. Building on these insights the practical end result of this more technology-oriented research was the current focus on blockchain, cryptocurrencies, and other emerging technologies that have continued to form the basis of my academic and professional reputation.

What Comes Next?

Given the context of this book, and the fact that you are most likely considering making a pivot and shift toward academia from industry or some other non-academic sector, this emphasis and focus of this book may seem to be the period leading up to the transition itself. That, however tempting and simple, only represents a portion of the conversation that should be had as it relates to switching over or transitioning to higher education from other types of financial services roles. After the job is actually obtained, and no matter what type of position is ultimately obtained—lecturer, tenure track, or contract-based faculty. After landing the job, onboarding, and meeting your faculty and staff colleagues, there are a few components of the workload and dealing with higher education that I encourage you to pay special attention.

Discussed previously to some extent, it is also important to keep in mind that the workload for academics is going to be different than pretty much anything else you had previously had to contend with in the workforce. Put simply, there is very little in common between the workload down by normal academic practitioners and those individuals employed in private industry. While in most organizations an individual or even department of individuals may only be responsible for a certain piece of a project or initiative, in the academic world the individual in question may be responsible for the entire scope of a project from start to finish. This is important to keep in mind when starting a project or proposing some areas of research to be discussed; you will most likely end up responsible for the completion of the project in its entirety.

Time management is something that I have mentioned several times throughout this text, and while that may seem like a relatively straightforward topic of conversation it is also something that should be acknowledged as extremely important. Specifically the importance of time management during the transition from industry to higher education cannot be overstated in the context of how you have to personally and professionally manage your time. Just like the work product and outputs are going to be different given the context of the institution and role you hold, the process by which that work is completed is also going to be different. Drilling down to the specifics of how the work is different, it basically boils down to the fact that much of the work completed by academics is going to be done independent of other people. Whether this is completed during an isolated fellowship, or even working in an office next to colleagues not in the office on the same day as you the end result is the same. No matter how the workload actually evolves or becomes iterated over time, any practitioner transitioning from industry to academia will have to get used to working in isolation for a higher percentage of time than previously.

There is also the element that a relatively larger percentage of the work that you will be completing will be done remotely, meaning that there will often be times that you are not in the physical office. To some, including myself, this is often seen as a welcome relief and benefit of being able to avoid a long commute, traffic, and the unpleasantness that often accompanies this commuting process. With every benefit, as with every aspect of life, there will inevitably be a downside that needs to be factored into the analysis, and this is where I have many aspiring individuals—be it in the corporate world or academia—struggle to adapt and fail. Taking a step back from this specific conversation for a second, it is worth noting that many organizations that have previously offered the flexibility for employees to work from home have subsequently withdrawn this privilege to many employees. This begs the question, if corporations are modifying or restricting the ability of employees to work from home due to any number of factors, what does this portend for the future of academia? We are going to be discussing the future of higher education and academia in more depth throughout this text, but that is one underlying narrative and theme that is worth examining in more detail.

Other Items to Consider

A question and topic that I am often asked is what specific steps I was able to take in order to make my specific transition simpler, more pleasant, and more doable in the context of everything else that is going in life and generally in the workplace. The first step that I would recommend, for anyone considering this transition—regardless of where an individual is in their professional career or where they plan to transition to—is to make sure that the people who will be impacted with you are aware of what is going on. While seemingly an obvious conversation to have, it is all too easy to get lost in the rabbit hole of job market research, doctoral course work, and focusing on your personal growth and journey, and not keep everyone else that will be impacted by your decision in the loop. Different people will have different people to get informed; family, friends, colleagues, or other subsets of your personal and professional circles are just some of the people who should be kept in the loop as to what this transition will entail.

Building on this, it's important to draw up a listing of pros, cons, positives, negatives, opportunities, and challenges, and truly understand just what items will have the greatest impact. Clearly the transition and shift from private industry to academia is not something to be undertaken lightly, and that is underlying item that should be communicated. On top of the day-to-day changes in terms of workload, engagement with peers, and everything else, this transition also means a change in lifestyle which may even include a change in physical location. So a question that I am asked, more and more, is whether or not it makes sense to relocate and move for an academic opportunity, which may or may not be as secure as the current opportunity. Depending on the person in question, the area of the country they are from, and the background they have with regard to work travel they may be more or less accustomed to travel and work while in a different environment.

What If You Have to Move?

Moving is never an easy task; just ask anyone who has tried to set up cable or WiFi at a new house. Compounding the stress embedded in the moving process itself will also be the reality that as you are relocating physically you are also changing jobs. A new job, simply by the nature that it involves new people, new workloads, and new expectations, is always going to be a stressful undertaking regardless of how good and opportunity is presented. Taking a step back from the high level, and drilling down to my personal experience there was an additional consideration that was important to take into account. Any map of demographics, population growth, or the inflows and outflows of people tells the same story; population and people are not growing nearly as quickly in the Northeast (my home) as is other areas of the U.S. Compounding this trend, the sheer number of colleges and universities located in the Northeast—reflective of historical trends and concentration of industry and education—means that the sheer number of college and university closing will inevitably continue to tick upward.

In other words, the possibility of having to move as a part of this transition to higher education is not as abstract an idea, or as radical a concept, as it might initially appear. Fortunately in my personal journey I have not had to relocate as of yet, but here is a place that I want to pause the main conversation of this text, and touch on another possibility that actually came my way as I was writing this book. In the spring of 2019 I had applied for a visiting research fellowship at an economic think tank, the American Institute for Economic Research. After following many of their fellows and publications for several years I thought that this might be the year where my areas of interest would overlap nicely. The idea of relocating often brings to mind a permanent move, but in the case of visiting fellowship or some other kind of short term engagement, the moving process itself might only be a short term necessity. We will revisit this idea in more detail later, but I felt it necessary to highlight this as legitimate option.

One other angle and perspective that seems worthy of inclusion at this juncture is the fact that as technology becomes mainstream, and virtual working shifts from a niche area to a facet of life. How this actually plays out might take any number of forms, but one of the clearest impacts of this shift toward increased remote or virtual work might be the ability of institutions and individuals to work from literally almost anywhere. This is going to be analyzed in more depth later on within this text, but it is worth introducing here simply for the fact that relocating for employment or career advancement may not be as frequent an occurrence going forward. While this might negatively impact some current areas of excellence that attract individuals and organizations, it will be a boon to individuals seeking to maximize career options while minimizing physical relocation.

Remote Work and Commuting

Even if the physical location that you end up working at does not require you to physically relocate there is a fairly good chance that your physical work location will end up being quite a bit further than a traditional corporate position might have been. This is an inevitable part of the deal when it comes to dealing with the transition from professional work to academia. Many faculty take positions that may be located quite a ways away from where they live, and this can occur for any number of reasons. It is important to recognize the fact that depending on the on-site requirements of a particular institution, i.e., how many days the institution wants the faculty on campus, a longer commute may or may not be appropriate. That said, common practice from everything I have seen seems to indicate that the majority of faculty members are required to be on campus for two or three days per week, with only a smallish percentage of institutions requiring faculty to be on-site for four of five days during the week. Returning to the point at hand, let's take a look at a few of the reasons why a faculty member may end up working further from home than might have been initially thought.

The institution that eventually hired the candidate is located far away from where the individual is located. Often times the simplest answer is also the most likely to be correct, and it may simply be that the institution in question happens to be located far away from where the applicant actually lives. Although this does tend to happen quite often, it is not something that is usually discussed in the normal course of most job application guides or how-to guides. For example, an institution I was employed at was about a 2 to 2:30 hour drive from where I lived, but that was where I had been hired. While for a more traditional or office job with more regular office hours the length of commute might be a make-or-break consideration, but if you are only coming into the office 2–3 days a week during the academic year, it may not be as important.

Hiring may have occurred, but it might not have taken the ideal form or final stage that that the applicant is seeking. Discussed throughout this book there is a range of potential jobs that can be applied for and received by an aspiring academic, and this is true regardless of where the institution is located. One scenario that could, and does, play out quite if often follows a pattern similar to this. Although an applicant may have received an offer and position, that position may not be the type or level of role that this individual ultimately is most interested in getting. In this case, it might make sense to put in a year or so at this most distant institution to establish oneself as a legitimate academic; after proving oneself in a specific role it might then make sense to leverage this experience to obtain a role closer to the desired position.

Something that should be noted, however, is that it is entirely possible—and not all that uncommon—for aspiring academics to leverage certain positions (even non-ideal ones) into positions at other institutions that might be more what the individual was ultimately seeking. This is something that occurred with myself, and I know that other individuals have been able to make work for themselves. While this might be frustrating or a non-ideal situation, the fact of the matter is that it might be the most practical ladder for non-academics to make a successful transition to higher education.

Specialization can be a double-edged sword, especially when it comes to fields such as financial services and accounting. As stated previously there is usually a premium associated with being specialized or hyper-focused in a particular area or subset of the profession, but this same specialization can make it difficult to find an academic position that is a just-right fit. Compounding this factor is the reality that for many academic institutions and faculty members the more specialized or focused an applicant appears the better the odds of obtaining and job opening may very well be. It is also important to note that this trend is not unique to higher education, nor is it unique to business overall. Medicine and professional medical services have long been subjected to a greater specialization during the last several decades. The causes of this increased specialization are multifaceted, but an underlying driving force is increased compensation associated with increased specialization.

This can be something that is difficult to avoid, especially as an individual completes a terminal degree; by its very nature that type of degree often requires some degree of increased specialization and focus. Regardless of the specific type of doctoral program that is considered or completed there will invariably be a shift and pivot toward increased specialization and focus versus a broader-based approach. It is true that a well-rounded, student, individual, and institution is the goal of any educational process, but the doctoral process itself seems to mitigate toward the opposite outcome. Now there is certainly a home for specialists and subject matter experts, but that does need to be offset by the appeal of a more generalized approach and knowledge base.

There may be a lack of openings or institutions in the local geographic area. This is something that hopefully my own experience can help illustrate. In my native New Jersey and New York City area it can feel like you are tripping over colleges, institutes, and universities wherever you look. Mirroring this set up, there is also an interesting phenomena that manifests itself even not in highly densely populated areas; the idea of a hub and spoke model. Take Ohio State University (or The Ohio State University), which routinely dominates local, regional, and national conversations in terms of sports, academics, fundraising, and numerous other aspects of higher education. What can fly under the radar in the shadow cast by OSU, however, are the numerous smaller institutions located around the behemoth of OSU.

These smaller institutions can actually offer more opportunities for some members of the academic community if these individuals focus in specialized areas. While these opportunities may exist, it is incumbent upon applicants to make sure that the financial situation of the institution in question is solid and healthy. Conversely it might be that these smaller institutions focus on certain specific goals, areas, or outcomes; this can be either a positive or negative development depending on the area of expertise and focus. In either case the increased density and academic presence in a certain geographic area will create more opportunities and openings virtually by default.

Things can always change, especially over the long term. Especially for mid-career professionals who, at the risk of generalizing, are usually in their 40s, it is important to realize that if everything goes according to plan, this employment may last for several decades. Academic institutions move at their own speed, but that does mean that nothing every changes. Especially viewed over years, if not decades, the expectation for faculty regarding on-site time, service, and office hours can certainly change over time. An 1.5 hour or 2 hour drive might be doable if its only 2 days a week, but if expectations change to be 4 days a week that commute can very quickly become unbearable.

Forecasting the future is always a fools errand, but if one had to hazard a guess as to the future of higher education it would be a blend or in-person, online, and hybrid type models; this points to a wide change and shift in the economic landscape that goes beyond higher education. Before diving into some of the alternative directions and opportunities for practitioners, including fellowship and the alternative academic career path, it seems relevant to also discuss how the shift toward decentralized learning and education is driving change both in the private sector and the higher education space. In order to understand the true importance and implications of just what these trends mean for business and education also means that education will have to develop and shift over time in terms of where it is located.

Decentralizing Higher Education

The trend of decentralizing higher education has long been evident to anyone who wishes to look and see just what the conversation is actually about in the context of how data is processed and communicated between interested counterparties. Outsourcing may have been the first and most obvious implication of decentralizing work and work processes, but that is merely the tip of the iceberg. More and more—across the financial services space as well as other industry sectors—there is a trend and push toward locating personnel and assets in areas outside of "traditional" centers of industry. Financial services have long been associated with Wall Street the physical location, and the greater New York region at large, but that reality is changing. High costs of living, infrastructure that simply has not kept up with the increases in population and transit volume, and local political machinations have made doing business in this traditional center of financial services and trading very costly and cumbersome. As a direct response to these broader trends is the fact that the fastest-growing offices for esteemed organizations such as Goldman Sachs have not been in New York or even New Jersey, but Salt Lake City, Utah.

Financial services is only one economic sector, but the trends and directions that exist in this sector are going to be evident in other sectors sooner rather than later. Unless the economic sector requires interpersonal contact and interaction there is a decreasing justification and need for individual to always have to be located in the same physical location or office. Higher education has been embracing this concept over time with the implementation of online learning and hybrid courses, but this trend is only going to accelerate due to the following two factors. First, the demographic dip in traditional college-aged students is going to put pressure on institutions across the board to think innovatively and creatively about how to address and fulfill the needs and expectations of students both current and incoming. These efforts are already underway in terms of the student experience, but it seems self-evident that over time there is going to be a need for more decentralized operations at a central and institutional level. Second, the impact of virtual learning, online learning, and distance learning opportunities tend to be more inclusive or conducive to an increasingly decentralized model of higher education. Decentralizing education is not going to be a simple task, but is actually already occurring in the K-12 space.

Fellowship Quick Take

Fellowships represent a very interesting type of academic opportunity for aspiring academics, and since during the writing of this book I was in the midst of one, it seemed logical to take a few minutes and break down just what exactly these can mean. The first thing to understand about fellowships is that not all fellowships are created equal, and that depending on the type of fellowship you are looking into there are different considerations that need to be taken into account. A common type of fellowship is the type of fellowship commonly reserved for graduate students or post-docs—individuals that recently completed a doctoral degree—to help these people ease into academia and higher education. Obviously unless you are actually finishing a doctoral degree as a part of your transition these types of fellowships are not going to be applicable to you. That said, there are several other types of fellowships and scholarship opportunities available for aspiring academics or practitioners looking to gain a toehold into the higher education space. One point to always keep in mind during the application process, especially if the applications are not initially successful, is that even going through the efforts to compile the application packet can be a worthwhile endeavor. For virtually any fellowship opportunity there is going to be an expectation on the side of the application to put together an application packet, package, or portfolio that does a good job at illustrating the work product and deliverables of the individual. This portfolio will certainly take different forms depending on the specifics of the position being applied for, but usually include the following. First out of the gate will be a CV (and an academic CV versus a professional CV) with a focus on research, scholarship, teaching, or whatever else will be the focus of the fellowship. In addition to this CV there will be a requirement that is connected to the work product itself, which can take the form of submitting published articles, articles, or working papers that are in process, full monographs (books), or other evidence of scholarly excellence.

Adding to these requirements, there is virtually almost a requirement or strongly suggested expectation that this application will also include an area where you will be asked to provide letters of reference, or at least contacts for letters of reference. In essence, this part of the application forces you to demonstrate that you have a mature and developed network of peers and colleagues, and that this network is willing to support you in your endeavors. For practitioners making a transition out of practice and into industry this might pose something of a challenge; do those peers exist? Former professional colleagues might be more than willing to assist, but might not meet the criteria of what the application expects. Conversely, if you remain relatively new to academia and higher education this network of appears might not exist as of yet.

In any event the process of putting together an academic package or portfolio such as the one outlined above does force you to assemble a robust academic portfolio, to organize your accomplishments, and to present your accomplishments in an organized manner. Seemingly a simple process, this might actually take more time and effort than is initially thought. In other words, this might give someone a good taste of what academia actually means from a practical point of view, versus just thinking about it in abstract. Since for every promotion or change in academic status usually requires such a package or packet to be assembled it stands to reason that even going through the process of assembling such a package generates its own benefits.

Fellowships connected to colleges and universities. Many of the larger or more prestigious universities in the country offer and have fellowships and opportunities linked to a certain school or area of study at the institution. These may be quite interesting to consider, but they might only be open to current faculty or students at the institution in question. Some of the fellowships that are either connected or sponsored by a college or university may, unsurprisingly, be offered primarily to students, graduate students, or current faculty members. That said, and especially for fellowships that are linked to some of the larger or more well-funded institutions, there are likely to be multiple fellowships available for external applicants. Competition is, again not surprisingly, rather intense for these externally available fellowships, but even going through the application process can be of benefit for individuals.

Fellowships at think tanks or research institutes. This is potentially a very lucrative and very engaging class of fellowship opportunities, but also a type of fellowships that can (1) be very competitive, (2) require relocation, or (3) only be for a certain period of time. That said, these can also provide tremendous opportunities for research, publication, and speaking engagements that are not necessarily going to come across your plate otherwise. The sheer number of think tanks of research institutes that are scattered around the country is hard to believe until you start really looking into during a search. Governmental fellowships. Virtually every major governmental agency has a recurring fellowship or research program sponsored and marketed during the year. While it might seem like these are only going to of interest for individuals seeking a career or opportunity in government, the reality is that these may be great opportunities for anyone seeking exposure to new ideas, career opportunities, or information. Particularly for individuals who have an interest in policy or other policy related issues, a governmental fellowship might be of greater interest to some of those individuals. One thing to keep in mind, however, is that not every politically oriented fellowship will be viewed as equivalent depending on who is doing the reviewing. Unfortunately, politics do tend to weave into many conversations, and decisions around fellowship opportunities are no exception to this rule.

One core thing to keep in mind as fellowships are analyzed and explored is that the compensation for these fellowships can vary wildly, and that depending on your personal financial situation, that can make or break the decision for you. For example, a fellowship at the Brookings Institute can pay up to $180,000 annually whereas others may only provide a modest living stipend for the duration of the program. Understanding that aspect may strike some as crass, but it is always more important to understand these factors before a decision is made rather than waiting until it is too late to make an effective decision. Like any job or opportunity there needs to be a level-headed assessment and analysis of key factors connected to the opening or openings. Regardless of what the institution is labeled as, and no matter if it is called a fellowship, a faculty line, or a full-time opportunity there are going to be expectations and requirements that have to be fulfilled as a part of the role.

Additional factors that need to be taken into account when analyzing various fellowship options or openings that might work for a certain individual in question is what the underlying goals of taking the fellowship actually is. What this actually means will mean different things for different individuals, but there are a few general guidelines that seem appropriate to take into account as various fellowship options are analyzed. One of the most quantifiable benefits of participating in a fellowship is the time that is allocated to work on different research and publication projects. Many academics actually participate or apply for fellowships for the express purpose of carving out time to work or expand current projects and start new projects. Especially since writing and publication can form such a large component of how faculty are judged and evaluated by fellow faculty members, as well as promotion committees, allocating and creating time to work on these types of projects is especially important. Coordinating and learning from other industry experts. Particularly important for individuals in the social sciences and business, the ability to collaborate, work with, and learn from other well respected and regarded industry experts and thought leaders is a definitive upside to participating in a fellowship opportunity. Many of the best ideas in the history of business or other fields have originated when equally motivated and focused individuals have had the ability to work together and collaborate on joint projects together. Being able to work together, bounce ideas off of each other, and work through the inevitable tricky issues that arise when attempting to analyze complex and multifaceted issues. Specifically, by collaborating with professionals and subject matter experts that may or may not be affiliated with the same specific areas or expertise, new ideas and ways of viewing things may very well emerge. Every problem or issue has multiple angles, and bringing these multiple perspectives to bear on the situation almost always leads to superior outcomes.

Ability to enhance or increase a professional profile with the institutional backing and support, especially if that institution is in close alignment with the professional topics and ideas that the individual wishes to pursue. Especially for individuals seeking to transition from industry to academia, and to break into academia, a position at a professional or industry affiliated think tank or research institute might provide the necessary boost and leg up so needed to establish and define a professional reputation. It is important to remember that many think tanks or institutes tend to operate in a quasi-academic and quasi-private industry, and so this might be a good way to get a taste of a semi-academic lifestyle.

Last but not least there is also something that can be a reason why professionals want to experiment with think tanks or research institutes; the pay and flexibility that comes with such a position. Stated earlier, think tanks and/or institutes usually provide competitive pay coupled with workplace flexibility that provides a good way to get a feel for more research or academically oriented work.

Fellowships can be an enjoyable and rewarding aspect of work for academics at any stage in their academic career, but can even be of more interest for those individuals that have transitioned recently. One note of caution that should be emphasized, however, is the simple reality that no matter how rewarding or enjoyable a fellowship might be, it is usually a temporary position rather than a definitive career path. This might be an interesting path to take, but it is always important to remember that these might not be a permanent position or role, but rather a short term position.

Institute Employment

Working an institutes, think tanks, and research consortia can closely mirror working in higher education, but it is important to fully acknowledge how they are different. Perhaps the most obvious difference is that many research institutes or think tanks do have a particular political or policy slant or angle. This is obviously something that might be more or less appealing to certain individuals, and should be weighed against the other opportunities in the marketplace, but that does not mean that all said institutes have such a policy. The core takeaway point to keep in mind, however, is that simply because an institute has a policy position on certain issues, or a reputation in such an area does not mean that this position or policies exist or all issues. This is an important piece of information to keep in mind if employment at an institute or research fellow does seem appealing; not every institute or research opportunity needs to have the same policy or position on every side.

What this means in practice, however, is that there are often research opportunities and fellowship opportunities that have employees and positions that may be often opposing. In addition to the intellectual curiosity and debates that can be generated by combining policies and positions that differ from each other it can also spark a new wave of creativity and interest for the individual. It is unlikely that an individual will end up working at an institute or think tank in the exact same professional capacity or role that they had held previously, and that is often a good thing. Being exposed to new ideas, thought patterns, and ways of analyzing information is something that lays the groundwork for new research interests, projects, and other content that lies at the core of what academics are actually supposed to produce. Taking these concepts out of the theoretical concept and realm and applying it to the practical and real-world methodology at the center of this text, the following scenario may very well play out.

Specific concepts and topics that may be analyzed at a research institute and think tank that lie outside of the specific research and expertise of the individual in question. For example, during my time at a research institute during the fall of 2019 I was exposed to a new lens and view of the current issues. While I might have otherwise been exposed to and worked on these issues previously, viewing them through the lens of economic theory and economics rather than accounting was an intriguing way to view and analyze said issues. Examining specific content and information issues from the perspective of economic theory provided me with a fresh and reinvigorated perspective through which I could write and discuss certain issues.

An ancillary benefit of working with or for an institute or think tank is the simple fact that by doing so, you are not usually going to be obligated to teach and perform institutional service. Particularly if your fellowship is a visiting or otherwise temporary occurrence it can also provide a welcome relief from the multifaceted demands and expectations of most faculty members. For newly transitioned faculty from a practitioner background having that opportunity to focus specifically on research and publications can be a much welcomes development.

1. Making new networks and contacts through the time on site or even, if in-person meetings and events are not happening, virtually or via some kind of remote connectivity. One of the most important ways that a fellowship creates value for both the visiting fellow and the sponsoring institute is the connections and conversations that occur during the fellowship process. Taking this into account, it is also important to remember that while networking and making connections is a good thing, that it is not as important as the opportunity to research and content production. While it may be tempting to relax and enjoy oneself in the moment, it is also important to remember why you are there. After the fact, the articles and other intellectual contributions you produced will be the proof and evidence or your time on site; be sure to maximize these opportunities.
2. Documentation is absolutely essential to the recognition and track record of your time at the institute or fellowship. Akin to how sometimes it is important to take a picture of a particular moment in time it is important to make sure that the record of your time on site is documented and maintained both during your time on site as well as afterward. In essence the only evidence or proof of your time at the institute in question are the articles and other content that you produce during your time on site. This may take different forms or documentation and production depending on both the institute in question and your particular form of production and area of interest. Whatever form it takes, however, there needs to be some form of evidence and proof of your time at the institute for it to have its largest impact. Taking care to do this from the beginning is, not only important in nature, but also something that should form a core component.

Wrapping Up

Coming back to what I considered when whether or not to move the answer is quite simple; I put that on the backburner and applied for any job that I felt aligned well with my background, expertise, and career goals. This entailed putting in for positions that inevitably would have required me to relocate substantially, but that was something I figured I could deal with at a later date. This is one of the things I would do differently if I could do it again; perform a more comprehensive analysis of the pros and cons of whether or not relocating actually makes sense for me given the context of my professionals situation.

This decision, whether or not to physically relocate, is going to be different depending on the individual in question, as well as the opportunity that is being discussed and analyzed. Clearly the rise of remote learning, collaboration tools that enable individuals and institutions to collaborate across geographic lines, and the improving connectivity enabled by these tools allow an increasing number of positions to be fulfilled in a fully remote manner. Fellowships, institutes, and other non-college opportunities for academically minded practitioners present another option for sure, but the true benefit of such a role does seem to be generated from the in-person conversations and connections that are enabled. Simply put, there does not yet seem to a viable substitute for the connections, conversations, and spontaneous sharing of information that is enabled by meeting, working, and collaborating in a face-to-face manner.

In other words, what this chapter tried to do in a concise manner is to simultaneously analyze the following two areas. First, the possibility of having to move and relocate is not something that came top of mind to me until I was fully invested in the transition from a practitioner role to more of an academic role. In hindsight, acknowledging this reality sooner in the process would have spared me some frustration and self-doubt; depending on where you are reading this book from this might be more or less applicable to you personally. In any event, the primary takeaway from this chapter should be as follows; there are multiple considerations that need to be taken into account during the transition from practice to academia. Realizing that, factoring that into whatever decision or career path is most appealing to you specifically, will make the transition and evolution of your career arc more fulfilling and satisfactory.

Reflection Questions

1. If you are transitioning, or know someone who is transitioning, from the private sector to higher education, what would be the single piece of advice you would give them?
2. What will effect be, if any, of increasing remote work and remote instruction be on the higher education space?
3. How should an individual best assess the opportunities for employment and engagement with think tanks and other types of institutes?

Additional Readings

1. Teach For America—Career Changers—https://www.teachforamerica.org/how-to-join/career-changers.
2. We Are Teachers—Should I Consider Teaching as a Second Career—https://www.weareteachers.com/teaching-as-a-second-career/.
3. Salary.com—Fellowships—https://www.salary.com/research/job-description/benchmark/research-fellow-job-description.
4. InsideHighered—College Must Attend to 3 Crucial Areas—https://www.insidehighered.com/views/2020/08/17/higher-ed-responds-covid-it-should-focus-three-areas-ensure-quality-and-equity.
5. InsideHighedEd—COVID-19: Boom or Bust For-Profits—https://www.insidehighered.com/news/2020/08/17/covid-19s-impact-profit-colleges-still-murky-second-quarter-earnings-arrive.

CHAPTER 7

Building Bridges

Introduction

It's always good to make friends, and that is doubly so when transiting from one professional area or subset to another. Higher education and private industry have not always worked in close collaboration, but that does not mean that there is a lack of opportunities for proactive professionals looking to cooperate, work together, and think of new and creative solutions. There are a few underlying trends and themes that do need to be analyzed and taken into account as this transition is considered and actually implemented.

There is something that can seem particularly unusual as it connects to the academic or higher education space, and that is just how much of your career success and development is dependent on other people having a favorable impression of you. Now, it is always a good idea to develop professional relationships, build out a network of peers, and generally be a good person and colleague. What makes higher education and academia a bit different, however, is just how critical it is to career success; the opinion that other people have of you can literally make or break your career. Coming from a practitioner background and mindset, this can seem unfair, illogical, and even somewhat of a bad thing for the industry at large. Taking a bigger picture view, however, and the importance and connection of building out a peer group makes perfect sense.

S. Stein Smith, *Shifting from Accounting Practitioner to Academia*, Palgrave Studies in Accounting and Finance Practice, https://doi.org/10.1007/978-3-030-67546-2_7

Education, and especially higher education, is on the one hand a collaborative effort but is also one that focuses quite a bit on individual achievements. For a department, school, or institution to succeed, however, there is much more required than simply an amalgamation or combination of individual efforts; it requires a team-based outlook and approach. Specifically, there needs to be an outlook and approach that not only emphasizes the accomplishments and achievements of faculty members but the accomplishments and achievements of the entire team and group. Framed in this context, the importance and emphasis on what peers think of your work product and deliverables are something that is connected to the current and future success of the institution and affiliated programs.

First, the cost pressures and competition from across the globe have driven private industry and higher education to work more closely together, and this is perhaps the most obvious with the education offerings put forward by private sector organizations. From Google to Amazon to IBM to more traditional (non-technology) firms offering credentials, badges, and other training programs, the trend toward organizations taking matters into their own hands is clear. Whether or not the management team is dissatisfied with college and university graduates, or the fact that things are moving so quickly in the marketplace that traditional educational practices do not suffice is not as important as the fact that the educational conversation has had to change. Specifically, in the course of a 4 year degree (although the average time taken to complete a degree is actually 6 years), it is realistic to expect that some of the educational content that has been covered will invariably be out of date.

This is both a challenge and an opportunity for private sector professionals to leverage some of their own experience and background connected to educational offerings, with one specific area in which that makes sense. Continuing education, regardless of the name that is given to it; continuing education, continuing professional development; or continuing training and education form a core component of how professionals are trained, educated, and kept up to date in the market. Analyzing how continuing education courses and products are offered a common format is that these courses are taught online or in a virtual format to make it as easy and simple for individuals to complete these courses as possible. Whether the courses are offered in real time or on a pre-recorded basis is not as important as the ease and convenience that these courses can be complete within. Certificate programs, schools of continuing education, and other educational offerings for mid-career professionals all operate in the same way; providing educational products that are developed with convenience, ease, and the results can be tracked and verified as they actually occur.

Second, the content and topics that are going to be covered in these innovative or creative ways are going to have to be different than traditional classes may. For example, it may make sense to keep some courses in a traditional format such as English or Chemistry 101, but for a large number of courses it may make sense to teach them in either a hybrid or fully online format. Regardless of the specific course in question, or the instructor that is being discussed, this is an opportunity for practitioners that have successfully transitioned to leverage professional experience and background to improve the educational products and outputs. This may seem like an innovative or difficult idea to push through to fruition, but upon further review it may not be as radical as originally thought. Course offerings by organizations such as Coursera and Udemy provide real-world examples of successful partnerships between the private sector and traditional higher educational organizations.

There are also opportunities connected to professional associations, such as the AICPA and IMA, that can and should be leveraged to help create and disseminate content to current and future students. Building off prior established track records and offerings, it also seems to make sense to leverage the enthusiasm and appetite for internships and cooperative learning. Career planning, guidance, and assisting students to develop career skills and knowledge necessary to succeed in the marketplace are increasingly core responsibilities of higher educational professionals, and anyone associated with academia. One other item that often goes overlooked, however, is the reality that the possibility and potential upside for collaboration between different functional groups are something increasingly expected of all professionals in the marketplace. Professionals can bring some real-world experience and examples of just how important collaboration and the willingness to work and learn together are in the modern workplace.

Of particular importance in a highly competitive higher education and academic landscape is the ability of schools and departments to be nimble and responsive to changes both in the marketplace and among competitive institutes. While tenure track faculty members may be the most involved in governance and other metrics of university activity and development, there are definitive roles and opportunities for faculty at all levels to develop courses and other offerings to make sure that the education taught and covered in the classroom is what the marketplace is desiring.

The Tenure Connection

It is important to note that every tenure journey, just like every individual and institution, is going to be different and will vary slightly from place to place, and this assessment of how this process works is simply based on my experience.

Something that else that often goes undiscussed in the context of tenure applications, promotion, and review of materials in general is the importance of having faculty contacts to assist with this process. At virtually every institution when tenure is on the table for an aspiring academic, the tenure process usually goes something as follows. It is important to note that every individual institution will operate slightly differently, but the same general themes do tend to be mirrored across institutional lines.

First, the tenure package or packet must be prepared and reviewed by the individual faculty member in general, and this is where the rubber hits the proverbial road. Echoing the previous comments and conversation on documentation and reporting this is why the documentation is so critically important. Even if a person is a well-prepared candidate, the correct paperwork and evidence must be prepared and communicated in a manner that is well understood. A network of faculty must be cultivated and prepared to assist with the reviewing of this faculty submission package. After the package and submission of the faculty members packet have been reviewed and approved by the internal review committees, they are ultimately sent out to a network of peers. This echoes the peer review process that is developed and underpins the publishing process; in order for publication or advancement to occur, it usually takes the support and approval of a peer network. Such dependence or connection to a peer network is ultimately why the importance of building a network and connections between other faculty members is so important.

After the review process has been completed and reviewed by this peer network, the decision reverts back to the institution in question. Linking back to the importance of networking, this importance is present both external to the institution in question and internally. Partaking in campus or university-wide programs is a recommended course of action to help both reinforce and construct a case for tenure, but it is also always equally important to make sure that the efforts invested and underway are worth the time and energy invested into the activities.

Developing a cohesive pattern and routine of publishing and other activities is also something that needs to be implemented built out during the tenure process. Whether or not the individual in question is indeed on the tenure track or not, the development of a cohesive story and publishing history is critical. One specific area in which this can be presented and discussed during the time of employment at an institution is the importance of publishing articles in appropriate journals.

The correct mix and blend of activities, services, and publications must be assembled, and this mix is going to be different and varies from institution to institution. Put simply, this is going to require that individuals seeking to make the transition from the private sector to higher education be proactive and active participants in this process. Being a passive actor, or not taking charge of the publication, service, and teaching process is a surefire way to miss opportunities and leave yourself open to critique.

Predatory Journals and Practices

The topic of predatory journals and practices is not a new occurrence, nor is it one that is unique to any specific subset of higher education or academia. In addition there is the case to be made that so-called predatory journals actually provide a valuable service to the faculty and higher education space. Depending on who is asked, what type of journals are assessed, and even the period of time that is examined, the nature of journals may shift and change over time. My personal perspective on this issue should be viewed as just that; my own personal opinion. Not meant to taken as authoritative or the singularly correct way of assessing this subset of academic publishing, this section on predatory journals and practice should simply be viewed as my take on this contentious, but fast growing area of academia.

Predatory journals and practices are unfortunately something that can derail or stall out even the most promising academic career arc or platform. The idea of a predatory journal, however, is not some nefarious or shadowy organization but is rather something that is a tangible and real-world threat to aspiring academics regardless of where their careers may have originated. In a 2020 magazine published by the Association of Certified Fraud Examiners, there was even an article documenting the very real threat and tangible concern for educators and institutions alike. Breaking down this dangerous and negative trend in the academic and higher education space, there are several components that need to be understood and factored into any plan.

Starting off the conversation, there is something that needs to be made clear from the get go; not every journal that is not a top tier or Rank 1 journal is a predatory journal or something that should be feared or protected against. The creation of a journal ranking and publication track record will always involve the biases of individuals and of their own personal background, and so not every ranking will be as applicable or as important to every individual. A quick google search will reveal just how many different listings and rankings will be involved in this conversation; every subject matter area is bound to have at least a few listings of journals and rankings. That said, and acknowledging the fact that there is always going to be some level of differentiation between various rankings, there will sometimes be predatory journals that exist in the marketplace, and as someone making a transition to higher education, it is always important to be on the lookout for such nefarious actors. Let's take a look at some of the factors and considerations that should always be part of how you analyze whether a journal is a good fit for you.

Kicking off the analysis is the importance of having a good understanding of just how much it is going to cost to have your article published. Taking aside for a minute the usual editorial process and timeline that is a part of every article that is submitted for publication and dissemination, there might also be a cost included as a component of this process. For example, a common practice is to have potential authors in a journal sign up for an annual membership, and this is a practice common across even the highest ranked and top tier journals. This can easily cost several hundred dollars; this is simply part of the academic publishing process. Aside from this relatively normal process, there is also something that should be watched out for—higher than normal fees for publishing articles in a journal. These fees and other costs can take the form of editorial fees, review fees, or other costs that can—in some cases—be quoted as high as $2,000–$5,000 per article. If that sounds like a wildly out of place cost for the publishing of an article, many of which might only ever be published online, that's because it is. How can this situation exist, with such intelligent individuals involved in the publishing and submission of articles for consideration? This can, and does occur, simply because of the pressure to either "publish or perish" that permeates and exists all throughout higher education and the academic landscape. In other words, and something that we have touched on before in this book, to advance and rise in the ranks of academia and higher education, faculty members must be able to consistently publish in quality venues.

Such pressure especially exists for those individuals that are on the tenure track because in order for any promotion or other development to take place and occur there needs to be a track record of publishing and distribution of written content. This pressure can be brought to bear by the individual itself, other members of the department, and the institution at large, but no matter what the source of this pressure is it can be quite powerful. What this means in the short term is that you might feel a tremendous amount of pressure and stress to publish articles, which can result in looking into journals and other venues that might be less than satisfactory in the longer term. While these publications might be a good fit in the short to medium term in terms of getting article counts up and padding the amount of content you can produce during any given time, it is also worth weighing the potential downside.

This might seem like something that might be a financially costly, but otherwise unimportant, piece of information to consider, but the implications of predatory journals can extend far beyond just a hit to your bank account. In the case of a tenure track application, for example, if the majority of your journals and publications are indeed associated with predatory journals or even journals that are suspected of being predatory in nature, this can lead to serious questions being asked at the last minute. In order to avoid this potential stumbling block, one additional consideration that should be taken into account is what the publication policies and frameworks are at your institution. Depending on the specifics that are outlined in whatever guidelines that are in place at the department or institution should also form the basis for whatever journals you are looking at publishing in. There have even been stories published about academics receiving research awards and grant funding that, as it turned out, were based in large part on predatory journals and other publications. Scandals aside, there are also the reputational damage and impact that publishing in such journals can have on your career; what this means for the institution at large is also something that should be considered carefully. As if this was not enough of a problem, there is also been recently some coverage of predatory conferences and other events that purport to feature research from aspiring academics.

These conferences, like the journals themselves, oftentimes have names that are similar in nature to legitimate and prestigious journals and other conferences which helps attract presenters and researchers to the conference itself. Conferences are often a part of the publication and research packages offered by these predatory outfits; they are often marked as opportunities to network and present with industry leaders, thought leaders, and other well recognized in the field of study in question. Reality, however, can be disappointing when the reality of these conferences is actually realized. One recent example, for instance, had a presumably international conference taking place in a hotel room for 2 hours on the first day and 1 hour on the second day, with multiple such conferences being held in these rooms on the same day. Taking into account the fees charged versus what is actually provided by the conference organizers, these can be very profitable enterprises for the organizers even if they are unsatisfactory for the participants. On top of the financial costs that are incurred by the attendees, however, there is also a startling fact; illegitimate conferences now outnumber—and have done so for several years—legitimate conferences and other appropriate venues for the discussion of research. So, in other words, there has sprung up an entirely parallel—and often unethical—universe of journals, conferences, and other such venues for aspiring academics to publish and present that can unfortunately attract many of the individuals who are most vulnerable to such practices. Like any other industry, there are bound to be bad actors and bad apples in the conversation but that does not reduce nor mitigate the impact of these unethical or otherwise nefarious actors.

The implications of predatory journals, conferences, or even editorial boards can have a devastating effect on the reputation of both scholars and institutions alike. For example, serving as an editor or editor in chief of an academic journal is something that can burnish the reputation of an academic as well as bringing high-level attention and rewards to the institution in question. Of course, serving as an editor or editor in chief of an academic journal is not something that can be taken on lightly or without a serious commitment of time and energy. Mirroring the prevalence of predatory journals or other publications, there is also the consistent risk of illegitimate editorial positions being handed out. This might seem like a minor problem or issue to be considered in the greater context of the predatory academic conversation, but that misses the broader perspective. Stuffing predatory boards with otherwise ethical academics can undermine the entire editorial process at large. Let's take a look at just how this stuffing of editorial boards can undermine and corrupt an entire part of the publishing and communication process in the higher education conversation.

Not only can otherwise aspiring and ethical academics be duped by the appeal of serving on an editorial board, but they may inadvertently find themselves "serving" on boards that they are not interested in, nor would they want to be associated with in general. There was actually a very interesting example as to how this played out from a practical perspective, and something that should be worth noting and analyzing for any academic involved in the educational discourse. A graduate student actually went ahead and constructed an entirely falsified resume, complete with a fake name, fake professional positions, and entirely falsified articles as part of a research project. Taking this completely falsified resume, this individual applied to hundreds of editorial positions blindly, with no communication nor outreach from the journals themselves. Even with a falsified resume and completely fake positions and everything else, this individual was able to obtain editorial board positions at nearly 50 journals, with 4 of those journals offering this individual the position of editor in chief. Compounding this already negative news, there were even some instances that offered this person the opportunity to organize and arrange a conference where this individual would be entitled to a cut of the proceeds.

This should be shocking and horrifying to anyone involved in the broader academic and higher education conversation for any number of reasons, but one in particular can seemingly be even more disturbing is the fact that this person also ended up awarded editorial positions on boards they had not even applied for. As if that was not bad enough, attempts to remove themselves from these positions was met with complete silence. In other words, this false resume had resulted in this individual being unethically placed on boards and positions that they were then unable to remove themselves from despite best efforts and attempts. If this sounds like something of a sticky situation that is because it definitely is! Not only can a situation like this be inconvenient to put it mildly, it can also make it difficult to ever obtain a legitimate position on an editorial board or other type of board or academic group. With all of this negative news and commentary, the rather obvious question that should be asked is how exactly these situations can be avoided; these are not idle concerns as these events do happen and have an impact on academics and institutions across the board. Let's take a look at a few methods and tactics that can and should be used by aspiring academics to avoid the trap of predatory journals, conferences, and editorial engagements. Not meant to an all-inclusive nor an exhausting listing, these factors and considerations should be a part of how journals and other writing and publishing opportunities are assessed.

First and foremost the best piece of advice is, like a lot of other situations, to be sure to do your homework and research before diving into the proverbial pool with either a journal, editorial position, or conference presentation. Now, this does not mean that every single submission or proposed position needs to undergo a full background check, but that means that before investing the time and energy into these efforts to be sure to make sure your investments will be rewarded. This can involve researching the journal itself, doing some research and investigation on the background of the editorial board members, and seeing whether or not what you are proposing is actually a good fit for the journal. These are all pretty standard research tactics for any academic or higher educational conversation, but seem to even be of more importance given the prevalence of predatory practices and journals in the marketplace.

Second, and here is where the difference begins to emerge, is that in addition to the regular research and investigation that should go into any research project it might be worth taking a few extra minutes to do some extra research about the reputation of the journal. This can take the form of some extra Google searches or more in-depth research and looking into the journal itself, or better yet, a little more of a hands-on approach—directly contacting some of the individuals listed on the website. This is actually something that I have done myself when I am looking into a new journal, new conference venue, or some other type of opportunity, to somewhat mixed results. Even if I do not hear back from everyone who I have contacted simply being able to contact these individuals or other people does reinforce the legitimacy of the journal or other endeavor. Sometimes you will actually hear back from these individuals, which can be a reassuring item when you are considering making an investment and allocation of time and capital.

Third, the pressure to publish or perish is something that needs to be taken into account in a very real manner when deciding which conference, journal, or other venues to disseminate information in. No matter what institution is in question, or what type of position has been obtained by an individual there is always going to be a need to publish information and get data out to the marketplace. Conference proposals, journal articles, or other types of information form the bread and butter of what academics are expected to produce in addition to their teaching and service. Sure, teaching and service have an important role to play in regard to how academics are assessed and evaluated, but the publishing and the communication of this information are going to play an important role in any academic or aspiring academic career. This pressure is something that will invariably be a part of the decision-making process, but should not override common sense, good judgment, or other evaluative techniques used to decide whether or not something should be pursued.

Predatory journals are, unfortunately, a part of the academic conversation and discourse that need to be guarded against even during the best of times, but are something that must be watched especially closely by aspiring academics or newly admitted academics to the profession. Even the most prominent industry practitioners with a long track record of expertise and success can fall sway to the allure of publishing and communication of information and other data; the tenure process and early career academics are particularly susceptible to the pressure of trying to get articles published. There is no guarantee of never being sucked into a predatory practice or other unethical event or venue, but being proactive and taking appropriate steps to only interact and publish with legitimate and ethical journals and other sources of information is always a good idea. Academia is not terribly unlike other economic sectors and industry groups in the fact that there are always going to be less than ethical or unscrupulous actors trying to take advantage of newer members of the profession, but that does not mean that it is inevitable. Taking proactive steps is always a recommended course of action, and that applies as equally to seeking our only quality homes for your data as anything other professional endeavors would.

Now, what to do if you do end being associated with a journal, conference, or other types of event? After the initial shock and potential horror that might come with being associated with having an article published in a predatory journal or being looped into a predatory conference, it is important to take steps to rectify the situation. The first step would be to immediately disassociate yourself from any further association or connection with any of the predatory or otherwise dubious sources of information or publication. This can take the form of spreading the information on social media, contacting your department or supervisors information them of what happened. Second is to, in writing, request that your article or other types of connection is immediately removed from any website, listing, or mail server that you had become associated as a result of this duplicitous behavior. Being proactive and fast moving about this is imperative; the longer that you and your information are listed and associated with these bad actors the more damage that will be created. Lastly, and connected to the first point, is the importance of sharing this information will your department and institution. Accidentally or not, the bad actors in the marketplace can wreak large amounts of damage; taking steps to mitigate this damage is your responsibility. In addition to sharing this data in public, it is also imperative that you take proactive and definitive steps—to control the narrative of your publication and professional engagement.

Real World Classroom

Especially in the context of business schools and business education, a common tool and tactic that is used to illustrate and highlight different points is the case study format. This is obviously a well-worn path that has served many aspiring business professionals and leaders quite well, but it is not the be all and end all of educational offerings. Developing a real-world environment and classroom space is an oft-cited goal of many educational programs, and this is an area in which professionals can certainly add value to the conversation and efforts already underway. Much has been written about the need for academic innovation and creativity in how courses are constructed and how the institution itself operates, but it can be difficult for traditional academics to innovate and think creatively in the context of course work and instruction outside of traditional metrics and methods.

Professionals, bringing in more recent professional experience, can certainly assist with the development of more professional-type classroom environments. Especially important for business professionals and aspiring business professionals (also known as students) is the reality that working with other people and individuals is something increasingly considered core to the mission of institutions. In other words, bringing the real world to the classroom is a core need for institutions of higher education as well as something that practitioners can directly assist with in the context of how academia and industry can successfully collaborate.

This is not merely a conceptual framework or idea; at nearly every professional conference, there is a recurring drumbeat of how important it is for accounting students and professionals needing to become more than just human calculators. Desiring to evolve into and become business partners and advisors has long been a desire and goal of accounting and financial services professional. While there will always be an important need and location for compliance, reporting and other traditional, it seems that the future of accounting and finance will be less focused on traditional areas of competence and more on a interdisciplinary team-based approach. Developing a more professionally aligned classroom and educational experience does not have to be limited to any one specific idea or concept, but instead should be focused on how students engage with each other, and how content is covered and delivered to students both in the classroom and outside of classroom interaction. Some examples of how the classroom can have a higher level of "professionalism" include, but are not limited to, the following:

Having students create and manage a business plan and model that interact with not only the other students in the class, but react to headline news stories as well. This may sound exceedingly complicated, but there are actually (and have been for quite some time) software packages and suites that allow students to virtually construct and compete with each other. While completing my MBA, and long before the current technologies making headlines were as commonplace, this is exactly what my classmates and I did as a part of our capstone class. It was fun, forced us to collaborate during the week—and even use Skype for in-between class meetings—and gave us real-world examples of how a business cycle can change rapidly.

If, instead, a professor is leading an investment or financial markets course, there are any number of ways to incorporate some real-world applications. Perhaps the most obvious and easy way to incorporate real-world topics and themes into the discussion and application of the classroom experience is to have students construct a paper portfolio. This can be accomplished either via a simple excel spreadsheet tracking and monitoring the performance of individual stocks (updated at the end of each day, for example), or can take advantage of some of the trading demos and "paper money" platforms offered by many brokerages in the marketplace. By forcing students to take decisions, such as by limiting the amount of cash that can be held in the portfolio to 10–15%, this can make students scan and incorporate headlines and new stories into how decisions are made.

Mandating that students collaborate and present to their peers is an underrated, but often unpopular, way to encourage students to engage in more professional behavior and activities. Presenting, in both written and oral formats, information, positions, and analyses is a critical skill that is often cited as underdeveloped in recent graduates. Forcing this to become a major part of the grade of student also gives the students the necessary motivation to complete what might seem like extra or additional work.

No matter what specific form this integration of real-world examples and case studies takes for the specific class, the underlying message and goal should be the same. A large part of the reason why individuals pursue education is to prepare themselves for the workforce, employment, and a successful career. It stands to reason, in that case, that at least a certain component of what is taught and covered within a course, programs, and degrees should reflect this reality. This is not to say that absorbing or being taught specific information simply for the sake of learning it is a waste of time, to the contrary. Rather, the emphasis should be on both the acquisition of knowledge and the subsequent application of this information.

This approach can even be framed within the context of Bloom's taxonomy by contextualizing these application-based exercises higher up on the taxonomy spectrum. In addition to adding some academic support and underpinnings to what may be viewed as unusual or non-traditional instructional techniques, this can also help reinforce and support the actual exercises themselves. Teaching students and providing them with the opportunity to apply the information they are being taught can also make all the difference between a program that thrives and one that merely survives. Benchmarks and metrics connected to employment following graduation, alumni salaries, and the like are by no means a perfect measurement mechanism, but they do establish consistency and comparability. A significant component of how this data is able to be measured is linked to (1) the information that is actually covered in the course and (2) what applications and use cases are also covered. Students and parents, reasonably so, expect that as a result of obtaining education and attending courses, students will leave the process well informed and prepared to succeed in the marketplace.

Collaboration Between Institutions

Work between institutions is also something that is becoming more important over time as resources become scarcer, competition increases, and the overall pivot from treating higher education as a pursuit and more like a business. This is also somewhere that an individual or group of individuals with a background in private industry may be able to add some ideas and creativity to help address the challenges facing the institutions. Let's take a step back and see why this might be more than might be initially believed, returning to the nature of academic work versus professional work and how that influences the decisions that individuals and institutions make and decide upon. Collaboration between competing organizations is not something that should be viewed as a radical, innovative, or especially disruptive idea; it exists in every industry and economic sector across the board.

Academic work, virtually by the nature of how the institution and how academics interact with each other and the institution in question, is more isolated and individual in nature than the collaborative efforts that continue to become more important in professional circles. Whether it is the article writing process, conference travel and presentations, or conducting service work at the institution itself, individual efforts do tend to form the basis for how academics are evaluated. Even in cases where increased cooperation between individuals and institutions would be encouraged and beneficial to all parties involved, it can be difficult to overcome the institutional inertia and competition that can hamstring even the most ambitious efforts. While this clearly presents a challenge for professionals seeking to enact change and institute new ideas at an institution in question, it also presents an opportunity for practitioners willing to be flexible and engage in this conversation.

Professional work, as highlighted and reinforced by the way in which business school courses are taught across the board (via case study and group analysis), does seem to operate in a manner opposite to academic work. Collaboration, cooperation, and the pooling of resources are—in the "real world"—actually how problems are addressed and solved. Bringing some of this market reality and experience to the academic conversation represents a definitive way in which academics can add value in this context. Launching or even suggesting greater cooperation between a number of institutions of even the individuals employed therein will be a process, but it is a process that is both necessary and will be helpful for both the individuals involved in the process and the institutions that are at the center of the cooperative efforts.

What may be becoming clearer is the shift and pivot necessary as to how higher education is treated, and the pivot toward treating higher education as a business is going to be needed in order for institutions to survive and thrive in globally competitive landscape. Obviously, the business of higher education is a big one, but it has not traditionally been treated as a for-profit business outside of the institutions operating on a for-profit model, many of which have come under fire and increased scrutiny during the last several decades and especially since the Great Recession during 2007–2009. The crackdown on for-profit institutions may have been partially motivated by politics, but it is also true that there was some merit to the accusations leveled against some of these players. In some instances, there indeed were cases where some institutions operated in a somewhat underhanded manner, essentially granting diplomas to anyone who was willing and able to pay. These crackdowns, however, ignored a bigger and more important point; higher education does have to change and evolve in order to compete effectively institutions of higher education will need to evolve and change.

Looking at the higher education landscape, the following issues and considerations become relatively obvious and straight forward to analyze and examine. If any other industry was being described or analyzed, there might be a few key terms and items that would be highlighted include, but would only include, the following: a highly competitive marketplace with thousands of entities in the market, rising costs across the board that has done so for decades, a customer base that is shrinking in some areas, and that overall is not happy with the cost/benefit trade-off of using the product. Does that sound like an industry or sector that is posed for significant growth and success moving forward? If this was any other industry sector or areas of the economy, such a confluence of factors would not be perceived as a successful model, but rather a set up for an industry to struggle. Given these structural factors, however, there are also opportunities for cross-institutional collaboration and cooperation, and this might take the form of something not entirely in alignment with what expectations may currently be set.

For example, in the case of major public (or private), but large research universities usually are hubs of innovation, research, funding, and all kinds of other activities related both to the academic mission of the institution and other goals. That said, and fully acknowledging that the larger the institution in question the larger the perceived benefits will be that can be delivered, there is a role that concept connected to either hub and spoke type of model or something akin to a solar system. If that sounds a little too abstract or somewhat confusing, let's break it down and see if this idea can be brought into clearer focus. Even the largest institutions cannot have expertise in every single area of research, literature, science, or management best practices; this is the core point. Specialized institutions have existed for hundreds of years, and this trend shows no sign of slowing down or becoming less important moving forward.

Practitioners, both those who are employed at larger institutions and those employed are smaller institutions, have an opportunity to spur and encourage cross-institutional collaboration and cooperation. Whether these initiatives take the form of jointly developed and offered programs, online courses and other educational offerings, or the sending of students to different locations for different courses, the underlying goal is the same. Just like organizations with different areas of strength will leverage the strengths of others to round out portfolios of content and product/service offerings. It certainly seems to make sense, viewed through the lens and concept of viewing higher education more like a business in nature, to strive to mirror some of the best practices connected to how private enterprises deal with gaps in skills and assets. Although this is somewhat already underway at any number of institutions, applying these concepts and ideas in a more comprehensive manner seems like an easy win with low hanging fruit for practitioners.

Bringing Business to Higher Education

This is a point that some people in higher education will have diametrically opposed views on; some believe that higher education should be treated differently than other lines of business to maintain academic integrity, whereas some others are embracing the more businesslike approach that some advocate. Either way, the trend toward more credentials, continuing education offerings, and more material designed for individuals already in the workforce indicates the trend toward the need for increased revenues. As discussed earlier in this chapter, there is a definitive need and point of collaborative possibility between institutions and practitioners transitioning to academia in terms of content development. Additionally, this is also an opportunity for those same practitioners to deliver top line growth to the institution in question. Growing revenue is necessary for every organization, no matter what industry vertical they inhabit, and it makes sense that higher education—in that sense—is not all that much from other industries. While there are a lot of opportunities for collaboration and growth as practitioners transition to higher education, it is also important that anyone considering such a move has the correct assortment of information and materials to make such a transition a success. The first step in such a process is building an academic portfolio and making sure that the right pieces of information are included therein.

Reflection Questions

1. Given the fact that there is so much pressure to publish for academics, do you feel there is a role for more "business-like" journal publishers, operating on something like a pay-to-play model?
2. Bringing real-world experience to the classroom is a major asset that former practitioners can deliver, but what are some of the skills coming over the horizon that students will need to know to succeed in the workforce of the future?
3. Since there are so many internal and external forces driving change in the higher education space, does it seem that there is a role to be played for colleges and universities to continue to operate more like a "traditional" business?

Additional Readings

1. Nature—Predatory-journal papers have little scientific impact—https://www.nature.com/articles/d41586-020-00031-6.
2. Beall's—List of potential predatory journals and publishers—https://beallslist.net/.
3. Real world classroom—https://www.rwc.school/.
4. Harvard Business Review—Why Companies And Universities Should Forge Long-Term Collaborations—https://hbr.org/2018/01/why-companies-and-universities-should-forge-long-term-collaborations.
5. American Progress—The Power of the Education-Industry Partnership—https://www.americanprogress.org/issues/economy/reports/2010/10/04/8518/the-power-of-the-education-industry-partnership/.

CHAPTER 8

Building an Academic Portfolio

Introduction

Putting together a resume or CV may seem like a relatively straightforward process, but that is a view that can trip up aspiring academics seeking to make a successful transition from private industry to academia. The type of CV that works in a corporate environment will not work for academia or higher education, because—linking back to the earlier conversations about the type of work to expect while employed in academia—the roles themselves are quite different from one another. With that in mind, there are a few initial steps to keep in mind as you are preparing for this transition.

The need for a new CV. Yes, even if there is a CV or resume that you have been using for decades with great success, that does not necessarily translate to a resume that is going to work in higher education. Realizing this, and being willing to construct an entirely new resume, is an important first step in this process. Simply put, the type of language and items that you want to highlight in an academic resume is going to be different than the language and content that you would have included on a corporate resume.

Willingness to travel. Commuting is no fun for anyone, no matter what region of the country you are traveling through. Delays, cancellations, and just the time that is consumed for commuting can make even

S. Stein Smith, *Shifting from Accounting Practitioner to Academia*, Palgrave Studies in Accounting and Finance Practice,
https://doi.org/10.1007/978-3-030-67546-2_8

the most enjoyable day a drag, but this needs to be analyzed through the context of how often this commute will actually be taking place. For example, a typical tenure track faculty member may only need to be on-site two or three days a week during the semester and usually is off for winter break and the majority of the summer as well. This lack of frequency can offset the length of the commute, which can lead to some faculty living an hour or even two from campus. Simple to say and conceptually understand, but is something that needs to be taken into account.

You may actually end up working more than at a 9–5 job. When an individual is employed at a corporate job, no matter how long the hours may be on a given day or during a certain time of year, when the day is over the work ends. Faculty members, and this is something that I had to get used to, tend to work on a different schedule than many professionals may be used to working. It may be difficult to reach certain people on a Tuesday afternoon, but those same individuals may be fully active and engaged on email and other work projects late into the evening. This may result, for some practitioners at the beginning, in confusion and frustration when a project or other deliverable is due.

There are certainly any number of items and factors that need to be assessed and integrated when a transition from private industry to academia is being discussed and assessed, but the point is that the workload has a different end goal. In addition to the changing nature and types of work that may be expected—presentations, written content, and service—the goal of much of this work is different than what may have been previously expected or associated with work. In the private sector, and this applies no matter what industry and individual are employed within, much of the goal of work is not self-promotion but is a component of a bigger project. Understanding this, and the role that practitioners often serve in the conversation, is a learning experience for many new entrants into the corporate workforce. Think back for a moment, to how odd it must seem to new professionals that are recent graduates as they first enter an office or professional environment. During the entire educational process, the emphasis and focus are always on individual performance and accomplishment; grades, GPA, honors, advanced placement classes, and any number of other academic benchmarks or tools are almost always affiliated or directed toward what an individual is able to accomplish.

Directly following this, and sometimes even following the bestowing of specific academic honors linked to individual performance, individuals are tossed into an environment where the goal is not linked to individual achievement but rather the goals of the department or company at large. In addition to some other critiques leveled against recent graduates—lack of communication skills, limited work ethic, narrow range of usable skills, and the inability to work together—many recent graduates are unused to not receiving consistent feedback and analysis on their work products. Stated slight differently the entire focus and purpose of work need to shift its focus from being honed in on individual achievement and become more closely linked to team or group-based outcomes. Academia from a career perspective, however, necessitates a pivot back toward increased focus and attention on the individual output and results achieved by the individual in question.

This is not to suggest or otherwise imply that academics do not cooperate with each other or are continuously engaged in politicking to receive credit (although this happens in academia as it does in every other industry). Rather, this should just serve as a reminder that both the type of work expected and the benchmarks by which individuals are evaluated and ranked will be different in academia versus other types of areas or professional backgrounds. What academia means will, of course, be different for every individual making this transition and shift from private industry to higher education, but in any case this does seem to point to being able to change and evolve in response to change criteria.

Putting this together into an actionable plan can be summarized as follows, although it is important to remember—as always—that plans are subject to change and evolution as it interacts with the marketplace. Putting a plan together and assembling an academic CV is one thing from an operational perspective, but it is also important to have an overarching plan in place to help guide and develop the process in response to changing market and academic conditions. Not meant to be an exhaustive or all-inclusive trip, these action points and suggestions should instead be viewed as a starting point to help develop a robust action plan linked to assembling a CV appropriate for both a practitioner and academic perspective.

First of all, it is important to have a plan in place at a high level that is connected to both the expertise of the individual and the specific type of content that is going to be generated by the aspiring academic. For example, if you have a history of written content in the form of a column, consistent articles, or other types of journal articles, it might make sense to leverage the experience in the context of your transition to academia.

If instead you are most well versed in presenting at trade shows, leading webinars, otherwise producing professional content that might make it easier and simpler for those skills to carry over into the higher education space. Lastly, if you are an actively engaged member of your professional community, it might make the most sense to see if those connections can be harnessed or repurposed for a higher education use case. This might be establishing collaborations and partnerships with external organizations, or simply using those connections to further certain goals of the institution in question. In any event, an effort should be made to take advantage of what you are already doing as you lay out your plan.

Building on this first step, it also seems logical to recognize that the focus and shift of said content and work product will need to evolve and change over time. Transitioning from quarterly reports and filings to academic articles might seem like an unusual pivot, but at the end of the day that is the one that will need to occur in order to effectively manage this shift and pivot underpins the entire attempted shift being managed. Shifting focus, or instead of focusing on company-specific details to more macroeconomic oriented viewpoints, can be more difficult than it might seem. While in most professional settings, the desired goal or outcome is to arrive at a definitive conclusion or answer that is not always the case with regards to higher education. Clearly, there are some instances where definitive answers are preferable to vague statements, but that does not mean it is always the case. For example, many of the most highly recommended and referenced academic pieces do not actually answer any of the questions posed by the researcher.

This lack of definitive answers and results at the end of the research and publication process can be extremely frustrating for newly minted or freshly transitioned academics. Of specific importance in this text is the frustration that cannot be underestimated as a result of this ambiguous approach to research and publishing. However, there are certainly tasks and research projects that do have a more structured process, including research that includes quantitative analysis, hypotheses, and results that do not mean that this is always the case. Qualitative or exploratory research might be types of research normally associated with a lack of definitive answer, but quantitative research can just as easily encourage such an outcome or results. Put simply not every question has a definitive answer, and not every question is able to answer within the context and with the rigor demanded of academic research.

Tenure Process—Frequently Asked Questions

This also seems to present an appropriate time to discuss just what exactly the tenure process entails, and why it seems so important to those entering academia. Tenure requirements and specific processes will vary from institution to institution, but there are a few core concepts to keep in mind when attempting to understand when analyzing what tenure is, why it is important, and how the academic landscape is changing. Prior to that, however, it always makes sense to understand that tenure will not be a viable option for every individual or institution, but that does not make these institutions or positions any less appealing or inviting.

What exactly is tenure, and why is it such a big deal? Tenure is considered, as discussed previously, to be the gold standard in academic circles in terms of prestige, ranking, and positions and ability to publish, raise funds, and launch programs. This prestige and ranking are often linked to the fact that tenured or tenure track faculty are thought of as permanent members of the institution that will be there for the duration of a career. In that context, it is reasonable to assume and state that tenure—in good situations—should be thought of as a partnership between faculty and the administration. Said partnership can take many different forms, but is most often characterized by corporate governance and shared governing structure that exists at many institutions. Tenure is thought of as the gold standard because of the importance and rank faculty members are granted in various aspects of university operations.

Why is tenure so important and so frequently discussed? Tenure is important, rather obviously, for the reasons listed previously, but is also important for several other reasons. Perhaps most obviously a reason that tenure is important is that it provides faculty with the ability to research, grant-write, and pursue other related endeavors without fear of being ostracized for any number of reasons. Such flexibility also allows faculty members to be engaged in governance, focuses on longer-term projects and initiatives, and not be as—for lack of a better term—obsessed with shorter-term publishing and teaching requirements.

How is the academic landscape is changing for faculty members, and the institutions they are employed within. The academic landscape is changing due to the array of forces mentioned within this text, including digitization, technology, internationalization, and the growing influence of corporate partners in the educational landscape. As a result of this confluence of changes and change in the educational landscape, it is also important to recognize that many of the old structures and relationships are being altered as well. Neither a good or bad occurrence, this is simply a reflection of the need for academia and higher education to change and evolve in response to both internal and external changes and forces. Unfortunately, one of the largest changes that are indicative of this change and force is the fact that as higher education becomes more businesslike many of the relationships and partners will also need to change and become more businesslike as well.

Even with the array of changes and forces coming to the higher education landscape, it is important to remember that, at least for the foreseeable future, the tenure process will continue to have a large effect and influence on the broader academic process. Acknowledging the fact that higher education is rapidly changing and evolving the importance and weight that the tenure process, tenure track faculty, and tenured faculty bring to bear on the academic discussion are unlikely to be reduced at any time soon. What this actually means in terms of institutional governance, teaching loads, and overall atmosphere will differ from institution to institution, but the fact remains that this will still be considered as the proverbial gold ring. Despite some dissatisfaction with the exact nature of how this process may play out, it would seem unreasonable to simply dispose of the entire current system in its entirety.

Revisiting the Importance of the Alternative Career Path

Given that the tenure process may not be as interesting, applicable, or possible for every practitioner entering the academic space, it is also important to be aware of, and see the value in, the possibility of an alternative academic career. As this book took shape, I did find myself struggling somewhat as to whether or not I should even include this section in this text; after all, this book was written with a specific audience in mind—accounting practitioners seeking to make a successful transition from private industry to higher education. To some, not including myself in any way, pursuing an alternative academic career can be seen as akin to failure, or a lack of success with regard to how this transition actually took place. This could not be further from the truth, however, and as higher education continues to evolve and change, it is evident that the educational conversation will continue to change and evolve alongside the profession. Higher education and the academic conversation, in general, are continuing to evolve and change far from the ivory tower that had once dominated the academic discourse and continues to move and shift more toward one more akin to a blended or hybrid approach.

While our conversation with this text may have focused primarily on the development and marketing of different courses, certificates, and programs from a professional perspective, there is also a broader conversation that needs to be had. Academia and higher education, in whatever form is discussed, have an impact and reach far beyond any classroom no matter what institution is being examined. Drilling down to understand just what exactly this means, however, is not a simple matter or something that can be summarized in a matter of a few pages; entire websites and publications are dedicated to discussing, presenting, and analyzing just what alternative academic careers mean from different individuals. Without purporting to represent an authoritative listing of potential careers from an alternative perspective, these options and conversations should, at the very least, provide an adequate starting point for an analysis of other options and alternatives that may very well exist.

Something is relatively close to what practitioners may have already dealt with and done, becoming an industry association or society head, which might be more familiar to some members of the academic community than others. Professional members of the accounting and financial services community often are already members of at least one association, and so moving out of the accounting-specific sectors and roles into a leadership or even simply an employment role at such an institution is not as outlandish as it might seem initially. Obtaining a role at such an institution may be simpler or easier for some individuals or people than others, but that also represents an opportunity and options for practitioners seeking to make this transition successful. Playing an active role in the profession is one thing, but this also represents an opportunity for individuals to establish and develop connections between institutions of higher education, professionals associations, corporate partners, and private sector actors.

1. Being employed at a role within a professional or private sector-oriented organization including those affiliated with advocacy or other goals. Whether the position is one assumed at an advocacy organization or one more oriented toward a specific policy objective, there is going to be an angle, perspective, or otherwise oriented toward a goal in mind. Depending on the goal or objective of the

organization in question, this may be more or less attuned to any personal objectives, but that misses the larger point. As a practitioner transitioning from private industry to academia, it will be upon you to be able to argue the multiple angles with which any topic is discussed. What this means is that you might have to analyze and discuss, and possibly advocate, positions and points of view that may not be inherently views that you possess. This leads us to the next point that is especially important, especially for individuals seeking an alt-academic career.

2. Understanding the different points of view and perspectives is an important thing that every practitioner transitioning the academia should keep in mind. Especially for those individuals that have been employed either in industry or in public accounting where there is always a problem to solve or issue to address it may be difficult or even unnerving to analyze and dissect a point of view or position that may be opposing or even just different than your own. Being able to understand, explain, and articulate the various points of view is the true marking of an academic willing to discuss and analyze issues that might not be intuitive. Discussing and analyzing these issues, which may or may not even if the area of expertise of a specific individual, is a role that must be fulfilled.

The rise of the alt-academic career, or alt-ac career path, is something that might have seemed to have risen prominence during the last several years, and this is for a very good reason; academia and the broader marketplace have changed and evolved in response to numerous market forces. This is not to say that this career path never existed previously, but there are several new iterations that have seemed to float to the surface more recently. Nonprofit associations have always been a draw for individuals that have been educated and motivated to do good, give back, but the importance of the associations continues to increase over time. What this means in reality is that there are any number of positions and opportunities that have emerged for aspiring academics and thought leaders that might not have existed or even been known about previously. Not every nonprofit association is going to operate in the exact same way, or be structured in a similar manner, but there do appear to be several traits, openings, and types of positions that aspiring academics can fill at these types of associations.

The first type of position and role that can be filled by an aspiring academic and practitioners that are moving into the nonprofit and academic space is the role of subject matter expert. No matter what the organization is actually oriented on, there are going to be forces outside of the firm that are going to drive change, innovation, and change within the nonprofit organization. Traditionally, the role of financial practitioner making a transition out of private industry has been to fill the role of CFO, Treasurer, or other types of financial analyst role, but that is a limited perspective on the potential in this arena. Instead of merely focusing on the specific financial analysis and reporting role, practitioners can bring other types of subject matter expertise to the conversation. Fundraising, helping to streamline the reporting process, bringing advanced technology tools to bear on the situation and internal processes, and being able to help integrate these technologies into current processes and workflows all represent areas in which practitioners can bring their array of information to bear.

On top of these operationally focused roles and positions, there is also always the possibility that practitioners making this transition can actually fill the role of subject matter expert, most knowledgeable person, or even some of the top leadership roles at the association. Assuming a leadership role may be or more or less of interest to some individual making the transition successfully, but that undersells the assets that these individuals can bring to bear on the conversation. Especially for industry associations and think tanks, it may actually make more sense to have a former private sector actor to assume a leadership-oriented role than to hire some individual that is located outside of the private sector. In the case of accounting professionals, the sheer number of associations, think tanks, and other types of institutes are nearly innumerable. Every professional field does have any number of professional associations and groups that practitioners can be a part of, but especially in accounting and finance there can be a large number of potential opportunities and openings for aspiring practitioners to be a part of state societies, national societies, and even international groups and associations. There are not all that many limits on what can actually be operationalized and implemented by practitioners, and this is an important point to always keep in mind during the process moving forward.

Simply because there are openings in these various institutions, however, does not mean that there are no competitors for these openings as well. For example, for every opening at a nonprofit or trade association, there will be several job applications; like any other field so this should not come as a surprise. The main difference in the field of alt-ac, or alternative academia, is that there are numerous other practitioners and individuals involved in these fields that can bring years, if not decades, or expertise and on the ground experience to bear on the conversation. Clearly, this can mean several results and things for aspiring academics and practitioners making the transition need to come prepared to compete for these positions. Without claiming to be an all exhaustive or inclusive listing, several considerations do need to be taken into account if an alt-ac career or even position is being analyzed or considered.

Make sure that the nonprofit or trade association that is being considered is actually a good fit for you and your background. Just because, for example, you have a background in accounting or financial services does not mean that every accounting or financial trade association or group is going to be a good fit for you and your interests. Doing due diligence should always be a part of any job application process, and the transition from private sector to either academia or an alt-ac position is no different. Especially with the rise of emerging technologies such as blockchain, robotic process automation, artificial intelligence, and cryptoassets, there are even more trade groups entering the landscape.

Ensure that your background and areas of interest are not already covered or otherwise addressed by current members of the association, which is something that might be occasionally overlooked. Professionals might assume, sometimes incorrectly, that the association or trade group is staffed by generalists or otherwise non-specialized individuals; this can be a mistake that can cost an interview or even position at an association or nonprofit. Many associations, particularly those that are more intertwined with professional or political angles, have in recent years become more connected and have embraced the importance of a professionally relevant team. Staffing up has obviously generated increased costs for these organizations, but do continue to pay dividends in the form of engagement, access, and professional influence.

Craft a pitch that makes sense in the context of the trade group, association, and other external factors that are relevant both from an advocacy; even if the association in question is a good fit on paper and you have made successful inroads to initiate conversation, there is a need to make sure that you craft the appropriate pitch. Developing a narrative and pitch is something that should always play a role in the broader transitional conversation. Researching the association, making sure that you are well positioned to make a successful introduction, and attempting to make sure that you are in a good spot to make a solid connection to this opportunity are vitally important.

Understand that a nonprofit association or industry advocacy association will have different goals than either a private sector organization or an institution of higher education. Private sector actors and organizations clearly have a profit goal and drive that underpin the majority of the choices made by management professionals; no matter what the specific industry is being analyzed and examined, the realities of profit and loss will always reassert themselves. Institutions of higher education, by contrast, tend to have several goals that overlap from both an operational and educational point of view. Maintaining accreditation, developing new courses and programs, and being proactive with regard to pursuing and retaining new students involve both sides of this equation.

A nonprofit or trade association, by contrast, tends to have multiple goals and objectives depending on the industry and goals of the association. Advocacy associations might focus on advocating several different areas of legislation, regulation, or other regulatory angles but that is only one of the options. Other associations, however, might focus more on pursuing professional goals such as education, training, and other practitioner-oriented objectives.

This potentially dual nature of the goals and directives of a nonprofit can create opportunities as well as challenges for practitioners seeking to make this transition work as planned. In practice, this can be a result of the potential political angle or slant that an association might become linked or connected to. The importance of this association means that this connection might only be perceived or not, but the association can become real depending on who believes that this connection is legitimate.

Attempting to work from the inside out of the association or nonprofit group is an angle and attempt that many practitioners think they can bring to bear; in other words, they can change the association from the inside out. Much like reforming the corporate culture at a private sector organization can be easier said than done, it can be just as difficult to reform or alter the culture at a nonprofit and advocacy group.

After understanding and linking together the various threads and potential objectives of this nonprofit association, it will be possible to make the best decision possible in terms of how to approach the variety of goals, the potential political ramifications of this array of goals, and where you might professionally fit in that conversation. The importance and possibility of alt-ac careers and job opportunities are something that is certainly worth exploring for any practitioner making a transition from the private sector to the nonprofit and higher education space.

Public Intellectual

The idea of an academic expert, a resident fellow, or other experts to be cited and referenced in a conversation is something that has been cited and referenced countless times throughout the decades, but in the modern era it does seem more appropriate than ever that academics, intellectuals, and otherwise educated people should take a leading voice in the public debate. Politics aside, it does seem that the idea of a public intellectual has been receiving increased favor over the last few years as the conversations and debates around policy and other issues have become more complicated. Understanding, analyzing, and having the ability to articulate different sides of issues, and issues across a range of perspectives is an important attribute for anyone seeking to become an academic or intellectual in any capacity. Although the title of public intellectual may seem a bit outdated or antiquated in the current discourse, it does seem, actually, more appropriate than ever. In the maelstrom that is modern media and politics, there should be a role for objective and level-headed analysis to be discussing the issues and items that occupy the current conversation. Despite the headlines that are generated by the believers on both sides, there still does remain a need for objective, level-headed, and reasonable conversation.

Academics occupy a unique position in the areas of public discourse, debate, and conversation in the fact that they are almost universally viewed as objective and impartial arbiters of conversation and debate. Such a position, however, is not one that is maintained with no effort of investment on the part of those involved in these conversations. For academics to maintain such an envied position and status among the endless talking heads and options that dominate the airwaves, those involved must be able to understand, discuss, and articulate the points of view of an array of audience members and individuals, even those that are not always in alignment with your personal perspective. The idea of a public intellectual might seem like something that is out of the mainstream, but these individuals and ideas probably occupy the majority of mainstream conversation and debate. In other words, being a public intellectual is not something that should be viewed as merely a tangential topic, but rather one that is going to be a primary role for many practitioners seeking to transition and move to academia. Drilling down to the idea of a public intellectual and what that actually means from a personal and professional perspective, there are a few areas that seem reasonable to include in this conversation. In other words, there are people that should serve as experts and sources of expertise in the ongoing conversations and debates, but these roles can take various forms.

The role of expert is something that not to be underestimated in terms of how important it is for the future of public discourse and debate. Oftentimes, if one turns on a major news network or media source and watches any news show for any length of time, there will invariably be an academic expert or source that is brought on to help enlighten, reinforce, or further push the conversation forward. Expertise is not equally distributed, however, and so it is important to remember that as a practitioner transitioning to academia that specific subject matter expertise or being able to discuss subject areas is almost always the role that academics are sought after to help fill. Depending on the role or area of expertise that an individual wishes to fill, this may be easier or more difficult, but it is something that needs to be assessed.

Serving as an arbiter or some other types of neutral and third party expert for the analysis and reporting of data. Playing the role of peacemaker or arbiter or otherwise some neutral or central third party is a common role for academics to fill—individuals often view academics as an objective and neutral source for information and data. This role is prevalent in virtually every form of media and conversation, from mainstream media outlets like CNN, CNBC, and Fox News to the more esoteric outlets such as ZeroHedge. Having the capability to analyze and discuss the multiple issues, and the individual facets that comprise these arguments and conversations, is a role that seems to be sorely needed in the current landscape. Playing the role of a referee and arbiter is a role and position that many academics do seem to find themselves in, and that is something that should be factored into conversation or analysis of just how the transition from private industry to academia happens.

Being or serving a role as a third party and objective expert to be brought in during times of crisis, uncertainty, or other potential issues that could cause conflict between different members of a group or people attempting to have a conversation. Such a role and position might seem to be close to that of a public intellectual or another neutral third party, but playing the role of mediator is significantly different. Playing the role of a mediator involves usually being on-site or otherwise meeting with potentially conflicting individuals or institutions, versus doing so from a remote basis. This role or expertise and mediation may seem like a simple combination of the first two roles. That said, this particular role and conversation basically represent a third option and opportunity for practitioners transitioning from that of industry expert to someone seeking to establish themselves more fully as a legitimate source of guidance and information.

The idea of a public intellectual might seem like something that is an esoteric concept, one that is not terribly relevant or important given the somewhat contentious nature of the current political, social, and business environments, but that misses the broader—and more important—point. Especially in such an environment, where changes and trends continue to permutate, evolve, and shift on a nearly continuous basis, having individuals at hand that are able to discuss, examine, and understand what these trends mean and how they are connected represent roles and ideas that are very interesting in nature in addition to being very important. Public intellectuals have long held a role of importance of expertise in different subject matter areas, and the names of said individuals are almost as familiar as actors may be. Authors and artists may be the most familiar and well-known members of the public intellectual class, but that does not mean that the role and positions of public intellectuals are not applicable for business-oriented or trained individuals. In fact, many of the most important issues that are driving change and influence across business and society at large are driven by underlying business trends.

Understanding the impact of automation, digitization, and increasing integration of technology into virtually every aspect of business, societal conversations, and economics, offers both tremendous opportunities and challenges for practitioners. Already possessing the necessary training and education to master and discuss these and numerous other trends makes it a relatively simple manner to leverage this expertise and knowledge to advise other stakeholders on a broader number of issues. For example, automation and digitization are two specific technical terms and forces that may have originated within the business or information technology community, but that are causing large amounts of disruption and debate among virtually almost every aspect of the conversational landscape. Being able to understand the following components of automation and any other trends represents an important role and position for aspiring academics and public intellectuals to embrace.

What exactly is the trend in question? This may seem to be an easy question to answer and address, but understanding just what exactly the trend in question is can be something that is more complicated than one might think. For example, automation in and of itself is not something that should be feared or otherwise perceived as a negative trend in and of itself. Regardless of whether the question in particular is focused on the academic or private sector angle of things, the ability to understand and accurately assess just what exactly is going on is just something that academics can play a definitive and objective role in assessing.

How does this impact the educational and private sector angles of the conversation? Education is clearly the focus of this text, but the evolving and developing role of academics and academia necessitates that the idea and concept of an academic will also need to evolve and change over time as well. Classroom instruction is one thing, obviously, but that only represents one angle and point of view of just what academics are increasingly tasked with doing. Coming from the private sector, the requirement and expectation that everyone wears multiple hats and does multiple different tasks will not be such a surprise, but this may actually come as something as a shock to more classically trained individuals. If this book can be one thing, or serve one role in this fast-moving conversation, it will hopefully help to illustrate and communicate the fact that higher education, academia, and the broader sector of higher education will need to change over time.

Should the educational conversation change and evolve to acknowledge these changing technology trends, or should the individuals associated with the educational conversation try to maintain current methodologies and techniques? Given the importance of equipping students with the necessary skill sets to successfully complete and navigate a business and economic landscape that continues to evolve and change over time requires, by necessity, the evolution and development of new techniques and ideas in order to do so, but that should not always involve a complete overhaul of every technique. As mentioned throughout this text, it is also important to be wary of overly focusing on the topic and trend of the moment versus more holistic and comprehensive education, i.e., only focusing on a specific technology or task at hand.

What should the role of the private sector or the public sector be in analyzing and discussing certain issues and the trends that are driving change in the economy, society, and broader society as a whole? Given the reality that the higher education sector is indeed influenced, sometimes overtly and sometimes less obviously, by the governmental and public sector, this is not simply an idle question or one of simple curiosity. The role of different economic sectors or actors will have an influence on how technology trends develop, and how these trends will drive broader change overall. The sheer pace and scope of change, both due to technology and other factors, will only continue to accelerate as time progresses, so balancing the influence of public and private sector actors will be important both now and going forward. Academics, in a role as instructor as well as public intellectuals, have a very potentially important role to play in both the public discourse and debates across areas of all importance.

Providing a balanced perspective and point of view and rationale for actions that might otherwise be hijacked, harnessed, or manipulated by any number of different actors and market participants. Especially given the contentious geo-political, societal, and economical conversations, providing an objective and level-headed assessment and examination of what exactly is going on in various areas generates a value that is difficult to overstate. Now, this assumes that those individuals providing said opinions and viewpoints on certain issues do so objectively, but that might not always be a case. Removing personal bias and perspective is important for every type of practitioner, and this is something that accounting and financial service professionals are already familiarized with doing anyway.

Defining and explaining the role and idea of a public intellectual or in-residence expert can be a complicated conversation for those that have not been otherwise introduced to this idea. Peeling back the layers, and inevitable political connotations that can be associated with some of the public statements made by academics and other prominent intellectual experts, the implications of this shift and development can represent a tremendous opportunity for aspiring practitioners. For those individuals that might not be as interested in writing and researching and teaching in a classroom, a role or position as a public intellectual is something that is very much worth considering. Is it for everyone? Absolutely not, but if it sounds like something that might be of interest to you this may be work inspecting and learning more about.

Why Not Do Both?

Attempting to navigate the vagaries of career paths and choices can be difficult even in the best of times, but can be even more complicated if one is attempting to do so in the context of entering a new career area of field. As tempting as it might be to transition entirely from the private sector of your previous role into higher education—after all that is why you are reading this book to begin with, I would assume—that may or may not be as practical depending on your situation. In that context, it actually might make more sense to instead focus on trying to find balance between your current role and potential future roles by keeping one foot in both camps. Striking a compromise is usually not an idea of a perfect or enjoyable time, but from a broader perspective that does actually make more sense. Especially since the spheres of higher education and private industry continue to overlap, and move closer together, there is a legitimate argument to be made that both of these areas are equally as appealing and interesting to large number of individuals. My personal experience, in my humble opinion, does seem to illustrate a potential pathway forward for individuals that are seeking to strike that balance while transitioning or moving from one sector to another. Let's take a look at how my example and path forward might be able to be of service and assistance to those individuals.

Before diving into specific examples, however, there is an important point that needs to be identified related to just how this balance should be developed and preserved over time. Like anything else, professional interests and areas of expertise will evolve and change over time, as well as the profile of said interests as they are viewed and valued by the rest of the professional landscape. My intersection and overlap of academic and professional interests have included working with the Sustainability Accounting Standards Board, my doctoral dissertation on the integrated financial reporting, analyzing and presenting on both the B-corp certification and benefit corporations at large, holding a position on a national commission committed to improving financial literacy, and finally pivoting to how emerging technology is driving change in the accounting and financial services space. Current roles that I hold that do present an overlap between my academic interests and professional areas of expertise include my work with the Wall Street Blockchain Alliance, the New Jersey Society of CPAs, the American Institute of CPAs, and Institute of Management Accountants, serving as a thought leader and expert as to how these associations can better interact and engage with all members of the stakeholder community.

The role of an academic, especially one that remains firmly grounded in reality, is a unique one for any industry, but especially for an industry like accounting and financial services. In many cases, an organization will only allow members of the C-suite to testify or comment on certain issues, and even those individuals will have to be carefully vetted and coached prior to appearing on any media platform. One need only to tune into and watch any mass media or business network to see how often these combinations do seem to manifest themselves. In that context, the entire conversation and debate around making the transition from private industry to academia are not as binary a choice as it might initially appear. Let's revisit the broader conversation around making this transition, as well as the number of alternative or other types of roles that are available to practitioners making a transition. There are any number of positions, associations, or other types of organizations available for these types of individuals to obtain and fill, but these do not mean that they are mutually exclusive.

Having an academic or an individual that has a blended background and approach to solving problems and issues can actually add to the credibility and authenticity of positions and policies undertaken at the organization. For example, would an opinion or viewpoint be examined from a better or worse perspective if it is presented from a private sector actor or someone who brings an objective and unbiased perspective to the conversation? This is not to suggest that an academic or member of higher education should be thought of as a token addition participant to a board of an organization; rather, this addition should be leveraged and maximized. Such an addition also ties directly into the second point as well.

Fundraising and grant writing is, as any association head will attest, an important but sometimes arduous part of running and managing such an association. The simple reality is that bills do need to get paid even if the group is organized as a nonprofit. This is also a good time to explain the following: simply because an organization is labeled or structured as a nonprofit does not mean that there is no profit, bill paying, or other financial motivation. Making good use of the connections, skills, or even just general awareness that someone in the nonprofit or academic space has with the fundraising and financial process is usually a much needed addition to the existing team.

Content, content, content. In order for any group to have a seat at the proverbial table or a voice in the conversation, this group needs to also have a voice that can be heard; the only way for a group to be heard and be active in the marketplace is via the information, content, and communications that it sends out. That said, the actual producing of content and making sure that this content is produced on a consistent and recurring basis may not be something that many of the other group members have experience with doing, or at least not be comfortable with. Additionally, if the rest of the members of the board are private sector employees, they might be able to comment on emerging issues like an academic member would be able to. This is not to say that every single academic or aspiring academic is going to be as equally good a fit for serving in an industry type of role, but this is something that needs to be acknowledged and factored into the career analysis and career planning. No matter what organization or association is actually in question, or is being analyzed as a prospective employer in the future this is something that needs to be taken into account. Academics and especially academics that have a track record or history of private sector experience have a unique value proposition that can and should be brought to the proverbial table. Whether it takes the form of managing content and other information to the marketplace, providing objective analysis and advice to both internal and external colleagues, or serving as a neutral arbiter in terms of moderating debate and dialogues attempting to straddle the gap and bridge the connection between different constituencies there are multiple roles that a practitioner-turned-academic can fulfill.

Now, this is not to say that attempting to bridge this gap and difference between private sector actors, governmental oversight bodies, and the higher education space is going to be simple or straightforward in nature. On the contrary, maintaining this balance and status as an objective and third party organization can be difficult for several reasons. First and most obviously is the difficulty that can be generated when trying to balance the needs and expectations of more than one supervisor, group, or external third party. As the saying goes, it is impossible to serve more than one master, and this can become painfully obvious if an aspiring academic is—for example—attempting to serve on multiple boards of advisory positions that may be competitive or conflicting in nature.

An additional consideration that needs to be taken into account is the simple fact that sometimes an institution of higher education might not like its faculty members to be in the employ of or even associated with a private sector or other market participants. This may take different forms at different institutions but can be categorized and positioned as a restriction on external employment, additional disclosures being required, or other forms of documentation and paperwork being required as a result of these additional roles and positions. From the point of view of the organization, this makes sense; they are paying you to perform a certain role for that organization versus paying you to do whatever it seems you might want to do. That said, it can be frustrating for individuals seeking to expand and develop additional networks and connections if these said activities seem to be artificially restricted. While this might or might not be something that you are particularly interested in pursuant at the given moment, it is important to take this into account if you are considering linking up or connecting with a variety of associations. Like almost anything else, having these conversations and maintaining an open line of communication and dialogue is important, and it is even more important to take into account that there may be others at the institutions that are not of like mind with either the organization or the positions taken by those organizations.

Trying to establish a position that enables you to straddle back and forth between the areas of academia and the private sector may not be the simplest or easiest methodology for someone to embark upon, but it may be one that is very interesting and engaging. Private sector individuals and practitioners clearly have a breadth of experience and on the ground experience, which can bring a much needed injection of practicality to the higher education conversation. What this specifically means is that as the higher education space will evolve and change over time, private sector individuals will have an important role to play in how it develops and emerge as a result of automation, digitization, and other changing factors. On the other hand, the rigor and objectivity that an academic professional can bring to any debate or conversation are a much needed and sought after perspective given in the current environment.

Recommendations for a Successful Transition

As you make the transition, and are preparing a new or retrofitted professional identity to do so, it is also important to remember that the roles and expectations of academics are different, and this is carried over to the work and tasks that are going to accompany the role or position.

Research, service, and presentations are—of course—a core part and role of what academics do on a daily basis, but it extends far beyond that higher level of view and to the nitty-gritty. One of the hardest hurdles to overcome for many practitioners is to get in the habit of writing and putting together content on a consistent basis. While this might seem different and something abstract compared to what previous tasks may have been focused on, the idea of writing and content creation may seem alien, different, or something entirely different out of the comfort zone of many people. A question that I have seen asked, over and over again, is how exactly to get started writing consistently when the longest writing assignment might have been an email or short memo. This may seem like a silly or basic question, but the importance of being able to produce and write consistently is important and cannot be overstated.

Hopefully as has been illustrated during the previous sections of this book, there are a number of alternative options and careers that should be discussed and examined during the transition from the private sector to the wider range of nonprofit, academic, and think tank options that do exist. Obviously, the specific career path that is chosen will vary from individual to individual but the underlying meaning is relatively easy to see and observe. Limiting oneself to a traditional model of higher education and instruction is not only a disservice to those people involved but also the wider discourse surrounding emerging trends and topics and the intersection of these topics and trends. Regardless of which specific track is selected and chosen by the people in question, there are several core steps that should be followed and integrated into the daily work and medium-term planning conversation.

Make Yourself Known

Perhaps the most important part of any career path that has been selected, alt-ac or not, it could be argued that the most important part of any selected option is the ability of those professionals to produce written content on a consistent basis. Multimedia options have certainly burst into the marketplace with the advent of YouTube, podcasts, and other such platforms but in terms of impact it does appear that written content—although perhaps complemented with other forms of information—seems to drive the majority of professional conversations. This is an important differentiation to understand up front. In early 2020, YouTube was, for the first time, broken out in terms of revenue from its parent company

Alphabet (basically Google plus some non-core operations); it's a $15 billion business on an annual basis. More on this later, but simply ignoring or discounting the value of such a platform is a recipe to undersell the impact content will have.

What academia actually means, in essence, is that you are going to transform from a process completion specialist to an individual that is going to be a content production and dissemination specialist. This may take different forms depending on the institution—be it a college, university, or other research institutes—but the underlying message is that any academic is going to be expected to produce content on a consistent basis. Research articles, practitioner articles, presentations, and multimedia appearances may form a larger or smaller component of this content, but the underlying message is consistent—as an academic you are going to be expected to produce appropriate content on a consistent basis.

How to Start Writing Consistently

Perhaps the first and most appropriate way to think of writing is to select a certain specific area of interest or expertise that you have, which should not seem abstract or difficult given the reality that you invariably have areas that you are more interested in than others as a result of your professional background and experiences. Simply being interested, however, is not enough when you are attempting to figure out how to craft and deliver content related to a certain subject area. In order to effectively write and be able to communicate information in either a written or verbal format, there needs to be additional focus brought to bear on the situation. What this usually translates into is a focus on a more niche area or a subset of certain other areas rather than discussing the concept or topic at a higher level. For example, an area of focus and expertise may be tax or even corporate taxation, but for most academic publications—or even more higher regarded practitioner publications—there is an expectation that the deliverable you produce will be focused on a specific business or use case that has dominated the marketplace.

Sticking with the tax subject area for a minute, an area of focus one area that might be of interest and appropriate for an academic perspective would be the possible implementation of a wealth tax, and the possible implications of that tax on the broader economy would be something like an appropriate topic for further discourse and discussion. This focusing and drilling down onto specific research topics are something common to academia across industry lines, but may represent something of a paradox for business professionals. In the marketplace, it is often stated that becoming too specialized or pigeon-holed may be detrimental to the individual in terms of career advancement or development, but in academia the more focused and specialized that a person becomes the better off their career path can be. Becoming more focused and conducting more exhaustive and comprehensive research on a particular topic is often the pathway to a successful career and publication record. Having this focus and subset of topics to research on, however, is merely the first step toward successfully writing, and drafting and putting together a writing pipeline and content creation plan.

The first place to start any successful writing project will inevitably be the outline and drafting stages, and that is not different for an academic writing project. Even after identifying the appropriate idea or subset of ideas that are going to be focused on, getting some concept statements, drafted subject lines, and proposed headlines all represent important first steps. In addition to helping craft the outline and framework of the proposed piece itself, it can also serve as a research aid; if certain headlines or topical ideas do not immediately return huge numbers of search results, this can be indicative of two distinct but equally important possibilities. First, the fact that there has not yet been a tremendous amount written on the topic can indicate that the interest in this topic is insignificant or still emerging in nature. Conversely, it can also mean that the topic is in need of additional research and analysis, placing you and your research in the enviable position of being able to contribute at the early stages.

Secondly, and arguably more important than developing a tremendous or groundbreaking idea is the importance of learning how to write consistently and how to make this a part of your everyday habits and life. Writing may not have been a large part of past duties or responsibilities, but it should quickly become evident just how important writing is to an academic career. Put simply, one of the few tangible deliverables created by a faculty member or other types of academic is the articles, books, and other written content that are produced. Podcasts and media appearances are certainly solid additions to a faculty portfolio and may even be sought after by some institutions, but by and large the gold standard for judging faculty productivity does include a healthy dose of written content and work. Researching and writing consistently, in other words, should form a core component of the workflow and work that is being conducted by academic professionals on a daily basis.

One trick that I started to implement to assist me with this, and it's important to note that I was not necessarily a prolific writer by any means, was to set a daily goal for myself in terms of how much I wanted to write. This book was actually written using this system, with my goal for daily word count being 500 words. This does not mean that I always hit word count, and there were some days that—due to my travel schedule or other flexibility—I was able to write more than 500 words a day, but setting that benchmark is beneficial for a few reasons. Most obviously, setting a benchmark like that allows me to see and understand how I am doing in terms of content production, and to understand whether or not I am on track to meet my writing and publishing goals. Secondly, by setting a writing goal that I knew—in all likelihood—that I can achieve on an average day kept myself from getting discouraged. That is something that is often overlooked; everyone who starts a large writing project always wants to be productive, do a good job, and complete the project as efficiently as possible. Acknowledging this, it is also important to set goals, frameworks, and deadlines that are also realistic in nature. Setting a word count goal of 2000 words per day may sound great on paper, but if that is not realistic there is no point in doing so; all that happens is that people get discouraged due to feeling like they are not keeping up with their own self-imposed deadlines. 500 words may not work for you, and a goal of 250 or even 100 words may suit your particular writing style or project. The point is not the specific word count, but rather the fact that writing and content production become ingrained and almost a default part of your daily routine and habit.

Everyone has a different writing style, clearly, so simply laying out a fixed goal no matter if it is linked to word count or page length might now work for everyone involved. During my fellowship during the fall of 2019, I had a very interesting conversation during lunch about the writing process, and that led me to think about how exactly the writing process is integrated within my day to day life, and raised some issues that I think may go under-examined by many professionals. Specifically, a question came to mind that on the one hand might seem a bit unusual, but on the other hand makes perfect sense: Is the writing process something that can be standardized or is it truly unique to every individual? Based on everything that I have seen, and especially the comments that I have seen in (ironically) written books and articles it appears, the answer is some of both.

Attempting to standardize certain processes and procedures is usually a well-known approach to attempt and gain operational efficiencies, time savings, and drive improvements throughout the process. That said, mandating and documenting a fixed goal is no guarantee of any success or progress along these issues; one needs simply to look at overly optimistic forecasts and estimates to see how easily these goals can crumble under closer examination. While fixed goals do bring to the table, however, are some discipline and accountability to the conversation, and this is something that is difficult to overstate. Accountability is something that is all too often lacking in the academic discourse and conversation, and that is almost a default result of the more decentralized nature of academic work in general. Establishing deadlines, benchmarks, and metrics can bring an invaluable sense of discipline to the conversation and content production, and there is something else that can—for lack of a better word—supercharge this accountability conversation.

Accountability is, by any definition of the term and idea, something that is often missing whether a person is employed in corporate industry or employed in academia or higher education. Deadlines by themselves are not going to spur an individual or group of individuals to hold themselves accountable, but when combined with a group mindset the applicability of deadlines becomes more amplified. An analogy that is often used across topics—personal finance, exercise, and even writing—is the idea and concept of the buddy system of network system. Let's drill down into just how important having a team or support network can be for academics, either struggling or succeeding, to tackle writing and other content production schedules.

The reality is that the academic calendar tends to alternate between frantic periods of activity and periods of much slower or lower activity. Fall semesters tend to generally be more active and engaging than spring semesters since the academic year is kicking into high gear on top of the usual chaos of the fall time of year. Winter session, usually in January, tends to be a quieter time of year no matter what institution is being analyzed, and so this usually frees up academics to focus on research no matter what format that research tends to manifest itself within. Even with this built-in period of lower activity, however, it is all too common for academics or aspiring academics to falter and not maximize time they have during these quieter periods. Following this quiet period, the academic calendar tends to reaccelerate headed into the spring semester, which while usually not as jam packed as the fall semester can still represent a very active and engaged time of the year.

Spring semesters, although not uniformly, do tend to be occupied with committee work and other service-related engagements and obligations. This situation creates a trade-off situation for professionals that do need to be assessed and weighed, focusing on whether or not individual research and publications take precedence over the needs of the department of college. Balancing these expectations and requirements also means that the individual faculty members in question must be able to effectively allocate time and mental energy across an array of projects without giving either personal scholarship or department service the proverbial short end of the stick. These busier times of the year are where having a set goal and support structure to help you achieve these goals might be of benefit to faculty members looking to keep themselves on track in terms of publication frequency.

After the academic year has ended, the academic summer can represent an alluring possibility. With many institutions wrapping up in the middle of May, and with many not returning to academic activity until the end of August, this seemingly endless period of time can be a golden opportunity to push ahead on any number of projects. Returning back to the danger of unstructured or loosely structured work and required outputs, the main issue here is that academics can lose focus or accountability over these long summer months. This is not to say that the only way to succeed is to barricade oneself in a den, office, or basement and dedicate the entire time to work. That, in addition to being somewhat odd behavior that might cause friends and family to worry, would not be productive; forcing a project or idea forward is only effective to a certain extent. In addition to the efforts necessary to push a project, it is also necessary to allocate time to unplug and relax. Academic summers provide opportunities for both items to be built into the schedule as required. The one downside that can insidiously sneak up on even the most dedicated and focused individual, however, is the risk that due to the summer itself the accountability and support networks that had been established during the year break down. Especially possible if colleagues travel, or are busily presenting at conferences during the summer, maintaining these connections and support during the summer is essential for maintaining momentum during this long stretch of "off time."

An additional tactic that I have employed to a certain extent is to take the approach of first putting word count and content onto paper, and then focusing on the editing at some future point. In other words, my approach is going to be to get word count and ideas on to the page first, typos and incomplete sentences in all, and then focus on the editing, proofreading, and finalizing of the content afterward. An analogy that I have used in the past is that in order to bake a cake or do any sort of project you need to have the raw materials to start with. You cannot carve a statue or put together any project or asset without the raw materials to work with; there needs to be a place to start in order to refine fine. The exact same concept applies to a paper or any other types of research project; in order to edit or refine a document to a final stage that is ready for publication, there needs to be a corpus that is ready to be edited down. Some people are not as comfortable simply dumping the information down onto the paper at first, to only come back later to refine and edit, but this is an approach that I have to be effective over time. Whichever tactic works best for you is the tactic that you should be using…

Presentations

One common refrain that I tend to hear, from colleagues employed both in industry and in academia, is that one of the reasons people go into accounting and finance is to avoid long writing tasks and the need to present publicly all that often. Even if that is the case, and it may or may not be equally as true depending on the individual, it is imperative to realize that presentations and presenting are core components of what academics are doing. From a career growth and development perspective, a successful transition and career advancement may actually hinge on the completion of conference presentations. That said, simply knowing that conference presentations are important, in and of themselves, is not enough to actually successfully present and attend said conferences. Much like any other types of engagement or gathering, there are a wide range of conferences that do need to be assessed and analyzed prior to actually attending and presenting at these events.

First and foremost is the application process, which by itself can be time consuming and stressful in and of itself. Every conference, regardless of the specific subset it inhabits, has a unique and differentiated application process that needs to be taken and completed on an individual basis. For example, for industry conferences—of which there are many—the application process usually opens right after the conclusion of the current year conference or event. What this means is that right after attending a conference, the application window for the coming year may be available for applications to submit to and apply for. This is how I first entered the presenting space and landscape; after attending some practitioner conferences, I wanted to be a bigger and more active part of those events. Looking at the conference website, I quickly realized how fast the portals opened up, and started submitting applications to these events; the first few applications did not go well. This also leads to another sub-topic and conversation that is important to take into account as aspiring academics attempt to accept to get into conferences to present.

Putting together conference applications can feel like a part-time, if not a full-time job, depending on how much effort is put into each application; therein lies a dilemma that needs to be assessed right away. Every conference is indeed different, and the conference goals, objectives, and topics need to be understood and taken into account during the application process. That said, it is also important to realize that there are general themes and trends that can be analyzed and understood as part of this application process. Conferences tend to post themes and topics that will headline the conversation up front, and these will ultimately drive the breakout sessions that will fill in the rest of the conference roster. These headline themes and topics are, in addition to driving additional conference content, also tend to be set and established relatively far in advance.

An additional component of the presentation circuit, or speaker circuit depending on who you ask, is the takeaway benefits and insights that can and should be generated from different speaking engagements. This is an area which on the one hand should be relatively straightforward but is often overlooked by speakers regardless of whether or not these people are grizzled academics or more recent entrants to the academic space. To illustrate how this might occur, let's take a look at a scenario that may be more or less typical, but certainly seems typical based on my experience as well as the conversations I have had with other junior or tenure track academics.

First things first, it is important to realize that most academic and trade conferences take place during the summer months, which can eat into some of that aforementioned free time that would have otherwise been leveraged to complete writing assignments. Realizing that is important for practitioners seeking to juggle both, because there are definitive benefits to both presenting at various conferences and publishing a robust mix of practitioner and academic publications. Setting these considerations aside for now, let's take a drill down at what might be a typical travel and presentation schedule, using an example from my own background from September of 2019. These presentations were for the Ohio Society of CPAs and Missouri Society of CPAs on back to back days, focusing on (not surprisingly) blockchain and cryptoassets and the implications of this technology for accounting professionals. Without further delay, let's get to it:

- September 25, wake up at 3:30 to pack and get to the airport for an 8:00 am flight to Cincinnati. If that seems excessive, remember that my "home" airport is in Newark, NJ (EWR)—a quick google search will explain why I need so much time.
- Land in Cincinnati around 10:30, grab something to eat at the airport, and make my way to Sharonville where the event is occurring.
- Arrive onsite around 11:30, catch up with a colleague of mine who presented early that morning, and then find some place to work until my session around 2:30.
- Present from approximately 2:30–4 pm and have a brief chat with the OSCPA staff, who have been very welcoming and friendly this entire year.
- Make my way to the Cincinnati airport hotel, which, to my initial surprise, was in Kentucky just like the airport!
- September 26. This is the marathon day, with a 2:45 am wakeup to catch the airport shuttle at 4 am. Then, the fun begins since there are no direct flights, or at least none that worked with my schedule, so in order to travel from Cincinnati to St. Louis I first have to fly to Chicago and transfer. After bouncing around the Midwest for several hours, I end up landing in St. Louis proper around 9:30 am in the morning.
- Making my way to the chic location that the MOCPA was holding this conference, I was able to spend the day and actually network/mingle with several colleagues who were also in attendance for the day.
- Immediately following my presentation which wrapped up around 3:30 in the afternoon I made my way back to the St. Louis airport.

Once again, there were no direct flights back to EWR that worked with my schedule, so I was connecting in Chicago along the way.
- With a very tight connection—45 minutes—I power walked through O'Hare and managed to catch my flight, eventually getting to bed around 2 am that night.

If that sounds like a little bit of a hectic couple of days, that is because it was. While there certainly were periods of less activity and less pressure sprinkled throughout the back to back days of presentations, there are a few core themes that appear to be present. The extremely long days, complete with early wakeups to make flights, will be familiar to anybody who has traveled for business. Compounding these long days is the reality that oftentimes a presentation is squeezed into these travel days. Adding these two factors together can result in an academic that is jet-lagged, rushed, and having to present while in that condition; it can be awfully difficult to network or mingle with colleagues in any meaningful way while in that state. Something else that often occurs is that even if an individual is able to get on-site with more time to spare, that usually also means that the turnaround after the presentation is also relatively quick. Having to leave immediately following a presentation can make it very difficult to obtain and digest anything but the most superficial feedback provided by attendees. So, what are some steps that can be taken to make the most of presentations, and the networking opportunities connected therein?

There is no definitive set of steps that can be taken across the board to help maximize presentation or time on the ground, but there are a few items that I have tried to utilize myself as well having seen in numerous publications across the board. First and foremost is to try and develop a game plan or strategy that you can realistically execute once you arrive on-site. The emphasis is on realistic because travel delays and other issues will inevitably occur, and the possibility of these delays can increase depending on the time of year in question. Putting together a short list of people to try and talk to, sessions to attend, and vendors to speak with all represent logical items to help maximize time on the ground. Second and building on the importance of the first point—try and make every effort possible to have materials and presentations complete before the last minute—and while this might seem like basic advice, it is surprising how often this does not occur. Oftentimes, and anyone who has traveled before can attest to this, flights and trains are full of people finalizing PowerPoint decks that are due to be presented or submitted in a few short hours.

It is also important to craft a strategy and narrative—notice how often that is coming up during this book—when crafting a presentation strategy and conversation. There are nearly limitless opportunities for professionals and experts to present, develop webinars, or participate in various media opportunities but that does not mean that all said opportunities are created equal. As cynical or as crass as it might sound there are some organizations that seek to leverage the ability and enthusiasm of market actors to take advantage of the interest to underpay or actually not even pay presenters for their efforts. Not to say that there is no place for volunteering or doing pro bono work; that is a very important part of both the accounting and educational conversation. It is, however, very important that if there is going to be significant effort and investments on your part on developing and presenting content, then there is either some sort of compensation or other remuneration provided to the presenter. Personally, I have been approached by at least two different organizations that looked perfectly ordinary on the surface, but that was only part of the story. Upon further review and conversation, however, it quickly became apparent that these organizations were—in essence—seeking to get something for nothing in terms of content production and presentation. Again, there is nothing wrong with doing volunteer work, but that has to be presented up front; crafting a narrative means that you must be proactive and in charge of what organizations you will be affiliated with going forward.

Regardless of what kind of presentation you are giving, or what type of association is being involved in these presentations, there are certain key traits that you should always be sure to include in any presentation or session. Traveling, incurring the time and cost of actually attending, and getting to a session, as well as the intellectual capital that you need to expend in order to assemble and eventually present your topic represent definitive and objective costs and opportunity costs that you have incurred. Clearly, the topic of an opportunity cost is something that anyone in the accounting and finance spaces will be comfortable and familiar with, but this exact same concept applies to the opportunity costs of presenting and attending various conferences. In essence, you need to make sure that the efforts you are expending are worth your time from both a brand building perspective and the takeaways that your audience will be able to—hopefully—use and leverage moving forward.

Without purporting to represent an all-inclusive or exhaustive list or how to prepare and deliver a robust and well-thought-out presentation, the following components should always be included in any presentation. Let's take a look at what some of these components are:

Make sure that your topic is reflective of both conference topics and what is actually going on in the marketplace. This is something that might seem like an obvious statement to make, but since many presentation topics and submissions are due long before the actual conference date it is possible that the topic themselves might have become outdated or obsolete. Making sure that the topic and session that are actually delivered on-site are still timely and relevant is an important part of the presentation and conference process.

For example, have you ever attended a session that—for whatever reason—seemed to be offkey, not in alignment with the conference at large, or seemed to be covering obsolete or outdated information? This can be a direct result of the time lag between when proposals are due and when the conference actually occurs.

Try and make sure that presentation has some takeaways, action items, or other tangible information for attendees to bring back to their organization; the session cannot simply be platitudes or generic statements. The best sessions, no matter what sub-sector or area is being examined or analyzed, are the sessions that deliver and present attendees with information that can actually use and apply to their everyday problems and situations. Rehashing previous talking points, covering ground that had already been examined in earlier sessions, or attempting to use the work of others as a basis for your own work will result in a subpar experience for you and your audience.

Make sure that the follow-up and follow through that are actually presented or covered in the session can be operationalized over time. There are few things worse than attending a session, finding the content interesting, but not leaving the session with any tangible takeaways that can actually be used. One of the definitive ways to make sure that your sessions are both well attended and popular with individuals and conferences going forward is to always give your audience something to take away and bring back to the office.

Provide additional resources and information that audience members can use and refer to during follow-up or future conversations. Sure, these people signed up for and have attended your talk and presentation, but it would be presumptuous to assume that you are the only expert in whatever subject matter area you happen to be focusing on. Be it technology, financial services, or some other area of information, there are always going to be other individuals that are talented and able to contribute value to the conversation. This is something that can be difficult to understand and take into account during the session or presentation process, but it is something that needs to be understood.

The sharing of credit, information, and content is something that may or may not come naturally to everyone; this is perfectly normal. In the private sector on persons or organizations, success usually comes at the expense of another individual or organization. Academia, certainly, has this component as well, but there also is an inherent shareability and transparency with regard to academic information that is also part of higher educational landscape.

Providing external resources, in addition to being something that just makes good business sense, is also something that highlights the willingness to collaborate with other individuals and organizations. No matter how productive an individual may be, how many previous works have been completed, or the level of expertise possessed by you, it is always important to collaborate and cooperate with other experts, individuals, and associations in your subject matter area.

Be open to sharing and collaborating both during the conference and after the conference. Networking is something that is constantly referred to as a benefit of attending and presenting at conferences, but actually doing so can be a bit more complicated than it might initially appear. Simply attempting to (in-person) cold call individuals at a conference can be quite complicated and an often frustrating experience that leaves no one happy. What actually makes more sense, in the vast majority of cases, is to attempt to find people and seek out connections that are either interested in the same subject as you or analyzing similar topics during their own sessions. Not everyone will always be open to this type of networking, however, and getting some initial pushback and resistance is all part of the process.

This also leads to another component and factor that needs to be taken into account; in order to present and go on the road as an expert is going to take the building of a relatively thick skin. Whenever you put an opinion out into the public sphere, there will invariably be pushback, comments, or just mean-spirited people that are looking to argue with you online. Personally, and at least up until the writing of this book, I have had the good fortune to not be on the receiving end of overtly hostile or mean-spirited comments. Rather, and sometimes harder to contend with from an intellectual perspective than just mean people, are the comments and critiques of your positions and opinions. Said feedback and comments can occur in an online environment, but can also take place in a face-to-face manner at conferences and other events. A factor that can make academic feedback seem worse than it might otherwise be is the simple following fact; educators and academics are highly educated and trained to construct and present arguments and analysis. In other words, this can mean that you are facing what can feel like scathing criticism from highly educated, articulate, and well research peers and colleagues! In any event, no matter the form nor the tone of the feedback itself, this is something that every academic is going to need to get used to. Discourse and vigorous debate is a core component of higher education and academia, so becoming more comfortable with this occurrence is something to start doing ASAP.

Multimedia

Linking back to the conversation around YouTube and other video/media platforms, the value of such platforms and tools is significant. Especially for millennials and Gen-Z, the majority of content that is produced and consumed tends to be focused on video platforms and other types of content versus traditional written information versus written content. Setting up a YouTube channel is a relatively straightforward process in concept, simply requiring a Gmail account, a headshot, and a description to get up and running, but that is only the first step of the process. In order to make a success of a YouTube channel or other video platform, however, any aspiring channel host needs to establish a consistent pattern of posting content. If the theme of consistency seems to be something that continues to be mentioned over and over again that is because that is a theme that is very important to any content production, brand building, or other types of information distribution. In addition to doing so, consistently, there are also the requirements specific to video content and channels; the fact that oftentimes this requires you to physically be present on screen. Let's take a look at several of the requirements and considerations that should also be factored in and taken into account if you are planning to construct a multimedia campaign.

Ensure that there is an audience for the type of content and information that you are planning to create and distribute. This might seem like an obvious first step in any content conversation, but it is especially important for a video or other kind of multimedia format. Considering the time and effort that it is going to take to create videos as well as the potential pushback that will inevitably result from creating a video campaign, it is important to make sure that you have an active and engaged audience. In practice, this is going to mean that you are going to conduct informal polls or other kinds of market research before launching the channel properly.

Building on this first point, a good recommendation and point of context to keep in mind is that you should always try to have a catalog or stable of content created up front and ready for distribution before the channel itself gets launched. There are few things worse than launching a multimedia campaign or video channel and then not keeping up the frequency or types of posting and distribution. Keeping up a consistent schedule is equally as important for other types of social media and content production, but given the unique nature of podcasts and video channels this importance is even more pronounced.

This has more to do with the algorithm embedded into many podcast channels, YouTube, and other media channels. In other words, the more frequently you post content or have content available to be uploaded the more likely it is that your channel and other information will be viewed by a wider audience.

Make sure that your lighting and camera angles are appropriate to the context and type of content you are attempting to distribute and communicate, both inside your specific circle of expertise and also outside of that specific circle as well. One of the primary benefits of participating in a multimedia campaign or other non-traditional content creation and distribution process is that it might enable you to participate and engage in broader conversations. In addition to engaging with a wider audience, this is also an opportunity to increase the possibility or potential of your role as a public intellectual. Assuming this role is not guaranteed by any means, but having a wider and more mainstream platform to be engaged does seem to make sense if the desire is to obtain such a position and role.

Maintaining objectivity is arguably even more important in an environment as contentious and potentially dangerous as the current geo-political one seems to be. Especially in a media landscape, being objective in both appearance and fact is of paramount importance. There have all too many cases of individuals who were initially put forward as objective and level-headed experts to later be revealed as someone more interested in sharing opinions rather than information. Now, everyone has opinions and personal points of view, and that is completely fine, but if someone is put forward as an unbiased expert source it is imperative that this individual does everything possible to act appropriately.

It is always important to be mindful of the fact that, over time, it might be necessary to change, tweak, or otherwise adjust views or positions on certain topics as the information and context around these events and assets evolve and change as well. Some do not label such behavior as flip-flopping or being inconsistent but that is an incomplete and partial perspective. Opinions can, and should, change and evolve as the underlying information that forms the basis for these opinions is updated, evolves, or otherwise changes over time. As logical as this sounds, and especially if there is a lengthy written or audio/visual record, this can result in some people saying that you are not a reliable source of information.

Professional Service

Professional service is perhaps one of the more interesting areas where practitioners can add leverage existing duties and activities for the benefit of the department, campus, and university system that they are a part of. By the same token, the very flexibility that this service component can deliver can also lead to some stumbles and potential missed opportunities on the part of aspiring or newly transitioned faculty members. Specifically, some of the very flexibility and options that service requirements can lead to or help facilitate can be confusing, so let's analyze just what exactly these different characteristics of service can represent. It is important to remember that every institution is different, and will most likely have different labels and names for different kinds of service opportunities, but the general categories and classification normally hold up as consistent across institutional lines.

Service to the professional community. Drilling down and revisiting this topic are worth doing because service to the professional community can mean different things depending on which professional community is being discussed or analyzed. For example, I have the great privilege of sitting on the advisory board of the Wall Street Blockchain Alliance, a trade and industry association focusing on driving the conversation forward as it connects to blockchain and the broader financial services space. Although this service is relatively narrow in scope, it certainly does provide me with a platform from which I can address and discuss the various issues driving change in the accounting and financial service space, while also focusing on a topic that is of personal and professional interest; blockchain and its affiliated services.

Service to the department. This can be a tricky line, and not because of any intentional confusion of obfuscation; simply because it can be hard to distinguish between service to the department and service to the institution at large. Obviously, every department or even school or college operates under the umbrella of the college or university that funds and supports these individual operating units. Understanding the different obligations and layers of institutional hierarchy is important not only for navigating the usual waters of paperwork and bureaucracy that characterize any large professional institution, but also to make sure that the efforts being expended related to service as being done so in an equitable manner that generates the most bang for your buck. Taking a look at my own personal experience, I was tasked with the development of an assessment protocol and program for the master of accounting. An initial review would seem to clearly indicate that this service is most clearly connected to the department, and while that is correct these service efforts and initiatives can also correctly be applied to a discussion connected to service to the college or university as a whole. Assessment, although not typically characterized as a fun or enjoyable experience by many of those involved, is an important part of the academic conversation and debate; this needs to be a part of the dialogue happening throughout the institution. Such an understanding and assessment—no pun intended—is necessary for professionals seeking to make the best decisions possible with regard to how time and effort are allocated.

Service to the institutions or university system is also an option and alternative that should be factored into how you, as an aspiring academic, plan and execute your service plan and strategy. The importance of having a plan and strategy for how your time and efforts are actually used is something that should be of the highest importance. Depending on the institution in question, there are going to be different opportunities for service at the institution level, and this can actually take many different forms when viewed through the lens of service, time. For example, if an institution has a strong or high profile athletic program or array of programs, there might be options to serve on athletic advisory councils. Student investment clubs, drama clubs, science clubs, and other student affiliated organizations on campus—or even off campus—may provide with the ability to not only give back to the institution, but to also do so in a manner that is of interest to you on a personal level.

Riches Are in the Niches

A phrase repeated often in the practitioner world or private sector is that due to changing technology forces and trends is that riches are in the niches in terms of profitability, growth, and sustainable firm development. While repeated often enough to have almost become a cliché, there does seem to be some significant truth in this phrase; due to the fragmentation and differentiation possible due to leveraging technology in the accounting and financial services space, there has been an increasing rise in the number of smaller and even one-person shops. Effectively leveraging technology and the attributes of these tools enable professionals to work more efficiently and continuously from anywhere regardless of physical location. These benefits and upsides are not limited to the private sector, however; there is no imaginable reason as to why these attributes and trends will not be applicable to higher education. Such a trend and directional shift are already clearly evident in several distinct yet related elements that have appeared and popped up across different levels and types of institutions.

First and foremost, something that has been discussed and documented thoroughly in the academic and media press is the underlying shift toward more specialized and focused courses. In 2019, Ohio State University made headlines and waves when it was announced that the institution would be developing an e-sports program and several accompanying courses. Something that immediately became part of the conversation was whether or not it made sense for an established institution to develop a program in an area that many consider to be a fad or of passing importance. Taking a step back and examining just why a well-established and high profile institution would be taking what might seem like drastic action, the rationale and plan behind this process may not seem as confusing as it might have initially. Analyzing this development and situation also reveals an area where practitioners and private sector participants can leverage embedded expertise and information to assist with the development and proliferation of new courses and programs.

Millennials may be getting a lot of coverage in the mainstream and educational media, but it also worth taking a look a just how millennials—as well as the generation following them (Gen-Z)—are changing the business and social landscape surrounding higher education. Starting with the shift away from mass media and traditional sources of information such as a television and more established media players uncovers an interesting trend. What this means, in plain and simple terms, is that the media dollars, viewership, and engagement are not simply evaporating into the ether. These dollars, engagement, and viewership are pivoting to other forms of media and entertainment; the explosion of streaming services is perhaps the clearest indicator of this shift and trend. E-sports and other streaming platforms such as YouTube, Twitch, and the rise of peer-to-peer media versus peer-to-establishment players play directly in the need of colleges and universities to develop applicable course materials.

While it is true that institutions of higher education need not move and respond to every change in the business landscape, it does seem to make sense that said institutions should monitor and factor into the decision-making process. After all, if private sector organizations are able to grow and succeed by focusing on a specific matter, it would make sense that a similar approach would work in academia. Linking back to an idea and concept discussed throughout this text, this concept already seems to exist throughout academia, and this seems to be represented with larger universities seemingly surrounded by smaller and more specialized institutions. Drawing a parallel to the broader accounting and financial services space, there does seem to be a growing market and need for more specialized and focused institutions and professionals going forward. Let's take a look at who this might work and actually play out in the marketplace:

An institution, which could either be a struggling institution or be a smallish institution that—for the time being seems to be doing well—develops a strategy and or plan that is focused around one or several narrower areas. Technology may certainly be taking the majority of media attention and analysis in the current environment but that does not mean that it is going to be the best fit for every institution. Depending on where the institution is physically located, makeup of faculty employed therein, and the student body attending the course, the specific area of focus will vary.

Developing an area of focus or specialization can take many different forms due to the rapidly changing nature and evolution of higher education both in the United States and abroad. Pilot courses, guest lectures and seminars, certificate programs, or online course offerings may be more or less applicable depending on the needs of students and strategy of the administration.

Regardless of the specific approach undertaken by the leadership of the institution, there does need to be a systemic plan in place to ensure that inputs and outputs can be measured and compared. Launching programs in and of themselves is not going to create a new narrative or direction for an institution by itself; there needs to be a feedback loop established and monitored to help make sure that lessons learned and then applied.

Obtaining the right kind of people to be a part of this new direction can also be a tricky proposition for the institution. No matter how well thought out or comprehensive the proposed changes are, there will inevitably be pushback and resistance to this change from at least some corners of the organization. This is a part of any change management project or process and should not be ignored, but rather incorporated into how the new ideas and plans are developed and matured over time. Understanding the type of people that are already in place at the institution and understanding the types of individuals that are necessary to successfully initiate and implement the proposed changes necessary are critical components of the process.

After making sure that the correct people are in place at the institution from a content and course production point of view, it may also be necessary to revisit and revise the marketing and other methods by which students are attracted to the institution. Like any other large organization with a long track record, there are invariably going to be a few things that most colleges and universities are associated with that may require revisions and updates. On the other hand, there are numerous colleges and universities whose specialty focus areas are boldly declared in the name of the institution. Changing the name of the entire college and university may not be necessary, but it is not beyond the realm of possibility to see the names and other categorizations of institutions changing.

Last but certainly not least any pivot, shift, or other changing of the course at any organization must have a quantifiable payoff and benefit to all parties involves. As the old adage goes, you do have to spend money to make money, but all too often the first part is enthusiastically embraced where the second part can be a bit more ambiguous. Horror stories abound about colleges and universities that have launched grand campaigns and restructurings, incurring costs along the way, only to stumble and fall short causing financial and operational damage along the way. Put simply, and as callous as this might initially seem, the dollars and cents of education need to also be a part of any new proposed programs or content.

There is something that should be noted after this conversation, however, and that is the danger of being pigeon-holed or artificially restricted to one specific niche or topic area. Especially when it comes to emerging areas of technology, it is easy to remain overly focused on one specific area, topic, theme, or other focus areas. Remaining flexible to a certain extent is important in order to be adaptable, even in fields that are considered to be relatively straightforward and conservative in nature such as accounting, finance, or other technocratic fields. Even if a niche is developed that is successful and remains relevant for a certain period of time that does not mean that such an area and expertise will always be relevant. For example, for a long period of time, the importance of neat handwriting, cursive script, and the ability to write neatly on a chalkboard were imperative for any successful teaching career or a career as a presenter at large. Clearly, there has changed during the last several decades as whiteboards, computers, and PowerPoint presentations have taken over the majority of classrooms, lecture halls, and the speak circuit. A relatively simple example, but the point remains the same; skills and areas of focus change over time.

Reflection Questions

1. As it relates to the future of higher education, and especially making sure that higher education remains competitive in nature, how important does it seem that tenure track opportunities are at large?
2. Given the increased competition around new types of learning and education, what do you think the percentage of "traditional" educational offerings will be compared to more niche-focused programs?
3. Since education and the higher education space continue to rapidly evolve and change, does the leadership of sector seem more aligned with traditional academic offerings or non-traditional project and initiatives.

Additional Readings

1. InsideHigherEd—Measures to Support Faculty During COVID19. https://www.insidehighered.com/advice/2020/09/04/advice-academic-administrators-how-best-support-faculty-during-pandemic-opinion.
2. American Association of University Professors—The Professors, The Press, The Think Tanks—And Their Problems. https://www.aaup.org/article/professors-press-think-tanks%E2%80%94and-their-problems#.X3N8lGhKjIU.
3. Purdue University—Stages of The Writing Process. https://owl.purdue.edu/owl/english_as_a_second_language/esl_students/key_concepts_for_writing_in_north_american_colleges/stages_of_the_writing_process.html.
4. APassEducation—The Process of Educational Content Development. https://apasseducation.com/education-blog/the-process-of-educational-content-development/.
5. The Chronicle of Higher Education—The Conference Circuit. https://www.chronicle.com/package/the-conference-circuit/.

CHAPTER 9

The Changing Higher Landscape of Education

Introduction

At the end of the day, the business of higher education is just that, a business, and like any other industry or business there are external forces that are driving disruption, change, and innovation that need to be analyzed by any practitioner seeking to break into the industry. While this is by no means an exhaustive or all-encompassing listing or the forces driving change in the higher education space, these buckets and general trends can be thought of as the major themes that are both creating opportunities and leading to some challenges to arise. Higher education is certainly changing in ways that are difficult to forecast, evaluate, and incorporate into an academic career. When these shifts happen there will inevitably be some friction, changes, and job losses as these changes occur but that does not mean that these negative externalities are permanent in nature. As an aspiring academic you are already embracing transitions, changes, and new ideas anyway, so why not leverage and apply these same concepts to analyzing higher education? Some of these changes will be different than other ones, but it is safe to say that the field will only continue to evolve, adjust, and develop over time.

S. Stein Smith, *Shifting from Accounting Practitioner to Academia*, Palgrave Studies in Accounting and Finance Practice,
https://doi.org/10.1007/978-3-030-67546-2_9

Content Production

The concept and idea of content production may not seem like a new or innovative or changing idea in the context of higher education, but this only represents a partial view of this conversation and situation. Faculty members, to be sure, have long been tasked with producing content and information in a variety of mediums including but not limited to oral presentations, shorter written content, academic articles, and long-form books. There are of course different requirements at different institutions across the educational spectrum but the underlying push to produce and disseminate content has long been a part of the faculty conversation. While this does not seem positioned to change, particularly for tenure track and tenured faculty, the implication and trend continues to be felt in virtually every aspect of the higher educational conversation. In essence, the entire higher education industry has gradually shifted and developed into something more akin to a content production industry more than anything else in particular.

Such a transition may seem like a contradictory or even paradoxical development in the educational space, but that misses the point. Underlying the entire economy, highlighted in the U.S. but present the world over, is the continued emphasis on the importance of content and other information versus other metrics or outcomes. Streaming services and subscription-based business models are dependent on a continuous stream (no pun intended) of fresh and engaging content to attract and retain customers. It seems logical to conclude that the same forces that are literally reshaping the entirety of the economy will also influence and drive change in the higher education space. As straightforward and reasonable as this might seem this does also appear to represent a sea change and dramatic shift in just how higher education operates and engages with the broader societal and business communities. Education framed in a traditional sense tended to focus on both the content and course work being covered in specific classes and programs but also the broader and more holistic concept of critical thinking. Taking a pause for a minute, this seems like an appropriate time to present a possible definition of just what critical thinking actually means.

> Critical thinking can be defined as the ability of an individual to assess and examine a problem or issue from a variety of angles, bringing multiple perspectives to propose a potential solution.

While that certainly sounds like an admirable goal, and is routinely cited as something that recent graduates often lack, the teaching of critical thinking is not something that can necessarily be nailed down to one course. Returning to the definition provided the idea of critical thinking need not be linked to any one technical concept, specific course, or even degree but should rather be thought of as the endgame or outcome of obtaining a college education or certification. In the current marketplace with the almost universal consensus that STEM and business degrees are worth more than liberal arts or humanities degrees, how are colleges and universities supposed to succeed? On the one hand, employers are constantly looking for new and recent graduates with the technical skills and knowledge to successful complete work tasks but on the other hand these same graduates must be more than just human calculators and need to be able to complete complex and multifaceted tasks. The answer to this question may lie in the very shift that some seem as undermining the traditional idea of higher education.

Content production, be it movies on any of the streaming services, relies on the continuous updating and refreshing of content and other information that is produced into the marketplace. Written content has also shifted more toward the idea of consistent and continuous production, partially as a result of the increased digitization of written content as well as the pace at which information is produced. The idea that textbooks, course materials, and entire academic programs can be created at a certain point in time, and then be set on autopilot simply is not an appropriate mindset going forward. From a technical perspective, this is relatively straightforward; technology and the applications built on top of these technology platforms continue to change at accelerating rates. This mindset, however, also is equally appropriate when connected to the idea and concept of critical thinking; how can students be expected to grapple with new ideas if those new ideas are not discussed in courses? This is exactly where practitioners can deliver a much needed proverbial shot in the arm linking together course content, program outcomes, and what potential employers are actually for in recent graduates.

Where Practitioners Fit in This Conversation

Whether the specific sub-trend being discussed is the transition from static content creation to a more continuous stream of information being produced, or the other items to be discussed in the coming pages, there is one common trend and theme that needs to be highlighted. In order for students to receive the best of both worlds—the ability to think critically and see the big picture while also receiving appropriate technical training—the methods and modalities of instruction need to evolve and develop to meet the needs of students. Taking a quick look at some of the approaches and concepts that can be used to combine both technical and holistic instruction methods, the following items seem to be appropriate

Debate style classes, or to be more non-confrontational, it could be phrased as a "make your case" style of analyzing and making ideas. An example of how this could play out could involve dividing the class into groups, and making them take opposing positions or stances on a number of issues or sets of facts. These decisions or issues could be related to make-or-buy, outsource or near source, expand into a new market or not, or to pursue a new strategy versus staying the course. The simplicity of this idea is also its strength; the same debate or make your case format could be used to discuss new technologies such as blockchain, or bigger picture views and ideas related to market development or strategic planning.

Case study analysis and assessment have long been a part of MBA and other graduate programs at institutions across the academic spectrum, but that does not mean these same tactics and tools cannot be used at different program levels. Analyzing a set of facts, having to do research, and leveraging existing technologies to help arrive at potential solutions, are all skills that can improve the critical thinking ability of students as well as engage them with new technologies. In addition to some of the more traditional case studies, there are also more modern questions that could form the basis for business courses taught by practitioners.

For example, a question could be posed in class as follows; what were the causes of the 2007–2008 financial crisis and what possible alternatives could have been put forward? This is a short question, but requires students to consider several issues simultaneously such as the role of government in housing markets, risk and reward of mortgage lending, incentives at financial institutions, and the desires of individuals to achieve home ownership. This type of case study model also highlights another important point that should be built into some courses.

There are often no single correct answers or responses to questions or problems in the real world, and that is something that should also be integrated into some courses. As nice as it might seem to always come to a solution or answer, the underlying reality can be much more complicated than that. In most business situations the majority of business context there is unlikely to a simple or straightforward answer available to end users. Stating this is one matter, but actually educating and preparing students to contend with these is an entirely separate issue. Now, even though there might not be a definitive answer or solution that does not mean that the work product or preparation can be less rigorous than in other situations. Stated another way, even if the ultimate result or outcome is not a definitive solution or answer there still needs to be sufficient preparation and efforts.

Collaborative Learning

It is important to realize that just because practitioners are coming into the higher education conversation does not mean that there is nothing to learn from traditional academics and higher education protocols. These practices and methodologies do exist for a reason; it is important to always recognize that higher education and academia is not like other businesses or fields. This is discussed throughout this text, but the one additional point that is going to be mentioned here is the following; it is always a good idea to come into any new environment with an appreciative and inquisitive mindset. Remember that as a practitioner transitioning to higher education you are basically reinventing yourself and starting from scratch for the most part. Asking questions, being willing to listen to the answers and the implications of those answers, and realizing that things are done a certain way for a reason should be part of your transition. Be it the way courses are taught, the way in which these courses are taught, and the methodology for constructing these courses there is usually a definitive reason behind even decisions that might seem unusual, inconsistent, or even illogical in nature. Having the patience and willingness to understand the reasoning behind certain choices being made is not something unique to academia, but is important nevertheless. This may seem like an easy or straightforward thing, but especially as it pertains to practitioners moving to higher education, there is always a risk that some practitioners may come in without an appreciation for what that actually means. Given the somewhat negative connotation some in the private sector have of higher education in the current political and societal environment, it is understandable why some new entrants to the space approach it with a jaded eye. Understandable for sure, but an incomplete and partial view of the situation.

One need only to turn on any news station, no matter what political affiliation they may be associated with, and it is likely that some guest, host, panel, or other event will discuss the many failings and shortcomings of higher education. Spiraling costs, decreased applicability of class materials to the marketplace at large, the general dissatisfaction with college and university at large, and—obviously—the trillions in student debt outstanding, make for good TV, conversation pieces, and create a rather critical lens through which most individuals view higher education and the people employed therein. That said, and no matter what your personal opinion of the situation may be, it is imperative that these personal views need not influence how you interact with your new colleagues, peers, and supervisors. What this means is that you need to understand the position you are applying for, what that means in the short term and long term, in addition to the influence that these choices will have on both your career and your personal brand. Higher education is not perfect that is sure, but there is a definitive value add to those individuals who actively participate and engage within the process.

Linking Inputs to Outcomes

An underlying trend that continues to permeate the entire higher education space and landscape is the increasing desire of institutions to connect the inputs of higher education; classes, faculty, and assessments, to the outcomes of various students. From a high-level perspective, this does not seem to be an unreasonable request. Students invest tens or even hundreds of thousands of dollars into higher education, and these funds need to come from somewhere. The total amount of student loans outstanding as of this writing are in excess of $1.5 trillion USD, and that amount looks set to continue to increase. In addition to serving as a significant financial burden and drag on a large segment of the working-age population, this also could present a systemic risk to the financial system. Without drilling too much into the details, a large provider of student loans—either directly or indirectly—is the federal government. So, in essence, the federal government may ultimately end up on the hook for trillions in loans that are paid back slowly, or possibly not at all. If one were seeking to create a lose-lose situation it would be difficult to create a more convoluted one. Financial implications aside, the importance of equipping students with the skills necessary to obtain employment in the marketplace is not a minor or irrelevant consideration. Avoiding becoming too philosophical on the matter, the connection between what is covered or taught in a classroom or educational setting, and the outcomes achieved by students is not a back burner or irrelevant issue. That said, it is important that educators at every level of institutions avoid the temptation to fall victim to a trend that continues to permeate the marketplace; the relegation of education to something that does not resemble true higher education.

Corporations and other institutions have long had training and educational programs that prepare individuals for specific roles at the institution in question. There is absolutely nothing wrong with this approach, and it has—and will certainly continue to—deliver value to both the individuals and institutions that are involved with these programs. That said, the increasing scrutiny with which institutions of higher education are judged and evaluated seems to have directly correlated with the rising interest and utilization of these types of training academies. One needs to simply look at the rise in coding schools, programming boot camps, or other accelerated educational courses linked to a discrete set of specific skills and direct outcomes to see how appealing this approach can be. For a few short weeks or months of concentrated effort, there can be a result of either guaranteed or strongly suggested employment options. In an economic landscape that—while much recovered from the Great Recession—still seems to be lagging in certain areas, these outcomes are extremely appealing. That is completely fine, but it is important to draw a clear line between job training programs or schools with more traditional drivers of higher education.

There is also an underlying fear that continues to exist in the higher education space at large; that as ever-increasing numbers of individuals seek out college education and training that there will be both explicit and unspoken pressures brought to bear on faculty members to assist with that process. This is nothing new. Diploma mills and other institutions with dubious (at best) credentials and accreditation have long been an unfortunate part of the educational landscape, and that there is no sign that these bad actors are going away. Especially as the trend toward micro-credentialing, or "do it yourself," education continues to increase and accelerate there is going to be ever-increasing pressure on educators and institutions to maintain academic standards. How this is actually maintained and implemented will, of course, vary from institution to institution, but that is something that needs to a point of emphasis from the highest levels of the institution.

Big Picture Trends

Digitization

Technology continues to infuse every business, industry, or subset of activity, and the higher education space is no exception to this trend. Distance learning, once conducted by mail and called correspondence school, has evolved and become a technology-driven aspect of education. The rise of online courses, certificates, and course has had a dramatic impact on the higher education space at large; entire institutions have, and continue to be, transformed as online courses continue to increase in popularity. Online courses, however, are only one part of the technology conversation in higher education; this integration of technology has also led to the possibility of increased concentration in academia. While this may sound contradictory—as online courses open more types of courses to a broader array of students—it also enables instructors to simultaneously address thousands of students at a time.

Given the ease with which online or remote courses can be constructed there is now literally no cap or limit on the number of students that an institution or instructor can interact with at once. From a practical perspective what this means is that a single instructor can record, or stream live, a lecture of a class simultaneously to students all over the world, potentially limiting the number of opportunities for new instructors seeking to break into the field. Since it does not seem that technology will not become less integrated over time, realizing the upside and downside of digitization is something that every institution and individual must be aware of. On the flip side, the ability of classes and certificates to be hosted remotely also means that the work and employment opportunities for aspiring academics are much broader now than may have previously been possible. Just as technology enables remote working in the private sector, these same technology forces can enable individuals to obtain employment at a wide range of locations.

On a practical basis, this means several things for aspiring academics seeking to break into academia. First and foremost, individuals must be comfortable working with technology whether that takes the form of an online class or leveraging technology tools for an in-person experience. An alternative trend that continues to make inroads into the broader higher education conversation is the shift and trend toward jumbo-sized courses, i.e., courses that may have in excess of 60 students. Clearly, the teaching style and aspect of a class this size will need to be different and evolve over time, but this is also an opportunity to take advantage of different technology tools. Examples of such tools include, but are not limited to, polling software and applications to be used during class, virtual meeting tools that seek to replicate office hours or in-person meetings. Whatever the specific case and application may be, the trend and shift toward greater technological integration is clear and must be factored into the plan for any aspiring academic.

There is also a shift and trend developing in the educational landscape in which professors and other educators host virtual classes where there is no actual classroom at all, and instruction is augmented with an audio-visual tool. Platform selection is not as important as it might initially seem; Zoom, Skype or an integrated option available with the institutional ERP generally has the same type of functionality at this point. Even with popular platforms such as Zoom or other enterprise-ready applications, there is a risk of negative repercussions such as Zoombombing. Quickly defining Zoombombing for the context of this text is as follows; a nefarious or other bad actor hacks or otherwise gains controls of a Zoom, or Zoom type, of meeting. Following this assumption of control, this user will share and post unethical, racist, or inappropriate content, forcing the other members of the meeting to leave the meeting. While there are controls and other ideas to help offset this risk this is something that needs to be accounted for moving forward.

Instructing a class in a purely virtual format may strike some as unusual or uncomfortable, but taken from a higher-level perspective this merely represents the most current iteration of a long-term trend. For years, professors have either pre-recorded lectures or had pre-prepared lectures delivered by graduate assistants or teaching aids. Delivering a lecture with a video, be it livestream or pre-recorded, seems like a logical next step in the process. Practitioners, many of which have assuredly been a part of innumerable meetings, are likely familiar and possibly even more comfortable addressing a large audience via such a platform than doing so in-person.

Internationalization

Internationalization has also been a fundamental sea change in how the higher education industry operates and interacts with current students, the labor market, and even accrediting bodies. Attracting and retaining talent and people, from students to faculty to staff, from the entire world undoubtedly makes the institution more comprehensive, better able to educate students with a global headset, and also benefit the institution from a revenue or earnings perspective. In addition, and linking back to our earlier conversation connected to international employment opportunities, it's important to remember this one overarching fact; the world is a big place and there are inevitably going to be more opportunities from areas you are not familiar with than areas you may have already had experience with previously. On the flip side, the trend toward increasing diversity and internationalization also highlights several other factors that represent both an opportunity and a challenge.

Leading off is the reality that when international factors are added to the mix increases the complexity and layers that need to be analyzed, including visas, passports, and simply the complexity that arises with international travel. Especially given the geopolitical conversations and factors that are included and embedded into every conversation, this is not something that can simply be brushed aside or relegated to the back burner. Turning back to the positive attributes of this conversation, international students and international opportunities can also provide a wide range of options and activities for academics to engage with going forward. Combining the international theme of many higher education conversations, and the digitization sweeping through higher education, these engagement and collaborative opportunities can also take the form of remote options if physical on-site activities are not as viable. The underlying truth is that the international trend and flavor of education is something that cannot be ignored, nor does it show signs of abating.

Business is clearly a global endeavor as is higher education, but that does not mean that every institution is equally as well prepared to deal with this global landscape. Particularly as the 2020s begin to move forward it is also worth knowing that the global business landscape is in the middle of transition, and that this transition is not always universally supportive of past practices. With the benefit of hindsight, which is always 20/20 of course, the unrestrained embracing of globalization may have had some unintended consequences or second- and third-order effects that are just now being addressed. Current political headwinds aside, the reality is that it is unlikely that business and the globe at large are likely to past practices and norms. Business classes, the faculty employed therein, and the institutions that employ and support these faculty and programs must be able to incorporate global trends and themes.

Seemingly this would be an obvious fact, but let's look under the hood with just one example that demonstrates just how short-sighted an analysis can be. If you asked one individual, be it out at dinner or in an MBA classroom, to name one company that dominates e-commerce, streaming video services, as well as other technology in general, and you would not be surprised to hear that Amazon would be mentioned quite a bit. Amazon dominates the airwaves, has completely transformed the e-commerce and logistics businesses, is competing with Netflix and Disney+ in the video streaming arena, and often finds itself in the crosshairs of U.S. politicians looking to either break up what are considered to be monopolies or that have unfair competitive advantages. With all of that coverage and analysis it would be easy to forgive some for assuming that Amazon has a similar presence the world over; that could not be further from the truth. The overwhelming majority of revenues and profits attributable to Amazon are generated in the United States. In other words, while Amazon may seem like a world-conquering juggernaut with no one able to even slow its ascent, the reality is far different. Alibaba, a direct competitor to Amazon headquartered and domiciled in mainland China, has a similar business model to Amazon, except even more comprehensive. Both e-commerce giants dominate their respective home markets, but so far have struggled to replicate that level of dominance once they lose home court advantage.

Uber might also be thought of as a world-beating organization; open the app on any smartphone and you are virtually guaranteed a ride will be available in a matter of minutes, but that is only true in the United States. In enormous markets such as China and India Uber has had to retrench and either sell off business or close shop entirely in the face of competition from local players. These comparisons are not to imply that U.S. organizations are inferior or unable to compete on a global basis; there is a plethora of evidence over decades proving that is simply not the case. Rather the point that should be taken away from this conversation is that member students, faculty members, and institutions should understand that business is global and that is something that needs to be integrated into any business class or conversation.

Changing Needs

The proverbial 800-pound gorilla in any room or conversation connected to higher education must reference the reality that the needs and expectations of students continue to change and evolve. As the job market continues to become more competitive and demanding of recent graduates, there is more that students and graduates will expect of the institution. Faculty, both those that are more established as well as those that are more recent entrants to the conversation, must be able to take into consideration as courses and curricula are developed. The debate around the value or worth of higher education in the modern business environment is not one that seems to be a passing fad, but rather indicative of a change in how education is factored into both personal and professional development.

One merely needs to tune into and mainstream media channel or business network and it will be evident that the topic of college affordability and worth of a college degree is a legitimate concern being raised by a number of different societal groups. The cost of a college education, in and of itself, is only one aspect of this conversation; the outcomes and results of students following college graduation is also something that increasingly needs to be addressed and factored into what specific content and curricula are covered. In addition to the institutional changes that these forces are driving, the needs and expectations of students must also be integrated into this conversation. Specifically, students are increasingly expecting that both the faculty and the courses themselves will equip them with the necessary skills and information to succeed in the job market. This represents a particularly interesting paradox for colleges and universities; how much responsibility should the individual faculty and institutions have for the job success of students? Such a question is beyond the scope of this book, but is definitely something that needs to be discussed more frequently, even acknowledging the volume of conversation that already exists. Something else that is related to the changing needs and expectations of students is the simple reality that many of these students are relocating and are located—sometimes—in completely different locations than many established institutions.

Population Shifts

A discussion of population and migration trends of individuals might not seem like a core topic for discussion among higher education officials, but it is one lying at the core of many of the challenges facing various institutions. Simply put, the population density and growth in the United States continues to shift from the Northeast region to the South and Southwest. Many of the fastest-growing metropolitan areas continue to be located in these regions, alongside announcement after announcement of corporations relocating to these different parts of the country. Why does this matter? It is certainly interesting from an intellectual perspective, but also has a direct influence and impact on the potential future success or failure of academic institutions. The density of colleges and universities in the Northeast and Mid-Atlantic regions is (INSERT), or there is an institution for every (INSERT) people.

Historically speaking the majority of U.S. residents were located in the Northeast/Mid-Atlantic region of the nation, and there are still over 100 million people residing in the corridor between Boston and Washington, DC. The fact that Amtrak (and Acela) railways are only consistently profitable in this region of the country speaks to the population density and activity in this area. Taking a step back, however, and the bigger picture tells a different story. Population and population centers continue to migrate from the North and East areas of the United States to the South and West regions of the country. The wide-ranging impacts of this dramatic shift will take years to truly understand and factor into a decision-making analysis, but the effect on higher education is not going to take nearly as long to understand and factor into the conversation. Let's take a short look at just how some of these effects and changes are already driving change, innovation, and disruption in the higher education conversation. The pressure on institutions of higher education across the United States as the number of students of high school age continues to decline at large. A smaller pool of potential customers and subscribers to a business model is not a recipe for long-term success, and this is something that everyone in the academic conversation needs to understand. Competing for students has always been something that colleges and universities have done in the past, but the pressure and nature of this competition will only become more intense and vitriolic over time. This will be bad news for some institutions, but overall the broader education landscape should emerge more competitive and robust over time as trends become entrenched. An increased emphasis on cost will permeate throughout the entire educational conversation, from the types of individuals that are hired to be on the faculty to the wider-ranging conversation around student debt. This is already an important conversation that is happening across many different bandwidths, but will only accelerate over time, which also provides an opening and opportunity for former practitioners making a transition. Bringing industry or public accounting experience to the conversation connected to budgets, cost-effectiveness, and other profitability measures is something that is set to become value added as the shift develops. While not the only reason why practitioners are valuable to this conversation, bringing a slightly more critical lens to these questions is something that should not be ignored.

A reimagining on just what higher education is and where it fits in the wider societal and business conversation. Higher education, as has hopefully been explained throughout this text and with examples, is in the midst of a dramatic reorientation and shift due to an almost endless range of external changes. Given the importance of education, and continuous education to be specific, this does seem to implicate that the current model of completing a degree and never returning to the classroom is not going to be sufficient. A point that has been made before to be sure, but it is especially important to ensure that everyone understands the ripple effects of what these changes mean for both current classes and institutions as well as implications for future. Far from remaining unmoving like a rock in a stream, education and educational professionals will need to evolve, shift, and take into account the changing nature of the workforce and education.

The Impact of Online Learning

Previously discussed, but worthy of additional analysis and consideration, are the effects that online education is already having on college and universities. Online courses have long been a part of the educational experience, but given the current marketplace, these trends and themes seem positioned to continue exerting outsized influence on the higher education space. Far from being a supplemental item and course offering in a few programs, there are currently online course and program offerings and every level of institutions in a variety of program offerings. Perhaps the most obvious sign of how thoroughly online learning continues to permeate the academic sector is the recent launch—as of this writing—of hybrid or fully online law school (JD) programs. Law school has long been heralded as a rigorous in-person experience forcing students to interact within the classroom, answer questions on the spot that are asked by intimidating professors, and present ideas to a peer group.

Not only is the impact and shift being felt in law school, but business schools are also feeling the effect and implications of increased online content. The MBA program at the University of North Carolina, for example, is consistently ranked in the top 25 programs in the country. That might not seem particularly interesting until one realizes that this program is entirely online, which just 10 or 15 years ago would have been impossible. Business schools and programs across the nation and world continue to add course and program offerings either via an online format or a hybrid format. Institutional benefits from offering courses or programs in a hybrid or online format include, but are not limited to, the following factors. Cost savings, increased flexibility in terms of times and locations that courses can be offered, reduced need to include full-time faculty in the process, and leverage adjunct or other non-tenured faculty. In addition to these operationally oriented benefits and savings, there are also the intangible benefits that come from being able to create and market course to a much larger and broader audience of students. Increasing the potential audience for courses and information generated by the institution will, of course, also potentially result in higher revenues but can also introduce the courses and content offered to a global audience.

Online courses, however, do have some drawbacks that need to be taken into account as the permeation of online learning and course creation are created at any number of institutions increases. Perhaps the most direct implication in question is the possibility that some students will lose access to the courses if they are not in possession, or relocated near, locations offerings high-speed Internet or other required technology. In addition to the potential disparity in student offerings, it is also worth noting that student performance may suffer in a hybrid or completely online course offerings. A lack of consistent interaction and engagement may not be appropriate for every type of course, such as those focused on a lab level or that are more dependent on the interaction between students and instructors than a straightforward lecture. These potential issues, however, are not just applicable for conversations linked to student success and engagement, but can also be applied to the impact these changes will have on institutions.

Concentration and consolidation are not necessarily a bad thing in any context, and can also help generate an economic benefit that is covered in every economic class; the benefits of scale. Scale is a concept pursued by virtually every organization in every industry vertical; financial services, health care, e-commerce, social media, retail, food production, and transportation filings are routinely populated with the desire of management to achieve scale to dominate a particular industry. Derived benefits associated with scale are relatively easy to document and find, as market leaders routinely point to the size of customer bases or geographic reach as core competitive strengths. That said, and realizing that no analysis is complete without viewing and examining both sides of the issue, scale for the sake of scale is not a sustainable business model. As of the writing of this text, during 2019 and 2020, there were any number of high profile corporate stumbles and failures that highlighted just how important remaining focused on fundamentals and delivering a valuable product are to the continued success of the organization.

Uber, Lyft, and WeWork all had one core theme running through both corporate messaging as well as how the business itself operated in any given context. Scale and the integration of technology to reinvigorate otherwise staid business models—taxi services and co-working spaces, respectively—were the key to an almost guaranteed path to profitability. Upon further analysis, however, and as these organizations either went public or attempted to go public (in the case of WeWork), the underlying realities of the situation and business cases were uncovered. No matter how much technology or cutting-edge tools are layered on top of existing or current business models or offerings, if the core business functionality and use case for the enterprise is not modified to keep pace, the organization and those who use or depend on its service will suffer. The same analysis and projection can, and should be, applied to initiatives that are connected to how technology can, and is, being integrated within the higher education conversation.

Attracting an ever-increasing number of students to a platform, service, or course will not generate any additional benefits for those involved in the quality of the instruction or "product" suffers as a result. Whether represented by the rise of mega-universities that combine in-person courses and online offerings to hundreds of thousands of students, the concentration of instruction in the hands of a much smaller number of superstar instructors, or the concentration of educational legitimacy in the hands of a smaller number of institutions the ultimate impact of this concentration will very likely mirror the effect other concentrations have had in other industries. Put another way, the very tool that can lead to dramatic growth can also undermine the traditional areas of value creation and course instruction that have for a long time dominated the higher education conversation.

Real-World Tools

It should be clear by this point that every practitioner and every organization is different, and that needs to be taken into account as the various career paths are analyzed and weighed against each other. Every practitioner brings to the proverbial table a different set of skills and background that can provide invaluable real-world experience and applications to the educational conversation. That said, it is equally as important for these practitioners to remember that the evaluative criteria and benchmarks that apply to the higher education conversation and landscape are going to be significantly different than those evaluated in the private industry. With all of that said, this seems like a logical time and to stop and attempt to categorize and summarize just where a particular practitioner may fit into the higher education conversation and which type of information may deliver the most value to the institution.

Zoom and Other Remote Working Tools

One of the biggest changes that have occurred in the overall business landscape over the last decade or so is the ease and frequency with which individuals can work remotely and in an off-site an remote site capacity. This is due to several different trends and broader directions that have dominated the business landscape, but it really can be summarized down into a few overarching trends and market forces. First and most obvious to understand and summarize is the fact that business is conducted on a global basis and that individuals need to be able to work and interact with colleagues and clients on an as-needed basis. This makes perfect sense given the fact that clients, colleagues, and other external subject matter experts can literally be located anywhere in the world; this means that people need to be able interact with these people on a continuous basis. Second, it is quite obviously cheaper and most cost-efficient to have employees working remotely and in lower-cost areas than requiring every employee to be physically located at a headquarters or regional location. Every organization is cost-conscious, which is both logical and a fiduciary duty of management to shareholders, employees, and the clients that depend on their advice and guidance. So, what does this have to do with higher education and online learning? It has to do quite a bit with it actually! Let's take a look at why trends and directions from the private sector have been making an ever-larger impact on higher education as online education.

Online interaction, especially via video platforms and other methodologies, is more and more common, particularly tools like Skype and Zoom, but with every new tool there are also new skill sets that need to be learned and acquired by faculty, students, and staff members alike. Not purporting to be an all-inclusive listing or summary of how to effectively run a zoom or other audio-visual business meeting, these should certainly be taken into account when planning and on running such a meeting. Something that might seem to be most obvious but something that has led to numerous amusing and potentially embarrassing situations is to always make sure that your camera is off unless you want it to be on. Cameras can be a tricky thing given the situation and context, and while they can certainly add value to the conversation and make the process more human, they do also create some drawbacks. Not everyone is comfortable on camera, different individuals might have more appropriate backgrounds and setups to appear on camera than others, and mundane matters such as WiFi connectivity and strength can amplify these already stressful issues. Keeping these issues in mind, as well as the fact that in higher education students are normally logging into online classes from home or some type of public space (and likely do not have the support or IT support staff) it might be simpler to just have the cameras off for the duration of the class.

Practitioner Specific Action Steps

Industry Background

Taking the clearest and most obvious place to start this analysis seems to be the easiest path, and so that is where this conversation will start. For example, if an individual has significant background and expertise in the tax arena, it might make sense to focus applications and letters of interest to schools and programs specializing in tax matters. A colleague of mine, not at my current institution, was previously an auditor with years of practical experience taking part in, and managing, audits at a wide range of clients for a Big 4 accounting firm. This individual was, after completing a doctoral degree, able to leverage both this doctoral degree and practical experience into a full-time tenure track position. Another colleague I have had the privilege to work with came to academia with a robust background and experience in the tax industry, specifically focusing in real estate tax transactions that culminated with leading a multi-billion transaction. No matter what the specific industry background is possessed by an aspiring academic, this should be leveraged to assist in this transition. Simply having a background, however, is only the first step, and in order to truly maximize this background for academic purposes, it might make more sense to focus on a single area or small areas of specialization/expertise.

Expertise is a tricky thing, and as has been discussed previously in this text it is often better to not become overly specialized in a professional or practitioner context, but the opposite may very well be true in academic circles. Drilling in and establishing yourself as an expert or leading thought leader in the context of a specific class of information can assist with publications, conferences, and other professional engagements. As it links back to the publishing requirement that is all too often a core requirement of tenure or even non-tenure job postings and successful advancement, becoming recognized as a thought leader or expert is a benefit. Making this shift and transition from a generalist or jack-of-all-trades to an individual focusing or honing in on specific tracks or research concepts can be a somewhat jarring shift and transition, but it does appear to be something necessary to succeed in a competitive academic marketplace. It is important to note that even as private sector unemployment continued to drop to nearly all-time lows during 2018 and 2019, the academic job market continued to show increased signs of competition.

Competition, of course, is not a bad thing, and realistically is something that the higher education industry most likely needed in a comprehensive way. That said, it is also worth noting that, as competition for resources, students, and well-prepared faculty continues to increase, the sheer number of academics also continues to increase. Much has been written and discussed related to the number of graduates and doctoral graduates—particularly in the humanities—that continue to be produced even as demand for those areas of expertise continues to dwindle. As these areas shrink, however, it is also worth pointing that STEM and business subsets continue to become more popular and in-demand in terms of resources as well as student enrollment. This also ties back to another area where, given the increased interest in these spaces, where practitioners and aspiring academics can deliver concrete examples of value additive information and content.

Remaining up to date on market information and news can be difficult under the best of circumstances, and doing so while attempting to balance the research, presentation, and service requirements common among academics can feel like an uphill struggle the entire time. Practitioners, or practitioners that are transitioning to academia, should definitely make sure to emphasize the fact that they remain up to date and "plugged in" to the marketplace as trends and topics evolve and shift over time. It is true that the further removed from industry an individual becomes the more challenging it may become to remain up to date and current, but this is also where practitioners possess an advantage over "traditional" academics. Even if an individual does transition to academia, if they are doing so from an industry position that individual is unlikely to simply stop paying attention to practitioner trends and publications. Put another way, if someone has been doing something, reading something, or listening to certain news broadcasts for years they are unlikely to abruptly simply because a new position has been obtained.

All of this truly ties back to what is often an underlying theme and reason driving practitioners to enter academia in the first place; they desire to give back, share knowledge, and help inspire the next generation of leaders and practitioners. Given this reality, the rest of the conversation and dialogue within this text fits rather neatly in a framework of how more current and applicable information is beneficial to institutions, faculty, and the students at various institutions. Ultimately the goal of any higher education institution is to provide information and value to the students enrolled at the institution and that carries through between the whole range of individuals associated with the institution. Every individual brings to the proverbial table a unique set of skills, information, and attributes that can, and often, help create a well-rounded student body that is an excellent reflection on the institution itself.

Commercialization of Higher Education

One trend that also began to emerge during 2020 and the writing of this book was also something that mirrors trends in the business community at large; the idea of subscribing to goods or services versus paying a flat fee up-front or on some periodic basis. Taking a step back from the higher education bubble and conversation this is a development and shift that has already taken root and is accelerating across different industry verticals. Services such as Uber, Netflix, and even enterprise-level solutions such as those offered by Microsoft, Salesforce, and other technology organizations have shifted and re-oriented themselves from a flat fee or even a periodic revenue model to one closer to a subscription model of booking and earning revenue. This model generates flexibility for both the organization itself as well as the customers that are able to access services on an as-needed or on-demand basis. Many organizations have sought to move from "lumpy" revenue streams to one closer to a consistent steam of earnings of income.

How can this trend and development be connected to higher education, and more importantly should it be connected and applied to higher education and academia at large? At first glance it might seem like such a question is antithetical to all higher educational morals and mindsets, but that misses the bigger point. Higher education has incurred increased scrutiny during the last decade or so, and so it is important for that to always be in the background and on the back burner of any decision that is made with regard to how this business model (and yes, once again, higher education is a business), will be sustained going forward. As the rest of the economic landscape continues to shift and orient itself toward a more flexible and customer-oriented model of operation there is no doubt this is also something that needs to be factored into the decisions made at institutions of higher education. But how might this work in actuality, and what implications will be associated with the rest of education overall?

As far as the pricing model would go the mechanics of pricing on a per-course or per-class basis are not all that dissimilar from how some institutions are already operating in the current environment. In many places, students are told the price on either a per-credit or per-course basis anyway, so what is the big deal? Although there may be specific courses and other forms of content that are priced on per-credit or per-course basis this is not the norm or standard for how institutions price their offerings or how students pay for these offerings. In fact, the vast majority of students either pay the full sticker price for tuition, room, and board, or have access to discounted prices via financial aid, grants, or other aid packages. This also exposes one of the inherent paradoxes of higher education from a cost and pricing model, so let's dive into exactly what some of these implications are for the financial health both of individual institutions of higher education and academia at large.

Fist and foremost is the understanding that higher education at large does tend to be accompanied by a large amount of fixed costs, from faculty and administrative salaries, rent, interest, taxes, and other fixed costs are going to have to be covered even if the revenue side of the conversation is not as consistent. In other words, having a recurring revenue stream is an excellent thing, but it needs to be matched with equally a flexible cost model; this represents a fundamental problem with the business and financing model of higher education. When viewed through the lens of financial models and other metrics, the business model and cost model of higher education is a paradox. Large amounts of fixed costs are incurred on an annual basis, and these costs are going to have to be covered one way or the other, which is also why for the most part revenue lines and earnings have come in chunks versus periodic streams.

Matching revenue and costs is something that every business 101 class teaches, but it is ironic that many of the institutions that teach these concepts do not implement these as a part of how they operate. So, in order for a subscription-based model of higher education to actually come to fruition the way that revenues are earned at institutions alongside how the costs are incurred by that same institution. In other words, the entire business model of colleges and universities operate and function from a financial perspective will need to change and evolve in accordance with market forces. While the idea of subscription revenue is indeed appealing and reflective of broader directions in the economy at large, this is also going to lead to a reimagining of how education is treated from a student and institutional perspective.

The biggest upfront change might take the form of reducing the fixed costs of a college or university, and by and large, the number of fixed costs of any institution are usually connected to either the physical campus itself, and the faculty that instruct courses. Shrinking the physical size and scope of college and universities is an action that might make sense of paper, but can result in dislocations for the institution and the community at large. Specifically, it is common for larger or more well-established universities to play an engaged and active role in their respective communities via community outreach, donating resources and expertise to local organizations, and or even directly investing or sponsoring startups and other entrepreneurial ventures. If the college or university was to leave, relocate, or even just sell the physical campus property to another higher educational partner this will, without a doubt, have a definitive impact on these wider relationships. Removing or reducing the physical footprint and cost of an institute, however, is just the first step in how this reduction might impact the broader higher education conversation.

Online or virtual learning has already emerged as a trend that is set to dominate the conversation around higher education moving forward, but that is something that will have to evolve alongside the needs of the marketplace as well as student needs. With this transition, however, comes both positive and negative externalities that need to be taken into account and understood as far as how it will impact faculty, staff, and students. Perhaps the most obvious and clear-cut implication of this trend and shift is the need, or the expectation, that Internet connectivity is going to be considered less of a luxury and more of a necessity. Understanding this and building this into the higher education model may take several different forms, but the underlying expectation and need will not change. Given the reality on the ground there are a few different ways in which that this can begin to manifest itself; let's look at a few of these implications and ramifications here:

Online learning and education will increasingly become the norm rather than the exception, and this will fundamentally change the dialogue and interaction between students and faculty that at the current time take place via face-to-face meetings. Distance learning, or online education will not be something that is only the refuge of adult learners or other non-traditional students, but rather might actually be the default model for all college and university students.

Video conferencing and other collaborative tools will emerge as the primary way in which faculty, students, and other participants interact with each other; this is something that will need to be factored into the design of courses going forward. Clearly, video tools are already being used by individuals and institutions at an enterprise level, but integrating and incorporating these tools into how courses are taught and managed will represent a change and shift in how certain courses are taught.

For example, while a literature class—consisting of reading and discussing materials—might be conducive for a video or other online format, a class in economics, accounting, or finance might not be as easily transferable into a virtual or online format. This is not to say that certain types of courses are more intense or academically transferable than others, but the very nature of these courses may be more or less transferable to an online format than others.

Grading and recording attendance will need to evolve alongside the other changes to course development and implementation. While recording in-person attendance and class participation is a relatively straightforward manner for most classes, it is important to note that doing so in an online format might be more complicated or difficult in a fully or even mainly online environment. Specifically, and rather obviously, how can attendance be recorded? Can faculty and instructors actually record classes or does that constitute an infringement on the privacy of students? How should these issues and considerations be communicated to students?

From a more nuts and bolts perspective and operational point of view, it is also important to realize that the importance of flexibility is going to only increase in importance going forward. Let's take a look at a few of the considerations that will need to be assessed and understood by faculty and administrators as the push toward subscription-based education and learning continues to accelerate.

Different types of learning and instruction will become more or less popular as the shift toward subscription-based education accelerates, and this will mean different things for different institutions. For example, if a program or certificate program becomes more popular and widely attended this will draw away resources and individuals from other more established models of education and learning. This does not mean that existing courses and faculty will be rendered obsolete, but rather that the faculty, staff, and administrators will need to evolve and shift areas of focus and other information.

New products and educational offerings may not be as lucrative as existing tuition and fee structures. Existing tuition and fee structures often include at least a partial component of these revenues linked to room and board, but these might not always be necessary if more and more programs and courses are offered online or in a distance learning format. Some institutions that are increasingly dependent on tuition may find this transition to be more or less difficult to contend with, but this shift is coming regardless.

Content and course structure will need to be updated and modified on a more frequent basis than current class and course offerings. It is not uncommon for some faculty and some courses to not truly be updated at that often; how often does a biology or English class need to updated and changed? Contrasting this with the fast-changing nature of how technology and business continues to be and develop it is readily evident that such periodic updates are not sufficient in the current marketplace.

Accounting, finance, and technology are evolving and being influenced by an ever-increasing and growing number of outside forces. Students that are coming to institutions of higher education will—and reasonably so—expect that the courses they are being taught are actually conveying and delivering value to students and attendees.

Closer collaboration and a continuing education will need to be a part of the faculty development process, and this might be something that there is some pushback that might be generated on the part of the existing faculty members. The form of continuing education and training is something that is very familiar to members of the professional and practitioner community it might not be as comfortable or as familiar with the members of the faculty community. Making sure that these training and educational programs are both up to date and relevant to the faculty community at the institution is something that requires the cooperation between administrators and faculty members.

At the risk of entering a controversial aspect of the higher education conversation, there is a truth and reality that appears to be increasingly undeniable; higher education and the education business is being treated and evaluated more and more like a business. This might aggravate or irritate some more classic or traditional proponents of higher education, and that is not an entirely unrealistic perspective. That said, it is equally as important to recognize the fact that the increased business-like attitude toward education is an approach and perspective that needs to be granted a seat at the table. Change comes to every industry, and simply putting ones head down and ignoring it is not a viable approach moving forward. Instead, and something that has hopefully been communicated throughout this book, is that the competitive pressures and forces that continue to drive change in the educational space also provide opportunities for both the individuals and institutions willing to embrace the fast-moving nature of the technology space. Underpinning a significant amount of the angst and gnashing of teeth that so often accompanies higher education conversations is the following—and possibly uncomfortable truth—the status quo is unsustainable and most everyone knows it.

Industry practitioners can, and often do, bring a much-needed dose of market knowledge and awareness into the classroom, but this does of reality should also be extended to how the institution at large is managed. All too often the leadership of an academic institution is comprised of individuals that have either work in higher education for the entirety of their career, or at least have done so for the overwhelming majority of it. This approach has merit, and this is not to say that there is no place for traditional academics in the conversation; quite to the contrary, there is an important role for traditional academics to play in the management and leadership of an institution. Discussed previously within this text the rise of corporate-sponsored education the risk of education being coopted by corporate partners is a real and present consideration to be analyzed. Having an effective steward of institutional knowledge and information is arguably important in an environment where competition is increasing and differentiation is increasingly difficult to maintain.

Balancing out this need for some kind of steady leadership and consistency in approach, however, is the need to spur innovation, create new ideas, and drive the institution at large as well as individual programs forward into the future. Leveraging the expertise and experience that so many industry practitioners and professionals can bring to the proverbial table does seem to represent a fiduciary responsibility of any higher education leadership team and is something that should be part of the conversation. While it might seem unusual or even antithetical to traditional missions and goals associated with higher education it does seem that the future of education is increasingly going to be dependent on the development and integration of commercial resources and players into the educational landscape. At first glance, this might seem like an unusual situation, but upon further review these trends are already occurring and driving change within the broader higher education landscape. Let's recap just a few of the changes that have already occurred just in the last several years that indicate that closer collaboration between institutions and commercial partners is not as unusual or radical as it might appear.

The NCAA has already made changes during 2019 that will enable students to receive compensation for when their likeness and images are used for marketing and other advertising purposes. While the future of such relationships and possible compensation policies may change over time as a result of the ripple effects of COVID-19, the trend and direction of that debate appears to be clear. Not directly related or linked to the business of education conversation, this development is indeed indicative of the underlying shift of higher education from simply an educational conversation to a more comprehensive engagement between business, institutions, and other stakeholder groups.

Corporations already are developing, marketing, and attracting students to training opportunities, boot camps, and other intense student-company interactions to help drive the educational conversation forward. These intense boot camp experiences can take the form of coding and computer programming classes and opportunities—which tend to be the most popular—but need not only be concentrated in that space. Depending on the field in question there will always be different aspects that are more or less applicable but there will always be some aspects of the field that can be handled via a trade school or other short-term education.

Vocational trends and schools are on the rise for a number of reasons, and even if they trade school are not explicitly linked to any one corporate sponsor or partner it does seem evident that these institutions are supported and driven by a more commercial angle than other types of institutions. Trade or other vocational schools—which may also include some of the corporate-sponsored programs—provide a valuable service and link in the educational conversation. Be it because of the rising cost of college, the lack of applicability of course work to the job market, or the simple need for more technically trained people vocational schools do not appear to be fading away.

OER does not represent a simple fad or passing thought, but the current path forward is unsustainable. Expecting that either individuals or institutions are going to produce, edit, and disseminate content to the marketplace without any direct or indirect form of compensation is a fool's errand, to put it bluntly. Services that are otherwise provided for free to the marketplace, most commonly associated with social media or other virtual services, are not free at all. In cases where there is no charge for the utilization of products or services it should be understood that the consumers are the product.

External pressures will invariably make the conversation and debate around the higher education debate and conversation more connected to either the cost-benefit or risk-reward associated with higher education.

Ensuring that this is understood and integrated into the decision-making process.

No matter what ultimately comes out of the COVID-19 pandemic in terms of societal and economic changes there is one thing that is already starting to emerge as a paradigm shift in terms of higher education. Even as vast swaths of the U.S. and global economy are shut down and under mandated quarantine, people are still able to access online tools, resources, and other resources; this includes online education and online learning. Assessing the future of online education in the broader context of higher education also involves the analysis of just what types of institutions might survive and thrive in the current environment. Despite the health and economic crises that are a direct result of the global pandemic, there is this underlying reality; people are going to have to continue to develop and learn even in the face of physical locations being closed or otherwise restricted.

Life will go on despite the current dislocations and issues that are wrecking the world economy, and at the end of this crisis—raging as this book was being written and edited—there are going to be two possible outcomes. On the one hand, people are potentially out of work and authentically disturbed and frightened by the effects of the pandemic and so might not be incredibly motivated to participate in higher education. On the other hand, however, is the reality that after the direct and second-order effects of the pandemic receded from the headlines employers and other institutions will be looking for employees. Furloughs and firings are temporary reactions to the economic effects of the pandemic; afterward is always going to be a bounce-back in terms of employment and opportunity. All of that aside, it is important to try and foresee just how these different versions and types of institutions exist and are managed. Online education, which was already a trend and shift in the higher education space, is going to be supercharged by the ripple and long-lasting effects of having millions and millions of individuals unable to be a part of physical education space.

Traditionally there has been something of a bifurcation in the educational space that has resulted in some institutions as well as the faculty and administrators employed therein. Not to say that this is always the case or that every single employee that teaches primarily in-person classes feels this way, but the following statement is undeniable. Over previous years and periods, there has been a feeling that courses and other educational offerings are not—basically—as good as the in-person offerings that are otherwise offered. As someone who attended and completed a doctoral program that was primarily taught in a distance learning format, I can attest to hearing some of these comments, at least early on. While attitudes have changed as technology has become increasingly integrated into every aspect of our lives, the fact remains that this opinion might still exist to some extent. To speak nothing of the reluctance of some administrators, faculty, and staff to develop and maintain online courses, there might also be a feeling that teaching online is not as rewarding as or legitimate as in-person courses. These attitudes are surely changing, but it is worth mentioning that as more and more institutions are increasingly expected—and even required to offer the bulk of courses online there might be some resistance and pushback to these ideas. As always it is worth noting that any ideas or projects might generate similar pushback and reluctance, and so introducing any new ideas will create such attitudes. Online education is a part of the higher education landscape, and only seems poised to become more important going forward versus less so moving forward.

Fully online institutions—these are probably the most obvious implications and contenders as the educational space inevitably evolves, and will capitalize on the trend and shift from in-person to online education. There are innumerable options that are currently available, but it is also important to conduct due diligence on the providers of these online educational offerings. These institutions of higher education are going to invariably capitalize on the upswing in interest in distance learning due to this simple yet impactful question; how many people do you honestly think will want to spend hours in a crowded classroom?

Institutions that develop increasing online offerings—many of the largest institutions of higher education, despite the vast amount of resources and personnel employed at these places, only tend to offer a small amount of online or hybrid offerings. Developing and increasing the amounts of courses and other educational offerings delivered in an online format is something that every institution will need to get increasingly accustomed to doing. This might actually cause a shift in feelings between "traditional" institutions of higher education, and those that have only entered the space more recently. Specifically, there has traditionally been some different views related to higher education being taught in an online format. While online education still remains a "non-traditional" area versus face-to-face instruction, it would not seem incorrect to assume that online education will become more prominent going forward than it had been in the past.

New upstart online education firms that can potentially take advantage of the 1–2 pincer movement that is already underway in the higher education space. Costs associated with higher education will need to reprice, as has been discussed throughout this text, and new players in the space can introduce offerings and programs without having to deal with the legacy costs of other institutions.

Drilling down into this fact there is also the fact that without a physical campus or location a large amount of the fixed costs associated with managing a college or university will simply not exist.

Building on this, and even if the tuition charged on a per student basis is lower than some other more established players the institutions might actually be able to pay instructors more on a course by course basis.

This potential higher pay on a cost by cost basis could potentially attract candidates and applicants that might have otherwise applied to more established players.

Regulation and accreditation of higher education courses and programs taught in an online format will evolve and shift. Common questions that are asked for new courses or instructors teaching in an online format tend to revolve around

The commercial influence on higher education does not look like it will be waning or diminishing in importance over the next coming years; it actually appears that this trend and market shift will become more amplified and important as the years continue. Particularly given the global financial crisis that accompanied the COVID-19 pandemic that swept the world in 2020, it appears that the impact and influence of corporations and other private sector partners will be more involved in the development and dissemination of higher education products and services. What this ultimately means in terms of how interwoven these institutions become is difficult to foresee, although it does appear that a few trends and directions that will continue to emerge and mature in the medium and long terms are crystallizing.

First, the influence and integration of corporate partners and other non-traditional partners will continue to increase. The dramatic closure and shuttering of college and university campuses during the spring 2020 semester was—of course—done with the health and safety of students in mind. That said, there is a conversation to be had around the financial impact of these closures on the budgets and bottom-line performance of these institutions. For example, if an institution closed campuses for the remainder of a semester (let's say 50% of the way through), will students request refunds for the portion of tuition earmarked for dormitory and campuses fees/services? On the surface, this does not seem to be an unreasonable request, but the institution might have already made purchases or otherwise spent these funds.

Second, the business landscape is going to be fundamentally changed as a result of both the technological disruption that was already underway, and these changes will be amplified by the economic disruption caused by the outbreak ripple effects of spring 2020. Despite the individual specifications of the institution in question, there will be an increased need and expectation that institutions will have the expertise and personnel to navigate these fast-changing situations. Of course, there will be negative ripple effects and ramifications of these broader events, but this also opens the door for practitioners to leverage collective expertise and on-the-ground experience. Whether it takes the form of background with remote working tools, a background in dealing with unexpected changes to the business outlook, or simply experience in dealing with stressful situations, there is a definitive need growing for a more business-like and administrative approach to managing higher education.

Mentioned throughout this text, it will be incumbent upon these practitioners that join the ranks of faculty and other members of the higher education field to ensure that even as these events occur that the learning process is not undermined. Corporate expertise and background is great, but there is also a substantive argument to be made for the continued integration of liberal arts, critical thinking, and applying these analytical capabilities in a logical and objective manner. The ability to analyze problems and situations is not something that should be ignored or taken away from the situation no matter what

Reflection Questions

1. What role, if any, does it appear that commercial partners and publishers should play in the creation and dissemination of content in the higher education space?
2. The role of open educational resources (OER) has had a dramatic impact on the text and educational materials used by colleges and universities, but is model sustainable?

3. In the context of the bringing some market perspective to the classroom, are business practitioners uniquely qualified to bring this perspective, or can lessons be gleaned from other areas such as journalism and the sciences?

Additional Readings

1. OERcommons.org—"What are Open Educational Resources"—https://www.oercommons.org/.
2. Wharton Magazine—"The Most Important Trends in Online Education"—https://magazine.wharton.upenn.edu/digital/the-most-important-trends-in-online-education/.
3. Inside Higher Ed—"A Flexible Future"—https://www.insidehighered.com/news/2014/12/02/some-research-universities-flexibility-and-modularity-influence-long-term-plans.
4. United States Census—"Population Shift to The West and South"—https://www.census.gov/programs-surveys/sis/resources/visualizations/west-south.html.
5. Inside Higher Ed—"Online Education Start-Up, Backed by Research University Credit"—https://www.insidehighered.com/digital-learning/article/2019/08/21/new-online-ed-start-aims-community-college-market-university.

CHAPTER 10

Reflections and Observations

Introduction

It would be an understatement if I said that higher education is changing, and that is something that anybody that is going to enter the higher education space is going to have to understand and be aware of. Viewed through the traditional lens of analysis the higher education space could be best thought of as a staid and difficult to change field, but that could not be further from the truth. Education is something that needs to be a continuous part of the conversation for every professional or academic, and that is going to be something that will change how institutions and faculty members engage both with the educational community and fellow peers. The takeaways that I have observed from my transition from a private industry practitioner to a tenure track academic can be summarized as follows, but by no means is a listing that is comprehensive listing. Specifically, it is critical to remember that every single individual and institution is going to have to contend with a variety of forces related to the higher education and the economy in general. Let's take a look at my top (five) 5 takeaways from my transition before we move on to my reflections on my specific journey and what this means for other aspiring academics.

The transition was more difficult than I honestly thought it would be. Coming out of private industry and out of a doctoral program, I really assumed that I would be able to move easily and quickly to a

S. Stein Smith, *Shifting from Accounting Practitioner to Academia*, Palgrave Studies in Accounting and Finance Practice,
https://doi.org/10.1007/978-3-030-67546-2_10

higher education role. Perhaps it was me being naïve or inexperienced or some combination of the above, but I was surprised at the rigor with which this transition to academia required of me. After applying and being interviewed—including multiple on-site interviews at different institutions—it was surprising that I was not offered a role that I thought that I had earned. The takeaway—making the shift from full time to full time—might be more difficult than I initially thought.

Understanding is simultaneously going to be something that is well understood and relatively straightforward in nature, but can be difficult to absorb and understand for successful practitioners. Making a shift and pivot such as the one from working in the accounting sector to the higher education or academic sector will invariably be a difficult one, but that does not reflect poorly on either the individual, institution, or prior work history of that individual. The reality of the situation is simply that education or academia and the other types of accounting work are vastly different. This difference is what oftentimes forms a large part of the appeal of higher education, but can also make successfully pivoting and transitioning potentially more difficult.

Higher education is a business, and practitioners making this shift should incorporate this into the decision-making process. This does mean that the bottom-line mindset that is all too common in the business world needs to be copied on a word for word basis, but that this will influence how different projects are assessed, planned, and executed going forward. This is a topic and theme that we have discussed throughout this book, but the main takeaway is as follows; certificates, programs, and other non-traditional educational offerings are going to become an ever-larger part of the educational experience. Practitioners should seize on this potential opportunity.

As has hopefully been made clear throughout this book and commentary there are tremendous opportunities for practitioners that are attempting a pivot and transition from private industry to higher education. It is true that a large amount of the workload and expectations associated with either private industry and academia are going to be different, but that should be discouraging news for practitioners. For every obstacle or challenge, there is a corresponding opportunity for aspiring academics. Developing new programs, reinvigorating existing programs, and the ability to weave practical advice and experiential learning into the classroom are invaluable opportunities for the individuals and institutions alike.

The landscape for higher education is going to change dramatically over the coming years, and this is going to impact both current and future job prospects for anyone that is going to be involved in the education space. Institutions will close, new institutions will arise, and the importance of understanding what happens when these institutions close is an imperative aspect of how the higher education space will evolve moving forward.

Disruption and disruptive innovation are topics that are covered and taught at virtually every business program, department, or school, but are topics that have—to date—not always been implemented by those very same institutions. Put simply, and in order to survive and thrive moving forward the same institutions that are so commonly associated with conservative operating guidelines will have to pivot and evolve rapidly and in response to market changes and developments. Once again, however, the pressures and stresses that can so often accompany disruptive innovation and disruption at large are an opportunity for practitioners to bring to bear some of the much need practical experience and processes to higher education.

If someone had said to me back in 2010 that I would eventually end up on the tenure track at a major public institution I would have thought you were speaking about somebody else, or some alternate reality. Looking back, however, the transition and journey from my perspective is not as surprising as it might have originally appeared. Some of the stress and anxiety generated as a direct result of this transition and shift from private practice and higher education were at least partially a result of the lack of preparation on my side for this pivot and career shift. With the benefit of hindsight, there are several items that I would have done a little differently that I believe would have benefitted my transition and pivot from.

First and foremost, I would have mapped out my transition and pivot from private industry to academia in a little more of an organized manner. To that end, and coming back to several points raised throughout this text, I would have certainly attempted to link my doctoral education to job openings, to the application timeline itself. Specifically, I would have tried to take into account just how long the job interview and application actually takes; the process from end to end takes months to complete. Timing, as is often stated, is everything, and the job market for recent doctoral graduates and other potential higher education roles. While it is true that there is no such thing as a perfect plan or strategy, some sort of plan or timeline is key to further success. Even under the best of circumstances an academic job hunt and conversation can be a tedious and long process that, most of the time, do not result in a successful job landing. By having a plan, and trying to ensure that the plan is realistic and actually possible to successfully execute, some of the stress and anxiety linked to this dramatic shift can be offset or reduced.

Second, the creation of a new persona and CV is something that should have taken a front seat as I took the transition in stride, and that is something that should take a leading and primary role in the transition process. While every professional certainly has a resume, CV, or some other summarization of professional accomplishments it is necessary that every professional needs to plan for and execute. It is clear that resumes and CVs do have common elements no matter of what the focus actually is, but it is something that needs to be customized and personalized as this pivot or transition entails. Viewed from a higher-level perspective and bigger picture view the requirement for this revised and new publication and professional reservations that are necessary to successfully make the transition from a private industry background to academia.

CV's are always important for any job application process or conversation, and so it should not come to a surprise that academic CVs play an important role in the job seeking, job promotion, and job retention conversation, but are arguably even more important in a higher education context than a practitioner context. Whereas in a practitioner or professional accounting/financial services landscape the CV can be used as a baseline for further conversation (a highlight reel, basically), an academic CV can be the only way that an individual's information gets communicated to external participants.

Third, and this is arguably the most important piece of advice and reflective assessment that I could provide to any potential application seeking to make the transition a successful, smooth, and relatively painless endeavor, is the adjustment in mindset that is critical to the higher education field. On the one hand, the competitive nature of academia, and especially the increasingly solo nature of most publishing and writing projects can make the collaborative nature of academia seem paradoxical. What this means is that at the same time that individuals and institutions are competing strongly for resources and personnel.

My Revised Action Plan

The action plan that I entered into this transition with was, for lack of a better word, made up as I went along. A set up like that generated all of the pitfalls and obstacles that you would expect with a plan that was put together on the fly, and basically held together with duct tape and silly string. All kidding aside, the manner in which I approached this transition was obviously not the best or most comprehensive plan that had ever been invented, and this is a good opportunity for both some self-reflection and to reassess what advice I might have given my future self. That said, this action step and framework should not be considered the go-to listing or listing of steps, but simply my reflections and pieces of advice that I would try my best to recommend to any professional making an academic transition. Such a transition is not an easy matter, but that does not mean that is impossible not too difficult to attempt; just because something or an idea is difficult does not mean there is no framework that could be applied. The listing or action steps include, but are not limited to, the following:

1. Figure out exactly what the outcome of this academic transition is. Much like how many recent graduates enter the job market with only a vague idea of what exactly they want to accomplish in terms of employment and career path, the same affliction can befall recently hired academics. No matter how qualified or high profile a professional may in a corporate or private sector setting, it is important to remember that this is a new career path for virtually all involved.
2. Do your homework and research on the entity involved linked to the department, college, or university before even submitting an application. A mistake that I have seen time and again, in both the professional and academic setting, is that individuals go into job interviews without sufficient knowledge of either the institution, or the specific sector/position they are applying. Nothing signals an unprepared applicant more than the inability to answer even basic questions about the position, role, or why you even applied for the position. This echoes back to the earlier comments about doing your research and homework about the place or team that are trying to make into your future home and employer.
3. This point builds on the second point, the importance of doing your research and homework prior to even applying for a specific

position. Every interview process invariably includes a question that goes something along the following lines; where do you see yourself in 5, 7, or 10 years? If an individual is unable to answer such a question in reasonable manner that is usually a highly negative sign for the remainder of the interview. Not only does this point to a lack of planning on the part of the interviewee it always illustrates the fact that the candidate did not adequately prepare in terms of researching the institution in question.

This is not to say that these are the only items or factors that I would change, but at the very least it should give anyone attempting this transition a more holistic and well-rounded approach for what to expect, how to answer the questions and inquiries that will invariably arise during the interview process, and be able to do so in a productive and proactive manner. It might seem like the importance of research, performing due diligence, and planning out answers to questions is emphasized quite often throughout this text, and that is because this is such an important step in the application process.

Something else that I would also keep in mind, or at least try to address and better incorporate into my planning moving forward is the reality that, like any other industry (and yes higher education is an economic sector and industry), there are both structural and temporary shifts that need to be taken into account. Understanding these changing trends and forces necessitates both an understanding of the specific institution and sector in question as well as understanding what external forces are driving these changes. The concept and idea of the ivory tower may be what many individuals think of when they think of higher education, and that model still does exist in some cases. Institutions do exist where the focus is primarily on research, publishing peer-reviewed articles, and pursuing an intellectual agenda forward regardless of the specific outcome. This approach certainly does generate some significant impact and continues to drive forward many research topics that continue to be of interest to the public sector, private sector, and governmental community. Basic research, as this process is known, is associated with a longer term and usually meandering path on research projects toward an uncertain outcome or direction. Such a focus and mindset is rewarding, but is increasingly unsustainable and unsuited for the globally interconnected business landscape.

Revisiting the Dual Mandate of Higher Education

Before diving into a visitation of the different types of higher educational institutions and employment options it is worth restating and analyzing the dual role and dual mandate that many institutions have to fulfill as part of broader duties and responsibilities. No matter what type of college or university is being examined or analyzed these different institutions virtually always have a dual responsibility or role to the students and broader community that they serve; educate and empower. Education, a seemingly obvious role and duty associated with an institution of higher education, can take several different forms depending on the situation. On the one hand, it can mean something more akin to traditional education, encompassing required and elective courses to produce a well-rounded graduate with a humanistic outlook. On the other hand, and has been covered and discussed throughout this text, is the increasing expectation that colleges and universities are going to equip students with the practical and immediately applicable skills to obtain and retain jobs in the modern workplace.

Higher education has long had a dual mandate of both performing research and educating students for the future of the specific industries in question. Both roles and mandates are fulfilled to different levels depending on the institution in question, but the differentiation between the array of institutions appears to only be becoming clearer as the higher education landscape evolves. Instead of maintaining the dual mandate across different institutional lines, it does seem that a fragmentation of the higher education landscape is going to continue if not even accelerate. At one level there is going to certainly be a renewed market for vocational, trade, and corporate-specific training and educational opportunities due in no small part to the need for the retraining, re-educating, and reskilling of the current workforce. It is also worth noting that it is as corporations continue to increase in size, scope, and influence the desire to have employees trained in a customized framework is neither unreasonable nor unexpected. Even with that acknowledgment however, it is worth noting that such corporate- or company-specific training models may not have significant tangible value outside of that organization.

Moving to another tier of the educational landscape the importance of community college is unlikely to wane in the face of growing needs for increased college education. Community colleges provide an important stepping stone and step forward into the higher educational landscape, and also serves as an important bridge between high schools and more traditional 4-year institutions. Especially since many of community colleges also offer, or are associated with, trade schools or other vocational programs the value of community college is not only quite tangible but also directly related to the current needs of the marketplace.

Public universities are perhaps in the most unique situation of all types of institutions since they traditionally come from the most obvious positions of strengths and success of all university models. Since the founding of the modern university and higher education system in the United States, public universities have occupied a prominent position in the educational conversation. Be they land grant universities, research universities, public universities oriented toward educating residents of a particular state, or a combination of states pooling resources—such as in the case of Western Governors University—the impact of public universities is felt throughout the economy at large. From these commanding heights of the educational landscape, public universities and research institutions lead the way in research, education, and pursuing the educational conversation as it relates to economic development and connection to broader policy goals. That said, and despite these strengths that have endured for so long, the public university model is coming under increasing strain.

Public universities are tasked with, simultaneously, educating residents from within state, accommodating students from outside of the state, and conducting cutting-edge research all at the same time. Such a triple mandate necessitates a massive increase in scale, resources, and scope that many universities have embraced with gusto during the last several decades, but this very same scale is also proving to be a struggle. Akin to how some of the largest and most complex organizations in the world face challenges integrating different systems and internal cultures, universities beyond a certain size face similar issues. The term and idea of a conglomerate discount that has long been applied to private sector corporations and actors is also being applied—in a certain manner—to large educational organizations. Although the labels and specific iterations that are referenced will be different than those used to characterize and evaluate private sector organizations the outcomes and implications will be the same. As organizations continue to grow ever-larger and more complicated they continue to deal with the same range of issues that plague and bedevil private sector counterparts. This should not come as such a surprise as it might initially appear; as stated throughout this piece it is important to recognize the reality that higher education is a big business in addition to being an academic matter.

To thrive and succeed in an increasingly competitive environment it will be increasingly necessary for institutions to adapt, become more nimble, agile, and responsive to change as they occur in the broader marketplace. If institutions do not respond to the changing demographic, societal, technological, and global shifts occurring outside of the educational environment they will continuously find themselves on the back foot of changes happening outside of their institution. The very size and scope of many of the largest institutions in the public university sector are hamstrung by the very same size, scope, and resources that make them so successful. Touching once again on the parallel between higher education and private sector organizations it is also obviously necessary for institutions to evolve and change over time.

It is not clear what direction some of the largest organizations will eventually evolve into, but it does appear clear that there are going to sometimes where organizations are broken up, differentiated, and redefined over time. First and foremost, there is a tangible and very real potential that some public institutions or universities will become increasingly focused on exclusively research going forward. Funding and maintaining such a high level and caliber of research is obviously something that is not possible nor realistic for every public university to undertake. Even in the conversation around public universities, there is a large range of them in terms of student size, resources, and faculty engagement. It would be, for example, unfair to compare the public university system of a state like California versus the public university system in the state of Maine or Vermont. Scale aside, it does appear that there is an increasing shift, albeit one that may be happening under the surface, for renewed interest in research and intellectual property development at universities. The technologies and industries that are, and will continue to, redefine and drive the economy forward appear increasingly aligned with technology and technological research. Some public universities may be very well suited to capitalize on this increasing need.

Another potential pathway forward is closer collaboration and cooperation between public university systems and community colleges. Building pipelines and other collaborative opportunities have already accelerated in response to several external forces. The rising cost of college is clearly a force, but there is also a greater understanding and acknowledgment that some classes are better taken at a lower cost institution, which allows students to focus time, energy, and resources on "major courses" or more highly specialized classes. Establishing and strengthening these partnerships and relationships also makes sense from an institutional point of view. Education is a business, but there is a relationship and symbiotic connection between different classes of institutions. Physically represented by the typical hub and spoke, or connected institutions with a large public university at the center of the network there is certainly a need and manifestation of how students, resources, and people move back and forth as well as work together across institutional lines.

Private universities are in a unique position vis-a-vis the other types of institutions mentioned within this text. Some of the private universities in the United States are some of the wealthiest, well established, and well recognized in the world, but that is merely a surface-level analysis. Peeling back the layers connected to the private university conversation it is also important to realize that many private institutions are struggling and suffering from financial hardships due to the numerous external factors driving change in the educational landscape. This situation can lead to any number of outcomes, several of which we will analyze here.

Broaden Your Scope

An additional point of view and perspective that I would definitely try to bring to the conversation would be to not enter the higher education and academic conversation with as narrow a perspective as I initially had done. This is clearly easier said than done in most cases, but certainly is something that I always try to emphasize for anyone entering the academic conversation. Every individual is different, clearly, but there are a few areas where in which individuals and even institutions can broaden the proverbial scope and lens through which an opportunity, challenge, or other item is viewed or analyzed. Acknowledging that no list will even be all inclusive or even close to complete, there are a few items that should form the basis for additional analysis and conversation.

1. Do not limit yourself to what you have grown up with as the mindset as to what academia or higher education actually means. This may take the form of expanding the geographic search area in which an individual looks for a job, considering taking different positions, or even applying to a wider array of firms and organizations. However this manifests itself, especially in higher education,

it is important to realize just how many and how varied the opportunities for practitioners moving into academia are.

2. Consider different types of institutions and roles outside of teaching, research, and service. In other words, and especially for practitioners that have more experience and real-world expertise, employment as a fellow, think tank, or research type of institute might be an excellent place to start and perhaps stay. Academia and the research side of the employment landscape and outlook are much broader than simply teaching in classrooms or developing courses. Embracing the breadth and depth of this work and the opportunities that come with affiliated breadth and depth is something that every practitioner should realize as soon as possible.
3. Be creative and innovative. My career and areas of focus and interest have developed and evolved much like anyone else's does over the course of exposure and interaction with new ideas and concepts. That said, it is important to always keep an eye peeled and open for new ideas and concepts that are originating in the marketplace that can have dramatic effects on business and other conversations now and going forward. For example, my own personal career arc and journey have touched upon the areas of integrated reporting, benefit corporations, artificial intelligence, robotic process automation, blockchain, and cryptoassets. These may seem like a disparate group of interests and ideas, and they are, but they also represent one underlying trend and idea as it relates to finance and accounting. How accounting and financial professionals can evolve and develop alongside the business environment.
4. Realize how much value and information that you can bring to the conversation. It is true that some individuals in academia may have more formal education and training than you might, in some cases, but that is only part of the conversation necessary for the successful transition from private industry to academia. Coming into the conversation as former industry expert or practitioner expert provides you a layer of expertise and working knowledge that can be applied to many of the questions and concerns that are increasingly coming to the forefront of higher education and academic conversations. Expertise comes in many different forms, and a lesson to keep in mind is that no matter what specific subset of expertise is being discussed is that there are equally as valuable.

5. Understanding that like every other industry or field higher education will change, and that you will have to change alongside. For example, my foray into education occurred initially during the years between 2016 and 2020, and even in that short time frame the conversation surrounding higher education completely changed. From a personal perspective, as well as the sector as a whole, several significant changes had a large impact on how I saw higher education as well as how education was perceived by many others. Presidential administrations changes, entirely new businesses rose, some of those same new models failed, but there was an unmistakable change in everything surrounding the educational conversation. Partially as a result of those external changes as well as changes in my own areas of interest and expertise, the topics and themes I discussed evolved and further developed.
6. Be patient with both yourself and the application process. As someone who is trying to make a major career pivot and transition, it should not come as a surprise that this process might take longer than you would expect. Specifically, the timelines and seemingly endless waiting between meetings and other events can be extremely frustrating even for the most patient individual. This continues to change as institutions become more attuned to the marketplace at large, but generally speaking it can still take longer to complete certain processes than it might take in other settings. That said, simply because a process takes slightly longer does not mean it will never be completed. To the contrary, understanding this fact about both the process and yourself during the process can give applicants a leg-up over more easily frustrated or discouraged potential applications.
7. Realize that hits might not be a permanent shift. If there is one thing that is constant, that is that change continues to come to every segment of the economy and workplace; higher education is no exception. This will play out differently for every individual and every institution, but just like how landing a job at a private sector organization is not a job for life guarantee. Even though the academic landscape might be evolving and changing, however, there is some kind of increased certainty that continues to accompany the higher education field that can be difficult to replicate in other economic sectors.

Topics and themes that I have discussed and studied during my transition from private industry to higher education have included but are not limited to financial literacy, sustainability, strategic planning, and more recently blockchain and cryptoassets. Mentioned before, but worth revisiting throughout this context, the primary driver behind these pivots and changes was the desire to keep up with external changes and forces in the marketplace. No matter what specific industry or subset you happen to be employed within there are always going to be changes and developments that need to be incorporated into what exactly you cover, research, and study. While it is important to not merely flit from topic to topic every time a headline changes it does remain important to keep into account that these changes and developments are important to understand. Specifically, it also helps with the crafting and development of a professional narrative over time by demonstrating the flexibility and adaptability to not only stay abreast of current trends and forces but to also factor these into presentations and research.

Taking this into account, it is increasingly imperative for individuals making the transition from a practitioner landscape to higher education and academia to keep abreast and up to date on the bigger picture trends and forces that are driving change in the accounting profession. It may be tempting, especially as practitioners shift and transition from private industry or public accounting into higher education, to not keep as up to date or on the cutting edge of emerging trends and topics as might otherwise have occurred, but that is an incomplete view of the situation. Maintaining professional relevance and competency is not simply good business practice, but is also part of the fiduciary responsibility that educators have to current and future students. The specifics of that this remaining up-to-date will vary from person to person, but it is increasingly expected that colleges, universities, and educational institutions will have personnel and resources to fully educate and equip students with both traditional and emerging technology information.

An additional factor that I would wish to take more into account, as well as continuing to offer as advice to any aspiring academics or practitioner, is to play a proactive role in ensuring that you have control and direction over your narrative. This will obviously mean different things for different people, but this is something that cannot be overstated as vitally important for any successful transition. Entire books have been written about the importance of making a good first impression, integrating yourself within your new team and workplace, and trying to make the best use of your first 90 or 100 days in a new position. Higher education might move at a slightly slower pace than some private industry organizations, but that does not mean that the importance of assuming control over the narrative is less important. Coming from a practitioner background where there is a large amount of structure and control it can be overwhelming, unnerving, and even a little bit scary for said individuals. That said, building a constructive and proactive narrative is important for any individual seeking to make a successful transition from industry to higher education.

Building a narrative, personality, and structure for yourself is of the utmost importance for higher education and academia, and this embedded flexibility is also something that makes the transition so appealing for some practitioners. Figuring out what topics to cover, how to present and analyze these topics, and what to incorporate into the content that is produced forms the basis for academic reputations, career arcs, and numerous other types of academic engagement. Seizing control is something that sounds easy on paper, but can be a bit tricky to actually develop and implement for a member of the academic community. What this might actually require will vary from individual to individual, and will also differ depending on the institution in question, but there are a few options and factors that should form the basis for the structure and composition of an academic narrative and content plan.

The concept of building a narrative and market persona might strike some as an unusual item to return to at this point, but something that crossed my radar during the wrapping up phase of this book made me revisit this topic. Specifically, there is a common phenomenon in which celebrities, actors, and other high profile individuals mentally create an alternative persona or identity through which they engage with either their specific subject matter, marketplace, or audience in question. While this might seem like something not particularly relevant to the transition of an individual from accounting to higher education, the truth is actually much closer to reality.

As a practitioner, there are going to be times where it might be easier to adopt an educator or educational identity for embracing and learning new topics and trends, as opposed to relying on past persona and identity. This might seem like an odd approach to things, but consider the following; how many times have you seen or heard that someone needs to get "hyped up" or "prepare," or get into "stage mode" before starting a project or initiative. Entering this good headspace and mindset is something that is shared and applicable across economic and industry lines; creating an educational or thought leadership persona is not all that different. To add some personal context to this conversation this is actually something that I have done for myself; an identity and "stage name" that I have adopted and been assigned is Dr. Blockchain. This does reflect both the subject matter that I specialize in as well as the role that this person fulfills, a technology-focused educator. In addition to creating a broader academic narrative and structure, this development of a persona and identity can also assist with honing in on what specific subset area you are planning to focus on.

First and most importantly is to decide what kind of academic you actually want to be, and this can vary depending on your personal goals and perspectives. A focus on research, an emphasis on service, or a desire to be a public intellectual will all require different forms of time and investment from the point of view of an academic. Second, and building on the construction and decision related to what type of academic you wish to become there needs to be a logical and well thought out plan in terms of content production and delivery to help make sure that this plan actually comes to fruition. Content production is always important, and it is equally more important to maintain and update a comprehensive mix of types and forms of content over time. Academic articles, practitioner articles, presentations, podcasts, TV appearances, and assortment of other platforms all have a role to play, but the mix of resources and number of presentations and content formats will need to play an important role in any academic portfolio.

The Path Forward

The field of higher education is changing and rapidly evolving, and this is not something that can be ignored relegated to the back burner, but rather should form the basis for how any planned career shift or career arc. Disruption, developing new ideas, programs, and possibly entirely curricula are going to be things that increasingly form the basis and core for how educators and institutions are going to need to embrace to move forward successfully. That said, it is important to understand that with every potential challenge or obstacle that these dramatic changes might create there will invariably be opportunities for engaged and proactive professionals.

Higher education is rich and rewarding profession for virtually everyone involved in the creation, distribution, and delivery of educational products to the marketplace, but that does not mean that the industry can afford to rest on its laurels or not be proactive in addressing and meeting the needs of student, faculty, and the staff that are involved in various aspects of the educational process. It can be said with great confidence that the higher education landscape as it is currently constituted does seem well positioned to thrive and succeed moving forward into a rapidly changing and developing landscape. Instead of being thought of as a negative trend or something to be feared, however, this rapidly changing and evolving educational landscape can and should be thought of as an opportunity for proactive individuals to embrace new technologies, leverage the ability of new tools entering the marketplace, and seeking to bring some best practices from the corporate sector to the higher education space. What this actually means in terms of individual adoption and integration of new technology remains uncertain in terms of outcomes, but it seems appropriate to speculate that the educational conversation will continue to move forward. The form that this path forward ultimately takes, however, is not something that seems easy or simple to forecast, but there do appear to be a few core areas and trends well positioned to continuously drive change and innovation in higher education. Of special importance, building on these changes and major forces, are also what the role of practitioners can be in this fast-moving environment.

From my perspective, own experience, and conversations with other members of the academic and practitioner community, one of the clearest benefits that practitioners can bring to the conversation is the ability to assess and analyze higher education from a fresh perspective. Many academic types, despite best intentions, might not have the correct mindset or perspective to critically review and modify existing content and course offerings. Individuals that have recently transitioned from industry have this point of view and can assist in delivering insights that are arguably more necessary than ever before in the current landscape. This assistance can take the form of real-world examples in the classroom, helping administrators develop and market new programs, or simply refreshing the way in which an institution is organized and makes decisions. Regardless of how specifically the organization makes use of practitioner experience and expertise the reality is that more and more industry and practitioner individuals can, and should, be involved in the educational process.

Combining the expertise and backgrounds of practitioners and traditional academics also creates a true opportunity and space for education to, for lack of a better word, rehabilitate the image that has become recently tarnished in the course of robust public debate. Open up any educational publication, podcast, or other venues for discussion, and there is bound to be a conversation about whether higher education is worth the cost, opportunity cost, and other ancillary items that are going to arise. While it is not necessary to radically redefine or completely transform the educational landscape, there is going to be a reorganization of the role of education in the broader economic or societal conversation. This is precisely where the importance of merging together the expertise and role of practitioners and more traditionally oriented academics. Combining the practical and theoretical is a powerful combination, and one that is both increasingly expected of institutions and required by potential future employers.

Collaboration and Consolidation

Second, higher education at the core of idea will need to change and evolve over time in order to keep pace with the fast-changing and evolving nature and this can take different forms depending on the type of institution that is being analyzed. Demographic challenges will inevitably continue to be something that institutions need to contend with and factor into how programs and courses are developed, edited over time, and marketed to current and future students. Additionally, there is going to need to be a reassessment as to how different institutions cooperate and partner with each other over time. Whether this takes the form of increased inter-institution cooperation along different lines, development of complementary programs, or consists of increased specialization, it seems evident that education will continue to change and evolve to contend with market forces over time.

Cooperation will not only be something is desirable, but a trend and fact that is required for institutions to compete. Think about the big picture for a second; there is no one area, country, or region, that has monopoly on the educational market or space. Over the last several decades this has become increasingly apparent, as the ranking for top business programs and colleges at large continue to represent a more global and diverse set of institutions rather than only those located in either the United States or Europe. This is not a bad thing, nor should it be viewed as a negative development or existential threat; rather it should be viewed as yet another sign, iteration, and indication of how interconnected the economy has become. Since organizations, individuals, and the cultural interactions that underpin these organizations and individuals reflect these realities, it should be apparent that the education preparing individuals should reflect this.

An additional way that higher education will need to change and evolve over time is the simple reality that institutions will need to develop and create different types of educational offerings for different student bodies. It used to be that an individual could obtain a college degree and then—for lack of a better word—coast on that education throughout an entire career. Given the tremendous rate of speed with which technology tools continue to change and evolve it seems increasingly evident that individuals will need to be continuously learning and educating themselves versus thinking of education as a one-time or static event. To contend with just how quickly the environment shifts and evolves it seems that education will continue to more closely mirror the continuing education process so many professionals are familiar with.

Higher education and academia at large is a multifaceted, complex, and fast-changing economic sector that generates hundreds of billions in revenues on an annual basis, and that is something worth stating again. If this book was about any other sector or business model it would be different, but higher education is additionally complicated because even though there are customers the relationship and dynamics at play are slightly more complicated than other businesses. Professionals obviously have experience and practice dealing with changing business requirements and needs but it also important to understand how higher education is different as well as how where practitioners seeking to transition and enter into the higher education and academic conversation.

Hopefully, my anecdotes and stories throughout this text have helped you better understand the opportunities and challenges that can come from anyone transitioning from corporate industry to higher education. Amusing as they may have been, they were included with the intent to assist, educate, and hopefully illuminate this topic for individuals that may be grappling with the same questions I did during the process. One additional takeaway that I would always encourage everyone to keep in mind is that there is always a time and a place for every type of career shift and change, and that if higher education seems appealing, it is worth taking a closer look. Education and educational services are the backbone of any profession, workforce, or economy; being a part of this segment and area is a privilege and fantastic opportunity. In any event, if you have any questions or comments on the book, on my journey, or specific items linked to your personal transitions, please feel free to reach out. All the best, and best of luck on your personal journey.

Concluding Thoughts

Attempting to conclude a book such as this is always going to be a difficult task for any number of reasons. Firstly it is important to emphasize and always keep in mind that every journey is different, and that there are literally thousands of variables that need to be taken into account with such an endeavor. Having the courage, and being willing to make such a bold choice as making the switch from practitioner to educator is arguably the most important step. Making such a dramatic change is always bound to be difficult, but going in there with a plan in mind is the most important step. Secondly, economic forces and trends are notoriously hard to forecast correctly, accurately, or even in a timely nature, and these bigger picture forces and developments can have a dramatic impact on career specifics. Now, it might seem like the current trends are the most important, relevant, or impactful for the higher education sector, but it is also important to remember that industries do adapt and evolve over time; education should not be thought of as any different. Lastly, the future may seem to be more uncertain now than it has been in years prior, but there is always uncertainty in every economy and every era. To sum up, my parting thoughts would be best summarized as follows; education and educating the future professionals and leaders of the world are noble goals, are rewarding, and can truly be an enjoyable career arc.

Go forth, be adventurous, and do great things.

Index

S. Stein Smith, *Shifting from Accounting Practitioner to Academia*, Palgrave Studies in Accounting and Finance Practice,
https://doi.org/10.1007/978-3-030-67546-2

O

P

Q

R

S

T

The manufacturer's authorised representative in the EU is Springer Nature Customer Service Centre GmbH, Europaplatz 3, 69115 Heidelberg, Germany. If you have any concerns regarding our products, please contact ProductSafety@springernature.com

Printed and bound by CPI Group (UK) Ltd, Croydon, CR0 4YY

30/09/2026

02225661-0009